CHINA'S GREAT ROAD

CHINA'S GREAT ROAD
LESSONS FOR MARXIST
THEORY AND SOCIALIST
PRACTICES
ARTICLES 2010-2021

BY JOHN ROSS

INTERNATIONAL PUBLISHERS, New York

&

1804 Books at the People's Forum, New York

1804 Books at the People's Forum, NY 10018
Copyright © 2021 John Ross
All rights reserved Printed in the United States

Particular thanks must be given to two institutions. First to Chongyang Institute for Financial Studies, Renmin University of China of which I have been a Senior Fellow since 2013. This is one of China's most important Think Tanks known not only in that country but internationally. Without the stimulus of working with my colleagues there, with its Executive Dean Wang Wen, many of the ideas in what follows could not have been generated. Second to Guancha.cn, one of China's key websites, which published in Chinese the majority of the articles which follow. My new articles which are published in English may be found at LearningfromChina.net.

John Ross, January 2021

Library of Congress Cataloging-in-Publication Data

Names: Ross, John, author.
Title: China's Great Road: Lessons for Marxist Theory and Socialist Practices / John Ross.

Identifiers: LCCN 2021905060 |ISBN 978-1-7368500-0-8
Subjects: Political Science| Economics

Typeset by Amnet

Table of Contents

CHINA'S GREAT ROAD

Introduction

China in 42 years, 1978-2020, far less than a single lifetime, has gone from one of the world's poorest countries, with more than 850 million people living in internationally defined poverty, to the brink of becoming a high-income economy by World Bank standards. It has achieved total elimination of absolute poverty and the world's fastest rise in average living standards – with life expectancy figures showing that its social conditions are even better than this economic result. This achievement, by a wide margin, has improved the position of by far the largest proportion of humanity of any event in human history. (Section 1)

Furthermore, both Marxist theory and practical experience shows that other countries can learn from this strategy with similar results – as particularly shown in Vietnam, Laos and Cambodia and, in a more partial form, in Latin America, in Bolivia. The most successful economies in the world in terms of development over the last decades are socialist economies. Learning the lessons of China – not mechanically copying it but studying its key features – is therefore of the utmost importance for developing countries and socialists in all states. (Section 2)

China has achieved this economic success not by departing from Marx but by a systematic application of Marx's theories. (Section 3)

China's present foreign policy is also based on an application of Marx's concepts. (Section 4)

Learning from China's development is therefore of urgent practical interest for all in developing countries. It shows in practice that it is possible to take developing economies and transform them into developed countries by socialist methods in a way far more successful than adopting the path of capitalism - with all the huge gains this means for the life of the people in these countries. Furthermore, China's success has created a huge potential partner for the Global South. In particular, in the coming period 'South-South relations' between China and developing countries will be the progressive pole of world development. The US will continue to pursue an aggressive policy against China with some imperialist countries likely to fall in behind this. China-Global South relations will therefore strengthen with mutual benefit. (Section 5)

While China's economic policy was developed in Marxist terms, in order to create broad united front bases for politics, it is also possible to explain China's economic policy in terms of Western 'Keynesian' economics. (Section 6)

One of the most striking proofs of the superiority of the socialist character of China's economy compared to capitalism is its performance when faced with global economic crises. The is due to the core of the socialist character of its economy – its large state sector. This allows China to regulate its overall investment level – whereas in a capitalist economy the overall investment level is determined by private capital. This lesson applies to all economies - not just developing ones. (Section 7)

Section *1*

The scale of China's social and economic achievement

Part 1: China's is the Greatest Economic Achievement in World History

Introductory Note – this is Chapter 2 of my book 'The Great Chess Game' published in April 2016

The first way to grasp the true magnitude of China's economic development is to understand that the statement made in the introduction to this book that China's is the greatest economic achievement in world history is no over-heated nationalist exaggeration but simply an objective measurable fact.[1] As will be shown in detail, even growth in the US, the previous economically dominant state, or in the USSR, was on a qualitatively smaller scale than China. It is this scale of economic development which alone makes possible the achievement of prosperity by China.

The percentage of world population affected

The simplest and clearest gauge of the historically unparalleled scale of China's economic achievement is the number of people directly benefitting from it as they lived within China's borders – this being measured not only in absolute numbers but as a proportion of the world's population. Table 1 therefore shows the percentage of global population in the world's largest economies at the time they commenced rapid sustained growth.[2]

6 CHINA'S GREAT ROAD

Table 1

% of World Population in Countries at Beginning of Sustained Rapid Economic Growth		
Country	Year	% of world population
UK	1820	2.0%
US	1870	3.2%
Germany	1870	3.1%
USSR[1]	1929	8.4%
Japan	1950	3.3%
Asian 'Tiger' economies[2]	1960	1.4%
China	1978	22.3%
India - potential	circa 1993	16.0%
1. Average of 1920 (8.3%) and 1940 (8.5%) 2. Total for South Korea (0.8%), Taiwan Province (0.4%), Hong Kong (0.1%) and Singapore (0.1%) Source: Calculated from (Maddison, 2010)		

Analysing these historical examples:

- The first country to experience sustained rapid economic growth was the UK in the Industrial Revolution, with 2.0% of the world's population.
- Sustained rapid US economic growth, after its Civil War, was in a country with 3.2% of the world's population.
- When Soviet rapid industrialisation began at the end of the 1920s the USSR contained 8.4% of the world's population.[3]
- Japan's rapid post-World War II growth was in a country with 3.3% of the world's people.
- The growth of the four 'Asian Tigers' (Hong Kong, Singapore, South Korea, and Taiwan Province) was in economies which together only comprised 1.4% of the world's population.

Additional countries might be included – for example Italy from 1950 (1.9% of the world's population) or Spain from 1960 (1.0% of the world's population) - but introducing these makes no significant difference. No other economy commencing sustained rapid economic growth approaches the 22% of the world's population in China in 1978 at the beginning of its economic reform. China's, at the time of economic 'lift-off', was seven times the relative percentage of the world population of the US or Japan, and almost three times that of the USSR.[4]

Scale of economic growth

China's scale of economic development translated into equally dramatic and unprecedented figures for comparative output increases. Measured at internationally comparable prices (PPPs), and adjusted for inflation, the greatest absolute increase in GDP in a single year ever recorded outside China was by the US in 1999 when it added $567 billion in output. The highest increase in production ever achieved in a single year by Japan, frequently thought of as a post-war 'miracle' economy, was $212 billion. The single biggest GDP increase in a single year recorded by South Korea, the largest of the 'Asian Tiger' economies, was $90 billion. But in 2010 China added $1,126 billion in output.[5] The increase in China's GDP in a single year was therefore more than twice that ever achieved by the US and five times that of Japan. This again gives an index of the historically unprecedented scale of China's development.[6]

Comparison to the US

Turning to a bilateral comparison of China with the US, Angus Maddison, the world's pre-eminent authority on long term economic growth, calculated that the US overtook the UK in the early 1870s, and China in the 1880s, to become the world's largest economy.

Figure 1 therefore illustrates overall trends in China's and the US economies during the period since 1870.[7] Taking the main parameters, in 1950, a year after the creation of the People's Republic of China, the US economy was six-eight times larger than China's.[8] This gap closed during the 1950s, only to reopen again in the early 1960s after the failure of China's 'Great Leap Forward'.[9] Between then, and the beginning of its economic reform in 1978, China again closed the gap on the US. But from 1978 the distance between the two economies

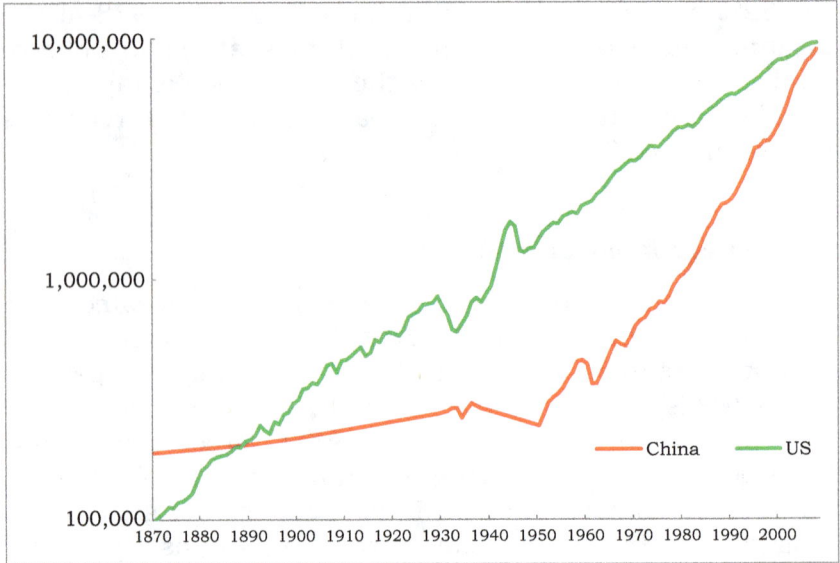

Figure 1: China & US GDP 1990 international
Geary-Khamis dollars.

Source: Maddison, World Population, GDP and Per Capita GDP.
1-2008 AD

began rapidly shrinking until, as already analysed, China's GDP is once more overtaking the US in PPP terms.[10]

Projection of growth rates

Figure 1 also shows a clear and contrasting pattern of economic development of the US and China, which fortunately makes qualitative short term projections regarding their respective growths relatively simple.[11] The US showed a steady growth rate over a prolonged 140 year period, with the only major disruption of the trend being in 1929-50, plus a milder tendency in the recent period to deceleration.

In contrast to the US's relatively consistent development, China's average economic growth from 1870 until the creation of the People's Republic of China in 1949 was extremely slow, after which dramatic acceleration occurred. It is also interesting to note that, contrary to certain myths, China's economic growth was relatively rapid during periods of expansion of its planned economy from 1949-78.[12] But China's average growth rate between 1949 and the commencement of economic reform in 1978 was substantially reduced by the setback caused by the Great Leap Forward, and a smaller one during the Cultural Revolution. China's average growth rate from 1950-78 was 4.9%.[13] In contrast from 1978-2014, after the launching of economic reform, China's annual average GDP growth was 9.8%, on World Bank data calculated in inflation adjusted US dollars, and from 1978-2013 it was 8.5% on the PPP data of the Conference Board.[14]

China's dramatic closing of the gap with the US after 1978 was therefore due to both avoidance of serious setbacks and to acceleration in underlying growth. As will be shown below, for China's GDP not to overtake the US, however measured, an unprecedentedly drastic deceleration of China's economy would have to take place in the near future. Without such a 'catastrophe' China's GDP will overtake the US – wishful thinking in light of this fact helping generate the prolific, if factually disreputable, genre of 'the coming China catastrophe' already referred to.[15]

China's transition from a poor to an upper-middle income economy

It is also important, with neither exaggeration nor understatement, to accurately understand the full degree to which China's extraordinarily rapid growth has already transformed its place in the world economy. Accurate understanding of this is indeed crucial for economic strategy. China has already made the transition, by international classifications, from a 'low' to an 'upper middle' income economy. As will be analysed below, within the coming decade a transition to a 'high income', that is prosperous, position will take place.[16] Nevertheless, the scale of China's transition is still underestimated, and perception of China's real position in the world economy frequently lags behind reality, due to common use of a misleading method of categorising and ranking countries without taking account their population. This method misleadingly gives the same weight to Monaco, a country with a population of under 40,000 and a higher per capita GDP than China, and India with a population of 1.2 billion, or Indonesia with a population of nearly 240 million, both of which have lower per capita GDPs than China. Such method of analysis has the effect of misrepresenting, not clarifying, China's real

position in the world economy. It also has negative consequences for analysing competitive economic strategy. Serious
calculations of China's position in the world economy must
take the population of different countries into account.

China's position in the world economy

To show the real scale of China's progress, in 1978, when
China's 'reform and opening up' began, less than 1% of the
world's population lived in countries with a per capita GDP
lower than China's measured at current dollar exchange
rates, while 74% lived in countries with a higher GDP per
capita.[17] By 2012 the situation was transformed. In current
dollars only 29% of the world's population lived in countries
with a higher per capita GDP than China and 51% lived in
countries with a lower per capita GDP. In PPP terms only
30% of the world population lived in countries with a higher
GDP per capita than China, while 50% lived in countries with
a lower one. [18] China had therefore moved into the top half
of the world's population in terms of economic development,
with less than a third of the world's population living in more
economically developed economies – see Figure 2. No such
dramatic improvement in the position of such a large proportion of the world's population has ever previously taken
place in human history. This is an index of the gigantic step
taken towards prosperity by China.

Level of development and economic strategy

The above fundamental facts are crucial bases not only for
analysing China's real position in the world economy but also
for China's economic and competitive strategy – as will be
extensively analysed in Chapter 8. It is misleading to think of
contemporary China as a 'poor' country: it is already a 'middle income' economy. As analysed in the next chapter, in less
than 10 years China will become a 'high income' economy
by international standards. The immediate consequence of
this is that it is already impossible for China to pursue any
successful economic strategy based primarily on low wages –
a number of competitor economies now have far lower wage
levels.[19] In particular China has a higher per capita GDP
than every developing economy in Asia except Malaysia – and

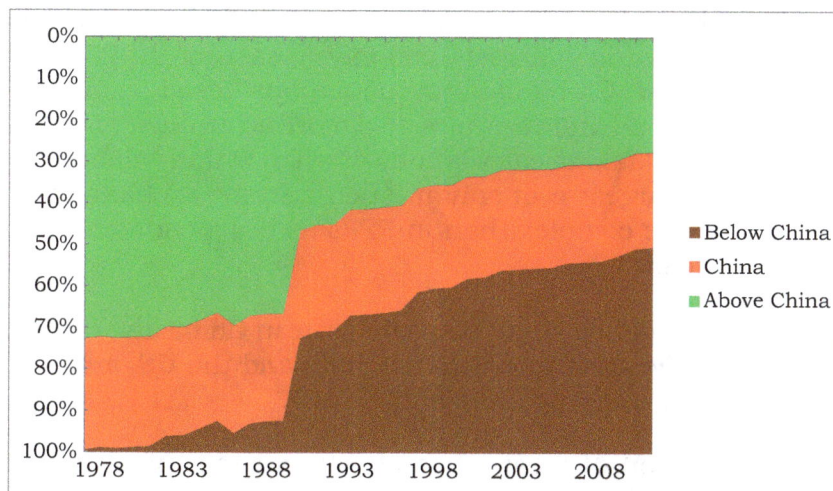

Figure 2: % of World Population Living in Countries with per Capita GDP Above and Below China - 1978-2012. Current US $ - countries for which data exists for all years 1978-2012.

Source: Calculated from World Bank World Development Indicators

China's wages show similar differences. According to the calculations of The Economist the average factory worker in China earns $27.50 per day, compared with $8.60 in Indonesia and $6.70 in Vietnam – that is, China's manufacturing wages are three times as high as Indonesia's and four times as high as Vietnam's. Nevertheless, for reasons analysed below, China's primary competitive advantage, in at least the coming decade, will necessarily still primarily be on price/value. But China's new level of development means that this price advantage must necessarily increasingly be gained not via low wages but by 'cost innovation' – use of high investment and innovations in technology and management to maintain a price advantage despite rising wages. It is for this fundamental reason that China must achieve an 'innovation driven' economy. The primary focus of China's innovations and R&D in the coming decade which this dictates will be analysed in Chapter 8 and Chapter 9.

When will China overtake the US?

Turning from China's overall position in the global economy to a narrower bilateral comparison with the US, it has already been seen that by World Bank calculations China became the world's largest economy, measured in PPPs, in 2014. However, China prefers calculations based on current exchange rates – and these are also more accurate for market calculations. Making calculations of when China will become the world's largest economy in such current exchange rate terms is more complex than in PPPs as it depends on three sets of variables

- the real inflation adjusted growth rate in China and the US;
- the relative inflation rates in China and the US, and
- the dollar exchange rate of the RMB.

For this reason of greater complexity, a range of estimates will be given. However, as will be seen, these do not alter time scales – China will become the world's largest economy at current exchange rates within a decade.

Analysing first the real growth figures to utilize to compare China and the US, it would be unreasonable to utilize the most recent US growth as this was severely depressed by the impact of the international financial crisis - in the last 10 years US annual average growth has been 1.7% and over the six years following the international financial crisis it was only slightly over 1%. To attain a more realistic figure, and to remove the effect of short term fluctuations, the 20 year moving average of annual US GDP growth is shown in Figure 3. This growth rate is 2.5%, rounded up the nearest half percentage point, and this figure will be used for calculations. Figure 3 also shows the US economy has a long term tendency to deceleration, so a 2.5% annual growth assumption is possibly slightly optimistic for the US.[20] Turning to inflation, since 2000 US inflation, the GDP deflator which must be used for such calculations, averages 2.1%. Taking this together with the real growth rate gives an annual average increase in US nominal GDP of 4.7%. Given the tendency of the US economy to deceleration this figure may be slightly optimistic.

If 4.7% growth in US nominal GDP is assumed, then China's growth in nominal dollar terms – that is China's real growth rate multiplied by the GDP deflator multiplied by the increase in the exchange rate of the RMB - would have to fall below 10.1% for China not to become the world's largest

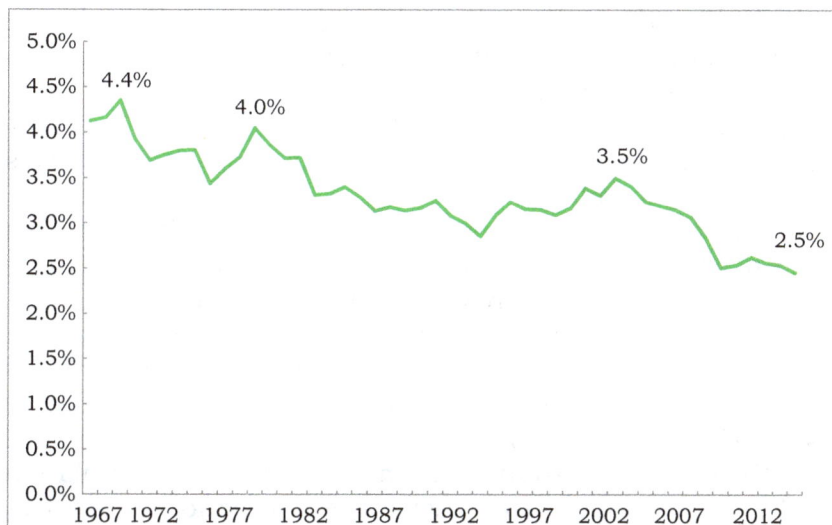

Figure 3: US GDP - Annual Average Growth Annual Average Growth Over a 20 Year Period

Source: Calculated from Bureau of Economic Analysis NIPA Table 1.1.3

economy by 2025. As a yardstick comparison it should be noted that in 1978-2013 China's average increase in nominal GDP was 12.5%. If the average 12.5% figure since 1979 were taken China would become the world's largest economy at current exchange rates in 2022. It is therefore clear that implausible assumptions would have to be made for China not to become the world's largest economy at current exchange rates in the next decade. The only factor that would break this trend would be severe deceleration of China's economy – the risks of which are analysed in Section 4 of this book.

Neither optimism nor pessimism but realism

The implications of the above assumptions should be clearly understood. They do not express 'optimism' or 'pessimism' on China's economy but necessary quantitative relations. If it is argued that China did not already become the world's largest economy in PPPs in 2014, or that it will not become the world's largest economy at market exchange rates during the next decade, it needs to be explained what alternative numbers should be taken - it must be explained, for example, why the US will grow more rapidly than an average 2.5%. In such serious matters, however, there is no virtue in either 'optimism' or in 'pessimism' there is only virtue in realism. Realistically, China is already the world's largest economy in PPP terms and within a decade China will be the world's largest economy at market prices.

These facts therefore give an indication of the awesome scale of China's economic achievement – the one that creates the potential basis for 'prosperity'. In seven decades, China's economy will have gone from being only one sixth the size of the US to overtaking it. China is a country which contains almost seven times the percentage of the world's population as the US at the time the latter commenced rapid economic growth, with more than four times the present population of the US, has more than twice the population of the EU, more than twice that of Latin America, almost twice that of Europe including Russia, and greater than the entire African continent. In short, the title of this chapter is no rhetoric: China's is simply and measurably the greatest economic achievement in human history. This unparalleled economic achievement is therefore what any analysis must explain.

Part 2: China's Achievement in Living Standards

Introductory Note – this is Chapter 3 of my book 'The Great Chess Game' published in April 2016

While China's economic growth is without historical precedent it is, as stressed at the beginning of this book, only a means to a more comprehensive human and national end. The aim of economic policy is not GDP growth, investment, or exports, but improvement of living standards, the achievement of prosperity, and establishment of the numerous dimensions constituting comprehensive 'national renewal' – including ability to protect the country's way of living against external threat.[21] Economic development is simply an indispensable means to achieve the China Dream.

Given this fact it is therefore important to evaluate attempts to claim that China's 'economic growth miracle' is more than offset by negative trends in other fields. One example is the claim known in China as 'historical nihilism' – the assertion that prior to accelerated economic growth after 1978 China's achievements from 1949 until that date were negligible or even negative. A similar claim is that, despite China's rapid economic growth after 1978 this was outweighed by negative trends in social, environmental or other fields. Evidently the goal of 'prosperity' in the real human sense, cannot be considered achieved if simple economic growth, or even increase in consumption, were more than offset by severe deterioration in social, environmental or other fields.

The facts, however, clearly show the exact reverse of these negative claims is true. First, China's social achievements under Mao Zedong were the greatest in any country in human history – and that is stated by someone who explicitly supports, for reasons analysed below, China's post-1978 economic policies inaugurated by Deng Xiaoping not the pre-1978 centrally administered economy. The claims of 'historical nihilism' are therefore fallacious. Similarly, far from the consequences of social, environmental and other factors being negative for China's development after 1978, the facts show clearly that the combined effect of these indicators are significantly better than would be expected solely from China's level of economic development.

Such realities, self-evidently, do not mean China does not confront numerous real problems in the social or environmental fields - as, to take a single example, smog and bad air quality in China rather graphically and regularly bring to everyone's attention. But they constitute a reminder that economic development, per capita GDP, is not merely an 'economic' factor with socially neutral consequences, but that it is powerfully, positively and closely related with highly desirable social and human developments such as longer life expectancy, better health, greater leisure and environmental protection. In light of this correlation of per capita GDP with other desirable goals China's developments in social, environmental, cultural and other fields, as with every country, cannot be evaluated in abstraction from its level of economic development, but only in terms of comparison to other countries at similar levels of development. These comparative studies show not only that China's economic growth raised its living standards, both in domestic terms and in comparison with the rest of the world, but that the positive social consequences of China's economic transformations are, in a measurable and verifiable way, even greater than its economic achievements.[22]

These realities immediately eliminate false myths and distortions about China's development – for example that China
has a slow growth of consumption and living standards,
or that environmental and other problems are sufficiently
severe in China to more than offset growth in economic
prosperity. In fact, China has long had the fastest growth of
consumption of any country, while objective factual indicators, most sensitively life expectancy, show that compared
to other countries China's life quality is better than would
be expected from its present stage of economic development.
Such facts clearly establish that the overall balance of China's social, environmental, educational and other trends are
ahead of even its dramatic economic growth. Following the
general method of this book, first the facts will be established
and then the reasons for their development will be analysed.

Pre-1978 developments

The superior post-1978 economic growth of China compared to the pre-reform period was analysed in Chapter 2.
Nevertheless, it would be misleading not to comprehend
the gigantic social achievements of the 1949-78 pre-reform
period. Indeed, these saw the greatest social advances ever
achieved in a similar period by any major country in human
history – improving the living and social conditions of a far
greater number of people, and a far greater proportion of
humanity, than ever achieved in any other country. This evidently casts a decisive light on rounded evaluation of the
pre-reform period, as well as placing in correct perspective
various issues of China's history and providing an understanding of features of China's internal dynamics.

Life expectancy and human well being

The most comprehensive criteria for judging the overall
impact of social and environmental conditions in a country
is average life expectancy - as this sums up and balances the
combined effect of all positive and negative economic, social,
environmental, health, educational and other trends.[23] Life
expectancy is therefore a more adequate measure of social
well-being than purely per capita GDP - significant as the
latter is, and despite per capita GDP being the single biggest

determinant of life expectancy. As Nobel Prize winner Amartya Sen summarized regarding the relation between these variables:

'Personal income is unquestionably a basic determinant of survival and death, and more generally of the quality of life of a person. Nevertheless, income is only one variable among many that affect our chances of enjoying life... The gross national product per head may be a good indicator of the average real income of the nation, but the actual incomes enjoyed by the people will also depend on the distributional pattern of that national income. Also, the quality of life of a person depends not only on his or her personal income, but also on various physical and social conditions... The nature of health care and the nature of medical insurance – public as well a private – are among the most important influences on life and death. So are the other social services, including basic education and the orderliness of urban living and the access to modern medical knowledge. There are, thus, many factors not included in the accounting of personal incomes that can be importantly involved in the life and death of people.'[24]

Taking first the long term development in the People's Republic of China, the trend of life expectancy, in relation to the most relevant comparison of India, the other largest developing economy, is shown in Figure 4.[25] In 1947, the year India achieved independence, its life expectancy was 32. China's life expectancy in 1949, the year of the creation of the People's Republic of China, was 35 – a gap of three years compared to India. By 1978, the last year of pre-reform China, China's life expectancy was 67 and India's 55 – a gap of 12 years. This sharply growing difference was not because India had a bad record - as an increase of 22 years in life expectancy over a 31-year period graphically shows. It is simply that China's performance was sensational – life expectancy increasing by 32 years in a 29-year chronological period. This means that in pre-reform China life expectancy increased by more than a year for every chronological year that passed - an annual average increase of 2.3%.

To understand the true scale of such an achievement in comparative terms, it need simply be noted that China's rate of increase of life expectancy in the three decades after 1949 was the fastest ever recorded in a major country in human history. For comparison:

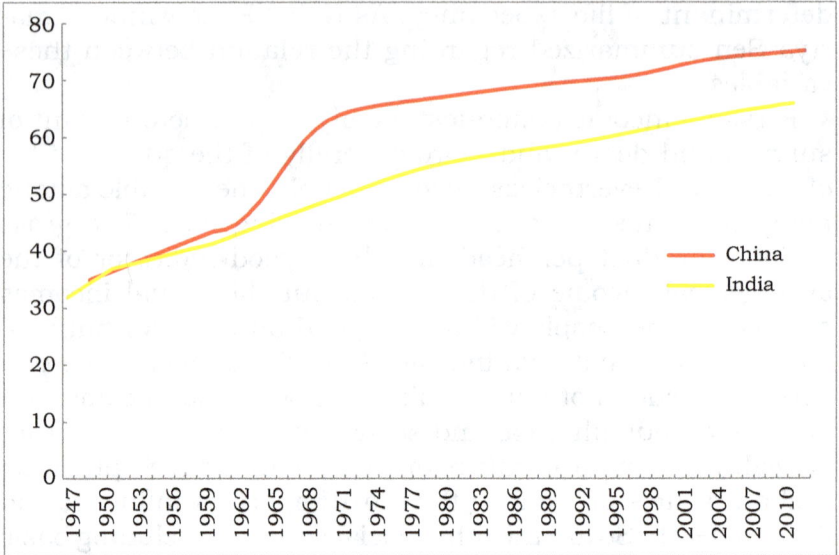

Figure 4: Life Expectancy – China and India in years

Sources: China 1949 Bergaglio 'Population Growth in China', India 1947 & 1951 Kuruganti 'Healthcare achievements of post-independent India,1960-2011 World Bank World Development Indicators

- The US in the thirty years after 1880, a period of sharp increase due to recovery from the Civil War, saw a 0.9% annual increase in life expectancy.[26]
- Life expectancy in the UK after 1871, a period of rapid growth, was under 1.0% a year.[27]
- Japan, a country considered to have an outstanding record in increasing life expectancy, and enjoying a rapid increase due to recovery from World War II, raised life expectancy by 1.3% a year in the 29 years after 1947.[28]
- China's 2.3% increase in life expectancy in 1949-78, therefore, far outperformed all these countries whose records, by normal standards, are considered exceptional.

When did life expectancy increase?

The period in which this spectacular increase in life expectancy was concentrated is highly interesting and casts a strong light on debates concerning China's historical development – and shows clearly the falsity of 'historical nihilism'. During the 1950s China made very creditable progress – life expectancy increasing by an average of slightly over nine months in each chronological year. India's performance in this period was comparable – between 1947 and 1960 its life expectancy increased by slightly less than nine months for each chronological year. India continued this progress in the period up to 1978, with life expectancy rising by slightly under nine months for each chronological year. But after the 1950s China's life expectancy began to rise extremely rapidly. Between 1960 and 1970 China's life expectancy increased by a dramatic one year and nine months per chronological year. Over the entire period 1960-78 China's life expectancy grew by an average one year and three months per chronological year.

This spectacular, indeed historically unprecedented, social achievement during 1949-78 does not overturn the analysis made in Chapter 2 of economic developments in this period, nor of political judgements concerning the Great Leap Forward and Cultural Revolution. But it shows clearly that attempts to present the pre-1978 period in an overall negative social light, as 'historical nihilism', and as represented in the West by a series of book attempting to present pre- reform China as socially disastrous, is, to put it straightforwardly, a blatant falsification.[29] In the 27 years between the establishment of the People's Republic of China in 1949, and the death of Mao Zedong in 1976, life expectancy in China increased by 31 years – or over a year per chronological year. In comparison, in the 27 years after India's independence average life expectancy increased by 19 years. Far from being negative, China's record in this period was one of history's most extraordinary social achievements.

Instead of engaging in factual falsification and myth making, foreigners can better understand the support for Mao Zedong in China, even leaving aside other issues, such as the achievement of real national independence, merely by the lived experience of this fact. If someone leads you to live an extra 31 years it is unsurprising you hold them in esteem!

In contrast to historical fabrications, Deng Xiaoping, who with his family suffered considerably during the Cultural Revolution, was therefore extremely balanced in his assessment of Mao Zedong, insisting not on taking individual episodes out of context but on taking the overall trajectory of the period, which saw immense steps forward for China. Historical accuracy certainly means clearly noting that economic growth was superior after 1978, but this should not lead to underestimation of the astonishing social achievements of the preceding pre-reform period. Xi Jinping put it very precisely on these two periods of China's post-1949 development:

'The two phases – at once related to and distinct from each other – are both pragmatic explorations in building socialism conducted by the people under the leadership of the Party. Chinese socialism was initiated after the launch of reform and opening up and based on more than 20 years of development since the socialist system was established in the 1950s after the People's Republic of China (PRC) was founded. Although the two historical phases are very different in their guiding thoughts, principles, policies, and practical work, they are by no means separated from or opposed to each other. We should neither negate the pre- reform-and-opening-up phase in comparison with the post-reform-and-opening-up phase, nor the converse.[30]'

China has the world's fastest growth in living standards

Turning to post-1978 development, analysis will start with the most direct impact of GDP growth on China's living standards and prosperity – increase in the population's consumption of goods and services. While consumption is not the only determinant of living standards, as is analysed later, nevertheless it is crucial for them. Table 2 therefore shows growth rates of consumption for the major economies – the G8 and BRIC. Both the increase of household consumption and that for total consumption (including not only household consumption but state expenditure on crucial factors for quality of life such as health and education) is given. The major economies are selected as, given China's size, the appropriate comparison is with these - not relatively small states for example in the Caribbean. Nevertheless, including small economies would make no difference, China would still be shown to have the world's fastest growth rate both of household and total consumption.

The fundamental period of comparison taken in Table 2 is from the beginning of China's reform in 1978 to 2012 - the latest date for which total consumption figures are available

Table 2

Annual % change - measured in inflation adjusted 2005 dollars				
	Household Consumption		Total Consumption	
	1978-2012	1990-2012	1978-2012	1990-2012
China	7.7%	8.1%	7.9%	8.5%
India	5.3%	5.9%	5.4%	5.9%
Russia	n/a	4.1%	n/a	3.2%
Brazil	3.2%	3.7%	3.2%	3.3%
US	3.0%	2.9%	2.7%	2.6%
Canada	2.7%	2.8%	2.4%	2.5%
UK	2.8%	2.4%	2.4%	2.3%
France	1.8%	1.5%	1.9%	1.6%
Germany	1.6%	1.2%	1.5%	1.3%
Japan	2.1%	1.1%	2.3%	1.4%
Italy	1.7%	0.8%	1.6%	0.8%
Source: Calculated from World Bank World Development Indicators				

for all countries. However, as data is not available for Russia before 1990, a comparison for 1990-2012 is also given.

The comparative trends shown in Table 2 are clear. China's average annual increase in total consumption was 7.9% in 1978-2012 and 8.5% in 1990-2012. The increase in household consumption in the same periods was 7.7% and 8.1%. China's are therefore easily the world's highest growth rates of both household and total consumption.

In particular, in comparison to China:

- India, which ranked second after China, had an annual rate of total consumption increase in the same periods of 5.4% and 5.9%, and its rates of increase of household consumption were 5.3% and 5.9%.
- The US had an annual growth rate of total consumption of 2.7% in 1978-2011 and 2.6% in 1990-2012. US growth rates of household consumption were 2.7% and 2.6% in the same periods. China's consumption growth rate was therefore almost three times as fast as the US.
- As it is illustrative to make a comparison between the economic reform path pursued in China and Russia, a

country which underwent full privatization, it is worth noting that Russia's growth in household consumption in 1990-2012 was only 4.1%, compared to China's 8.1%, and Russia's growth in total consumption was only 3.2% compared to China's 8.5%.

As China had the world's fastest growth of consumption, why does the entirely erroneous statement sometimes appear that China is weak in developing consumption? This claim commits the elementary economic mistake of confusing China's growth rate of consumption, the world's highest, with its percentage of consumption in GDP – which is low. However, what practically affects a population's living standards is how fast their real consumption grows, not the percentage of consumption in GDP. To demonstrate that it is merely necessary to note that the percentage of consumption in GDP of the Democratic Republic of the Congo is 89%, far above China's, but it is the world's poorest country for which data exists. No sane person would choose to exchange the 8.5% growth in consumption in China for the living standard of the Democratic People's Republic of the Congo on the grounds that the latter had a higher percentage of consumption in GDP!

Poverty

The above figures are for average changes in consumption. However, perhaps the most impressive of all China's statistics, from the point of view of human welfare, is its contribution to the reduction of human poverty - not only within its own borders but in terms of its impact on reduction of world poverty. The facts show that China has been responsible for the *entire* reduction in the number of people living in absolute poverty in the world. A point rightly emphasized by Professor Danny Quah.[31] This fact clearly demonstrates that while inequality in China, as is admitted domestically, has risen to levels which are excessive, and need to be corrected, it is entirely false to present any picture that China's economic development has only benefitted those at the top. It is the improvements at the bottom of society which, from an international viewpoint, and that of human welfare, are most striking.

To show this, Table 3 gives the numbers of those in China and the world living on expenditures which are less than the two standard criteria used by the World Bank to measure poverty. These are for extreme poverty, expenditure of less than $1.25 a day ($37.5 a month), and those living in poverty – expenditure of $2.00 a day ($60 a month).

In 1981, on World Bank data, 835 million people in China were living on expenditure of less than $1.25 a day. By 2008 this was reduced to 173 million while by 2009 it fell to 157 million. Therefore 662 million people were lifted out of extreme poverty in China in the 27 years up to 2008, and 678 million by 2009. In contrast, the number of people living in such extreme poverty outside China increased by 50 million between 1981 and 2008.[32] Consequently China was responsible for 100% of the world's reduction of the number

Table 3

Number living on expenditure of under $2 a day (million)					
	1981	2008	2010*	Change 1981-2008	Change 1981-2010*
China	972	395	362	-577	-610
East Asia excluding China	302	249	n/a	-53	n/a
Latin America	84	69	59	-15	-25
Eastern Europe	19	6	6	-13	-13
Middle East & North Africa	52	44	40	-8	-12
Sub-Saharan Africa	284	580	603	296	319
South Asia	807	1,109	1,072	302	265
Total	2,520	2,452	n/a	-68	n/a
Total excluding China	1,548	2,057	n/a	509	n/a
Number living on expenditure of under $1.25 a day (million)					
China	835	173	157	-662	-678
East Asia excluding China	229	105	n/a	-124	n/a
Latin America	42	36	31	-6	-11

Eastern Europe	4	1	2	-3	-2
Middle East & North Africa	17	9	8	-8	-9
Sub-Saharan Africa	202	563	418	361	216
South Asia	566	402	499	-164	-67
Total	1,895	1,289	n/a	-606	n/a
Total excluding China	1,060	1,116	n/a	56	n/a

*China figure is for 2009
Source: Calculated from World Bank World Development Indicators

of people living in extreme poverty. These trends are shown in Figure 5.

Analysing those living on $2 a day, still a very low figure, the trend was even more striking. The number of people in China living on an expenditure of this figure, or below, fell from 972 million in 1981, to 395 million in 2008, to 362 million in 2009. The number therefore fell by 577 million by 2008, and by 610 million by 2009 – see Figure 6. In contrast the number of those living at this level of poverty in the world outside China rose from 1,548 million in 1981 to 2,057 million in 2008 – an increase of 509 million. Again, China accounted for the entire reduction in the number of people in the world living at this level of poverty.

Indirect consequences of poverty reduction

Given these trends in income, consumption and living standards, it is almost impossible to exaggerate the contribution China's economic progress made not only to its own people but to the welfare of humanity. But it is also clear that the gigantic impact of this for human well-being is not only through its direct effect on personal income and expenditure, but in its indirect consequences for human welfare. Indeed these latter indirect factors are possibly as important as the direct increases in consumption. As Sen notes:

Life expectancy has a significantly positive relation with GNP per head, but... the relationship works mainly through the impact of GNP on (1) the incomes specifically of the poor,

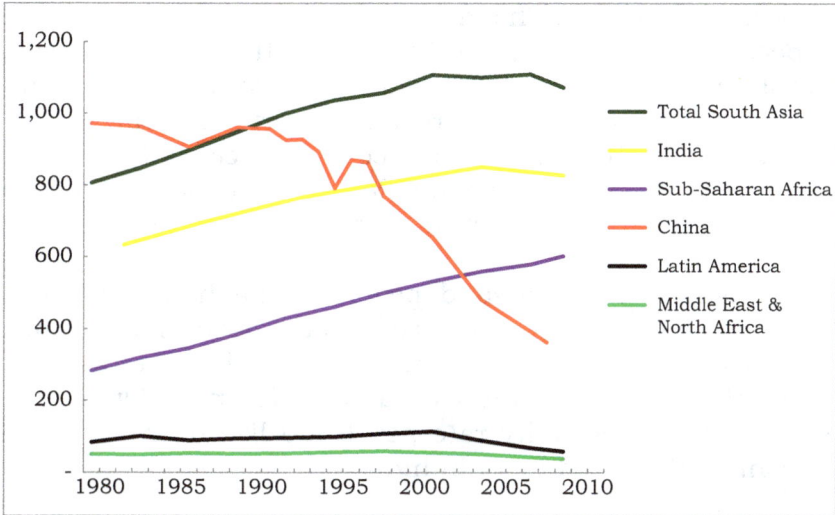

Figure 5: Number of People Living on Expenditure of $2 a Day or Less (million people -income measured in PPPs)

Source: Calculated from World Bank World Development Indicators

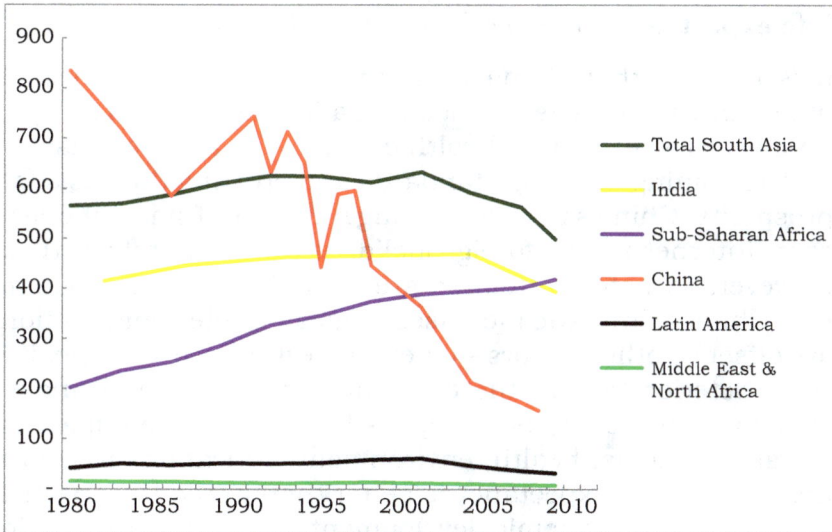

Figure 6: Number of People Living on Expenditure of $1.25 a Day or Less (million people - income measured in PPPs)

Source: Calculated from World Bank World Development Indicators

and (2) public expenditure, specifically on public health. In fact, once these two variables are included in the statistical relation, the connection between GNP and life expectancy altogether vanishes. This does not, of course, imply that life expectancy is not enhanced by the growth of GNP per head, but it does indicate that the connection works through public expenditure on health care, and poverty removal. [33]

The working through of these consequences in China may again be seen by simple examples, again making comparisons with the other largest developing country - India.

- Measured per thousand people China had 66% more nurses and midwives and 160% more doctors than India.
- In China the literacy rate for women aged 15-24 was 99%, on the latest World Bank data, while for India it was 74%.
- The infant mortality rate per 1,000 live births is 12 in China compared to 44 in India.

Evidently such facts substantially contributed to the dramatic improvement in social conditions reflected in the life expectancy data.

Life expectancy and overall social conditions

It is obvious that China's rise in consumption – reflected materially in increase in food quality, housing, holidays, phones, cars, furniture, health care etc. – is a decisive factor in determining its living standards and creating the basis for prosperity. China's rapidly growing numbers of smartphones, cars, internet users, foreign holidays trips etc. reflect this. However, as noted, attempts are sometimes made to claim that China's dramatic increases in measurable consumption are offset by other factors – for example weaknesses in health care, deterioration in the environment etc. Factual analysis shows the reality is the opposite. Data on the impact of social conditions, health, environment, education etc. show that China's life expectancy is better than would be expected purely from its economic development. This, evidently, again does not indicate that there are not negative factors, nor is this being argued, but that these are clearly and considerably outweighed in China by positive trends.

This fact can be tested objectively. As already noted, life expectancy provides the most sensitive indicator of overall living conditions. Earlier, to assess the pre-1978 period, a comparison was made of China with the second largest

developing country – India. Comprehensive comparative
data does not exist to allow a comparison for all countries
back to 1949, however for the post- 1978 period it is possible
to make a systematic comparison with most countries.

To provide an overall framework Figure 7 confirms clearly
the high degree globally to which life expectancy is primarily determined by the direct and indirect consequences of a
country's per capita GDP – prosperity makes you live longer!
It shows the correlation of per capita GDP and life expectancy
in 2011 - the latest year for which comprehensive international data exists. Coverage is for all 117 countries for which
annual records exist from 1980-2011 – these states include
the overwhelming majority of the world's population. It may
be seen differences in per capita GDP account for 71% of
differences in life expectancy.[34]

In order to explore this correlation with the most comprehensive data available Figure 8 shows the relation between
per capita GDP and life expectancy for every country for
every year between 1980 and 2011 in which World Bank
comparative statistics exist for even a single year. Taking

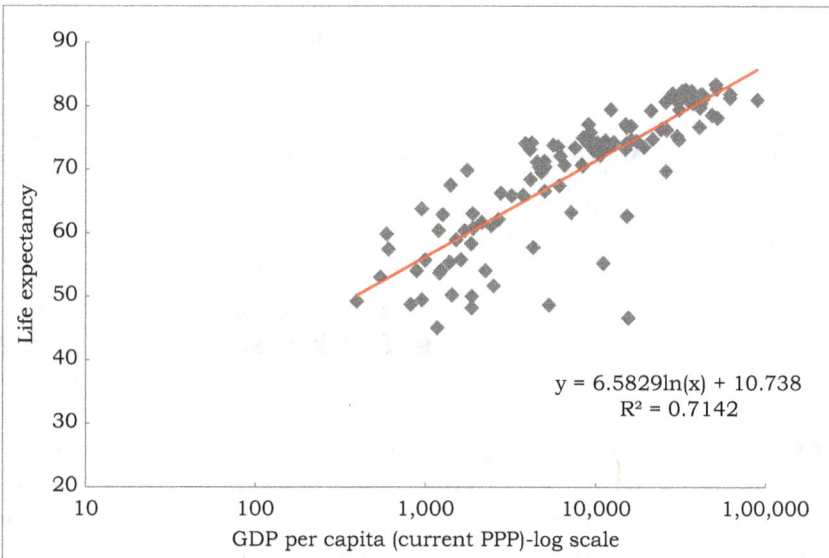

$$y = 6.5829\ln(x) + 10.738$$
$$R^2 = 0.7142$$

Figure 7: GDP Per Capita & Life Expectancy in 2011 GDP per
capita in current PPPs, life expectancy in years

Source: Calculated from World Bank World Developments Indiators, all
117 countries for which full annual data exists in 1960-2011

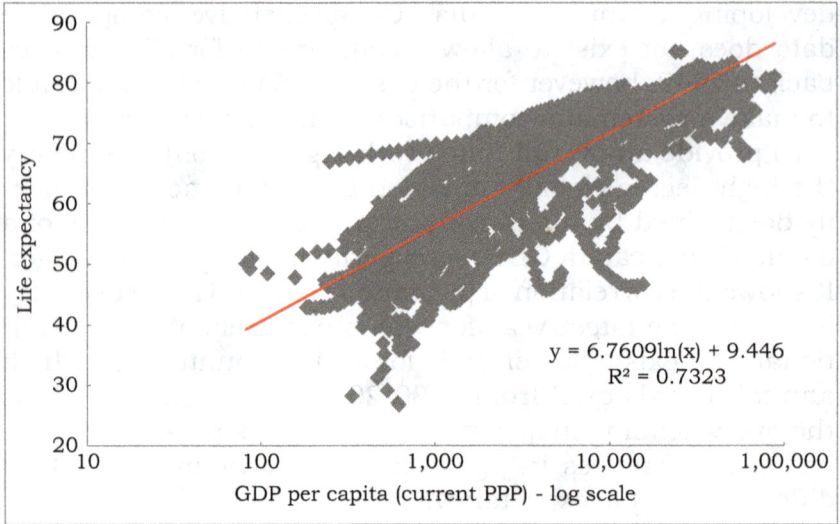

Figure 8: GDP Per Capita & Life Expectancy 1980-2011 GDP per
capita in current PPPs, life expectancy in years

Source: Calculated from World Bank World Developments Indiators, all
117 countries for which full annual data exists in 1960-2011

this larger sample, per capita GDP accounts for 73% of the
differences in life expectancy between countries. In short,
per capita GDP is the overwhelmingly decisive factor in life
expectancy.

Other factors in life expectancy than GDP

It may be seen immediately from the above data that life
expectancy rises rapidly with increases in per capita GDP –
internationally, on average, doubling GDP per capita adds
four years and six months to a man's life expectancy and five
years to a woman's. But this itself is a key fact for discussion of
international development as well as that of China. It shows it
is a fundamental mistake to present GDP growth as simply a
question of accumulating steel or chemicals, as is sometimes
suggested. Instead rising GDP has dramatic social and personal consequences – i.e. rising per capita GDP is not socially
'neutral' but is highly socially positive. An accurate judgement regarding China was therefore made by David Pilling in
the *Financial Times*: 'Life expectancy has more than doubled
from 35 in 1949 to 75 today, a miraculous achievement.'[35]

Nevertheless, although almost three quarters of differences in life expectancy between countries are explained by per capita GDP, this equally means that slightly over a quarter of such differences are determined by other factors – again indicating life expectancy is a sensitive indicator of overall social wellbeing.[36] These differences measure the positive or negative effects of environmental, health, education and other factors in addition to the quantitatively dominant one of per capita GDP.

In 2011, on the basis of international averages, China's life expectancy would be 70 based on its per capita GDP, but it was actually 73 on World Bank data. For comparison in the US life expectancy would be expected to be 81 but was actually 79. In China people live therefore three years longer than would be expected from its level of economic development, whereas in the US life expectancy is two years less than would be expected from its economic development level. China's data therefore clearly demonstrates that far from health services, environment, education etc. being negative factors they add to life expectancy, whereas in the US these other factors subtract from it.

What life expectancy shows about social conditions in China

A more comprehensive examination confirms these key trends. It is relatively simple to compare a country's economic development with its life expectancy. Comparing a country's rank in world per capita GDP with its rank in life expectancy shows whether factors other than per capita GDP are leading to a country's people living longer or less compared to what would be expected solely from its economic development level.[37]

Table 4 therefore shows the rank for per capita GDP and rank for life expectancy for the major economies – the G7 plus the BRIC developing economies. These are sub-divided into the 7 major advanced economies and the 4 major developing economies. As can be seen, China rates 86th in per capita GDP but 75th in life expectancy – i.e. China's life expectancy is 11 places higher than would be expected from its level of economic development.

Table 4

Comparison of World Rank in Life Expectancy and GDP per capita for G7 and BRIC economies in 2011		
Country	World life expectancy rank	Life expectancy rank compared to GDP per capita rank
	Developing Economies	
China	75	+11
Brazil	78	-10
Russia	104	-60
India	119	-3
	Advanced Economies	
Japan	3	+22
Italy	6	+20
France	12	+12
Canada	18	-1
UK	21	+2
Germany	23	-4
US	34	-23
Source: Calculated from World Bank World Development Indicators		

Considering first developed economies:

- Life expectancy in the UK and Germany is close to what would be expected from per capita GDP.
- France, Japan and Italy all have life expectancies which are significantly higher than would be expected from their per capita GDP.

The strikingly negative data is for the US. Life expectancy in the US is significantly shorter than would be expected from its level of economic development. The US has the highest per capita GDP of any major developed economy but the lowest life expectancy - life expectancy is 83 in Japan, 82 in Italy and France, 81 in the UK and Germany, 80 in Canada but only 79 in the US. The inhabitant of any other major developed country should therefore expect to live longer than in the US. US life expectancy rank is 23 places below where it would be expected to be judged only by per capita GDP. In the US there is therefore clearly a significantly negative effect of factors other than GDP per capita - such as health services, environment, education etc.

China and the BRICS

If the US has a far lower life expectancy than other major developed countries, the situation with China is the reverse. China has the longest life expectancy of any of the major developing BRIC economies, even although it does not yet have the highest of their per capita GDP's. Life expectancy was 66 in India, 69 in Russia, 73 years and 5 months in Brazil and 73 years and 6 months in China - despite Brazil's per capita GDP being 29% higher than China's and Russia's per capita GDP being more than double China's. Returning to bilateral comparisons with the US, therefore far from China's health services, environment, education etc. detracting from its social situation they clearly augment it compared to what would be expected purely from its per capita GDP, whereas in the US the effect of such factors are negative. In short the overall effect of social and environmental conditions, compared to per capita GDP, is negative in the US but positive in China!

This data evidently casts a clear light on discussions regarding China's economy and social conditions. As people in China live significantly longer than would be expected, given China's level of economic development, any claim China's rapid rise in GDP or consumption is more than offset, in terms of rising living standards, by health, environmental or other considerations is false – the reverse of reality. Overall China's life expectancy is three years higher than would be expected from per capita GDP - showing that the positive balance of health, environmental, educational and other factors significantly outweighs negative ones. The evidence is therefore clear that environmental, health and other factors affecting life quality are superior in China than would be expected for its level of economic development.

Such data is naturally not intended as grounds for complacency. What have been analysed here are growth rates, and position relative to economic development, not absolute levels. China's life expectancy on World Bank data (73.5 years) is still significantly behind the US (78.6 years) let alone Italy (82.1 years) or Japan (82.6 years). Consequently, China must still undergo a prolonged period of economic development before it achieves the highest levels of advanced economies. More precisely, for people in China to live even longer in the future, which in turn is a key indicator of quality of life, two things are required.

- Above all, China's GDP must continue to grow – this will contribute almost three quarters of any increase in life expectancy.
- China must maintain, and if possible improve still further, those factors which mean people in China already live longer than would be expected from its level of economic development.

As a long life would certainly be part of most people's 'China dream' seriously internalizing these facts in discussion of economic policy is rather important - indeed a literal 'life or death' question!

GDP growth and living standards

Finally, these social facts cast light on the discussion in the recent period in China that the goal of economic policy should be increase in living standards, not GDP growth. This point is correct but as formulated is misleading, as it neglects the fact that increase in per capita GDP is not socially neutral, but is highly correlated with desirable social trends reflected in increase in life expectancy. As shown above, other factors can reduce life expectancy below that which would be expected from per capita GDP – or can increase life expectancy above the level that would be expected from per capita GDP. Therefore, the goal of policy should, indeed, be the most rapid possible sustainable increase in living standards, not GDP growth. But it is necessary not to throw the baby out with the bathwater. It has to be clearly understood it is impossible to achieve high living standards *without* GDP growth. The fallacious idea that 'prosperity can be achieved by sharing out scarcity' used to be an argument of extreme 'leftist' views in China.[38] However a new 'rightest' variant has emerged in which it is argued that China does not need high GDP growth to achieve high living standards.

The fallacy of this argument can be illustrated simply. Figure 9 shows the correlation between GDP growth and total consumption growth for all countries for which World Bank data exists for the period 1978-2011 – the latest available statistics for most countries. Increases in GDP account for 81% of increases in consumption with a correlation of 0.86 – an extraordinarily close relation. In short, nothing else even comes close to accounting for increases in consumption as GDP growth. High living standards in China can only be achieved by high economic growth.

The consequences of this reality also may be illustrated by a bilateral comparison with the US. Despite China's economic growth, US per capita GDP is over four times China's even measured in PPPs. To simplify comparisons, if it is assumed both the US and China invested nothing, then even if the whole of China's existing GDP were shared out among its population the average person in China would only have per capita consumption less than one quarter that of the US. Anyone who believes China can content itself with a living standard less than one quarter that of the US clearly does not know what 'prosperity' constitutes.

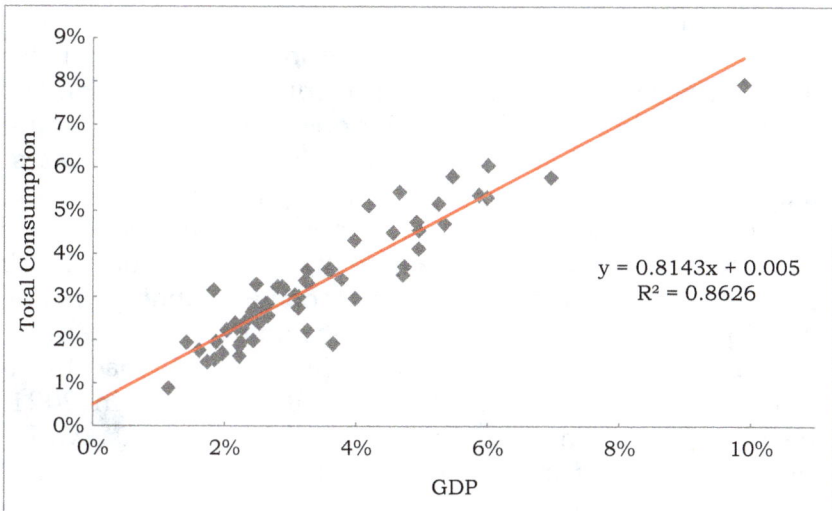

$$y = 0.8143x + 0.005$$
$$R^2 = 0.8626$$

Figure 9: All Countries - Correlation of GDP Growth & Total Consumption Growth 1978-2011 Annual % growth in inflation adjusted dollars

Source: Calculated from World Bank World Development Indicators

Taking into account the extremely close correlation between GDP growth and consumption, and the dominant effect of per capita GDP on life expectancy, China's long term goal cannot be less than living standards equal to the highest in the world. To achieve this aim, consequently, China must undergo rapid GDP growth continuing for several decades. High GDP growth is therefore not the aim of economic policy, that should be the maximum sustainable rate of growth of living standards and national regeneration - the economic policy consequences of this are considered in Chapter 15. But nevertheless it remains the case that prosperity cannot be achieved without a high rate of economic growth.

When will China become a high income economy?

Finally, to turn to future trends, if China has already made the transition from a poor to a middle income economy by international criteria, how long will it take to make the transition to a high income one – that is to achieve prosperity by global standards? As the timescale for achieving this is rather close if the correct policies are pursued, being 10 years or less, it is also rather easy to calculate.

The official World Bank definition of a high income economy in 2012 was one with a Gross National Income (GNI) per capita of more than $12,616 at current exchange rates. The percentage of the world's population living in such economies was 21.7% of the world's total population.[39] The latest comparable data for China, calculated by the specific method used by the World Bank for such rankings, was a GNI per capita for 2011 of $4,900.[40] Assuming that the World Bank increases its definition of a high income economy in line with China's inflation, and taking the same growth assumptions as in the previous chapter, China would become a high income economy by international standards in 2021. Following the method of this book, of taking conservative but reasonable assumptions, it may therefore be stated that within a decade China can become a high income economy by international standards.

The consequences of this achievement not only for China but for the world are of globally transforming dimensions. High income economies account for 21.7% of the world's population, and 22.8% of the world's population for which there exists Gross National Income data.[41] However China by itself accounted for 19.2% of the world's population. China's population is almost equal to the entire population already living in high income economies. China becoming a high income economy will therefore in one step almost double the number of people living in high income economies in the world. This will not only constitute a milestone in the 'China Dream' but is a further illustration of why the 'China Dream' will necessarily transform the global order.

In summary, with the correct policies prosperity is within China's grasp. But can it be achieved it, and what obstacles can those hostile to China's national rejuvenation and prosperity attempt to place in its path? This forms the subject matter of the rest of this book.

Section 2

Other countries can learn from China's socialist development strategy

Other countries can learn from China's socialist development strategy

15 August 2016

This article demonstrates that the 1st, 2nd, 3rd, and 4th fastest growing economies during the period since the putting forward of the neo-liberal 'Washington Consensus' all follow, or are highly influenced by, China's development model. These are the socialist states of China and Vietnam, Cambodia, and the Laos People's Democratic Republic. In contrast capitalist development models, including the Washington Consensus, have been a failure in comparison. China's anti-socialists do not wish these facts to be generally known – because it clearly destroys their claim that China should abandon its socialist path of development and adopt a capitalist one.

These facts also have international political implications. The socialist development model followed by China is the creation of the Communist Party of China (CPC). The Washington Consensus is the dominant economic strategy put forward by international economic institutions such as the IMF and World Bank and is taught in Western universities. The overwhelming economic superiority of the performance of countries following or highly influenced by China's socialist development model shows that China's economy not only outperformed capitalist alternatives but the CPC 'out thought' Western economic models.

A detailed theoretical analysis of the reasons that China's development model outperformed capitalist alternatives is made in my book 一盘大棋？中国新命运解析. It is therefore not dealt with here. The focus here is simply on establishing the facts – facts which clearly establish the outperformance by China's socialist development model of any capitalist alternative, and therefore which anti-socialists in China carefully wish to conceal.

*   *   *

This article compares factually the international results of two different economic development approaches – one which will be termed China's 'socialist development strategy' versus the 'neo-liberal' Washington Consensus. The latter is the dominant economic development strategy advocated by capitalist countries.

The reasons to make such a factual comparison should be clear. The wise Chinese phrase says 'seek truth from facts'. Put in international language this dictum asserts the only basis of scientific analysis: that if facts and theory do not coincide it is the theory that has to be abandoned not the facts suppressed. 'Dogmatism', a fundamentally anti-scientific approach, consists of clinging to a theory even when the facts entirely contradict it.

Despite this requirement for factual study supporters of the Washington Consensus appear to strongly dislike systematic factual comparisons of the two development approaches. The reasons for this will become evident from the data below. This shows that China's 'socialist development strategy' far outperforms the neo-liberal 'Washington Consensus'.

The term 'Washington Consensus' was first coined in 1989 by US based economist John Williamson - although the actual practical policies were commenced in the late 1970s/ early 1980s. The Washington Consensus is a classic form of 'neo-liberalism'. It advocates in terms of economic policy privatisation and minimisation of the state's economic role. Its social policy may be described as 'trickle down' – a belief that if there is economic growth all layers of society will automatically benefit as the benefits 'trickle down' from richest to poorest. Legally the Washington Consensus states the overriding goal is the strongest guarantees of private property. Politically, although claiming to be neutral, this combination of policies evidently favours capitalist and conservative political parties.

China's 'socialist development strategy,' which commenced with its 1978 economic reforms, is radically different in its entire framework and directly counterposed on key policy issues. China used, in Xi Jinping's phraseology on economic policy, both the 'visible' and the 'invisible hand' – not simply the private sector but also the state. Indeed, in China itself, as the 3rd Plenum of the Central Committee of the 18th Congress of the CPC insisted: 'We must unswervingly consolidate and develop the public economy, persist in the dominant position of public ownership, give full play to the leading role of the state-owned sector.'

In social policy, accompanying the economic dominance of the state sector, China did not rely on 'trickle down' but, in line with its socialist approach, China:

- undertook massive and conscious programmes deliberately aimed at eradicating poverty – these are to be completed in the 13th Five Year Plan by 2020 by lifting the remaining 70 million people out of poverty;
- China deliberately promotes development through urbanisation as a way of moving the population into higher productivity economic sectors;
- China deliberately sought to narrow the income gap between rural and urban areas;
- China does not rely exclusively on 'the market' but deliberately uses state infrastructure spending to raise the economic level of its less developed inland provinces;
- legally China guaranteed private property but a key economic role was assigned to the state sector,
- politically China was socialist.
- What, therefore, were the factual outcomes of these two radically different approaches to economic development? To assess this, for reasons which will become evident from the statistics, not only will China itself be analysed but three other countries will be considered. These are Vietnam, which defines itself as socialist and which in reality drew heavily from China's 'socialist market economy' approach, Cambodia, and the Lao People's Democratic Republic – the latter two also being highly influenced by China's development model.

The facts are summarised in Table 5 which shows the annual average rate of per capita GDP growth up to 2015 from 1978, when China began its economic reforms, from 1989, when

Table 5

Per Capita GDP Growth at Inflation Adjusted Prices			
	1978-2015	1989-2015	1993-2015
	Annual average % growth rate		
China	8.6%	8.8%	8.8%
Cambodia	n/a	n/a	5.5%
Vietnam	n/a	5.4%	5.4%
Laos PDR	n/a	4.8%	5.2%
Average all countries[1]	1.6%	1.8%	2.3%
Median all countries[1]	1.5%	1.6%	2.0%
	Rank		
China	1	1	1
Cambodia	n/a	n/a	2
Vietnam	n/a	2	3
Laos PDR	n/a	3	4
Total countries with data[1]	70	85	94

1. Non-oil dominated economies with populations of more than 5 million in 2015 with data for the period
Source: Calculated from World Bank World Development Indicators

the Washington Consensus was put forward, and from 1993 when data for Cambodia becomes available.

The data is of course extremely striking – indeed conclusive. From 1993-2015, when all four countries can be analysed China, Cambodia, Vietnam and Laos ranked respectively 1st, 2nd 3rd, and 4th in world per capita GDP growth – peripheral cases of countries with populations of less than 5 million or dominated by oil production are not included. From 1989, the date of the putting forward of the Washington Consensus, to 2015 China, Vietnam and Laos ranked respectively 1st, 2nd and 3rd in the world for countries in per capita GDP growth. From 1978 onwards China ranked 1st among all economies in terms of economic growth.

The degree to which economies influenced by the 'China development model' outgrew the world average was huge. From 1978 onwards China's rate of growth was almost six times the world average Since 1989 China again grew almost six times as fast as the world average while Vietnam and Laos grew over three times as fast as the world average.

The contrasts not only of average per capital GDP growth but in eradication of poverty were overwhelming. From 1981 China lifted 728 million people out of World Bank defined poverty. Another socialist country, Vietnam, lifted over 30 million from poverty by the same criteria. The whole of the rest of the world, in which the dominant model advocated by the IMF was the Washington Consensus, lifted only slightly 120 million people out of poverty. In summary 83% of the reduction of the number of those living in poverty was in China, 85% was in socialist countries, and only 15% of the reduction in the number of those living in poverty was in capitalist countries.

This data, of course, also destroys the claim that is 'capitalism' which has produced rapid economic growth and poverty reduction. If capitalism were the motor of rapid economic growth and poverty reduction then this growth would be most rapid, and poverty reduction greatest, in capitalist countries. Instead it is in socialist China and socialist Vietnam that the greatest poverty reduction has taken place Socialist China and socialist Vietnam, together with the countries they influence Cambodia and Laos, have seen the fastest economic growth.

China's 'socialist development model' therefore was a huge success while the Washington Consensus was a failure. Economic development remains the most fundamental issues for the overwhelming majority of the world's population- on the latest World Bank data, 84% of the world's population lives in developing countries. Any objective analysis based on aiming to maximise a countries development potential would therefore start with China's 'socialist development model.' The facts of world economic development show that China's development policies of a huge role for the state sector, large scale conscious policies to eradicate poverty, and a socialist political orientation were the most successful in producing both economic growth and poverty reduction.

The simple but decisive fact that the 1st, 2nd, 3rd and 4th most rapidly growing economies during the period of the Washington Consensus all use the 'China socialist development model' is the factual demonstration of the superiority of China's socialist development path to any capitalist alternative.

Appendix
Per Capita GDP growth rates

Annual Average Per Capita GDP Growth at Inflation Adjusted Prices						
	Rank			% growth		
	1978-2015	1989-2015	1993-2015	1978-2015	1989-2015	1993-2015
China	1	1	1	8.6%	8.8%	8.8%
Cambodia	n/a	n/a	2	n/a	n/a	5.5%
Vietnam	n/a	2	3	n/a	5.4%	5.4%
Lao PDR	n/a	3	4	n/a	4.8%	5.2%
India	5	4	5	4.0%	4.7%	5.2%
Mozambique	n/a	7	6	n/a	4.3%	5.2%
Ethiopia	n/a	16	7	n/a	3.3%	4.7%
Sri Lanka	6	5	8	4.0%	4.5%	4.6%
Belarus	n/a	n/a	9	n/a	n/a	4.3%
Poland	n/a	n/a	10	n/a	n/a	4.3%
Mali	11	13	11	2.8%	3.5%	4.2%
Korea, Rep.	2	6	12	5.2%	4.4%	4.0%
Slovak Republic	n/a	n/a	13	n/a	n/a	4.0%
Kazakhstan	n/a	n/a	14	n/a	n/a	3.9%
Uzbekistan	n/a	28	15	n/a	2.4%	3.9%
Bangladesh	13	10	16	2.8%	3.6%	3.8%
Dominican Republic	12	15	17	2.8%	3.3%	3.7%
Peru	41	20	18	1.4%	2.8%	3.6%
Romania	n/a	n/a	19	n/a	n/a	3.6%
Bulgaria	n/a	37	20	n/a	2.0%	3.5%
Total countries with data[1]	70	85	94			
Average all countries[1]				1.6%	1.8%	2.3%
Median all countries[1]				1.5%	1.6%	2.0%

1.Non-oil dominated economies with populations of more than 5million in 2015 with data for the period
Source: Calculated from World Bank World Development Indicators

Section 3

China is a socialist country in line with Marx

Part 1: Why China is a socialist country – China's theory is in line with Marx

12 September 2017
Introductory note 16 January 2021

This article does not deal with the argument that the total state ownership of the economy in the USSR after 1929, with the nationalisation of even small enterprises, was necessary for political reasons – the threat of Nazi attack. Politics must take precedence over economics. But it shows that the economic structure of the USSR after 1929 in economic terms was not in line with Marx's conceptions whereas the economic structure of China after 1978 was in line with the conceptions of Marx.

Deng Xiaoping is famous for the saying 'it doesn't matter whether a cat is black or white provided it catches mice.' As I am an unashamed Dengite in economic theory, the equivalent of this is that it is perfectly possible to understand China's socialist economy in terms of either Western or Marxist economic theory – an analysis in terms of both is given in this book at 'Deng Xiaoping and John Maynard Keynes'[42].

This reflects the fact that economics study a material reality and to accurately and factually analyse it is the most important issue. For this reason, most articles on this website, and others which I write, don't bother to quote any economist - they just study the facts – that is they don't bother to discuss whether the cat is black or white, they just focus on catching mice.

But posts on this website have created some discussion among readers of a socialist viewpoint who believe the myth that China's is a capitalist economy. This is the misunderstanding that constantly leads Western analysts to make fundamental mistakes regarding China's economic dynamics – a typical example of those errors, regularly updated, are collected together on this website at 'Wrong Analyses of China – Listed by Author and Date'[43].

This error arises among those of such a socialist viewpoint because they have a definition of socialism deriving from the post-1929 structure of the USSR rather than Marx – as will be shown below. To clarify the issues for them, this article is therefore a brief outline of the key foundations of China's economic theories and why they are entirely in line with Marx. Those who prefer to use Western categories can analyse China's socialist economy in those terms – as outlined in 'Deng Xiaoping and John Maynard Keynes'[44] – and not bother to read this article. Those who prefer just to have accurate economic analyses, without being overly concerned with what framework they are put forward in, can ignore whether the cat is black or white and just study China's economy.

China's economic theory

Deng Xiaoping as a Communist naturally explicitly formulated China's economic policy in Marxist terms – China's economic reform policies were seen as the integration of Marxism with the specific conditions in China. More precisely Deng stated: 'We were victorious in the Chinese revolution precisely because we applied the universal principles of Marxism-Leninism to our own realities.' (Deng, 28 August 1985) Consequently: 'Our principle is that we should integrate Marxism with Chinese practice and blaze a path of our own. That is what we call building socialism with Chinese characteristics.' (Deng, 21 August 1985)

Authors, including (Hsu, 1991), have contended that Deng's economic policies were not in accord with those of Marx. However, while China's economic policies clearly differed from those of the USSR after the introduction of the First Five Year Plan in 1929, which introduced comprehensive planning and essentially total state ownership, it is clear that China's economic policies were in line with those indicated by Marx. Whether people wish to formulate Chinese economic policy in Western or Marxist terms may be left to them. What is most crucial is not the colour of the cat but whether it catches mice – that is, the practical policy conclusions drawn. This appendix therefore briefly shows that Deng's concepts in launching China's economic reform in 1978 corresponded to Marx's.

The primary stage of socialism

Regarding China's economic reform policies Deng noted, as stated in Marxist terms, that China was in the socialist and not the (higher) communist stage of development. Large scale development of the productive forces/output was the prerequisite before China could make the transition to a communist society: 'A Communist society is one in which there is no exploitation of man by man, there is great material abundance, and the principle of from each according to their ability, to each according to his needs is applied. It is impossible to apply that principle without overwhelming material wealth. In order to realise communism, we have to accomplish the tasks set in the socialist stage. They are legion, but the fundamental one is to develop the productive forces.' (Deng, 28 August 1985)

More precisely, in a characterisation maintained to the present, China was in the 'primary stage' of socialism, which was fundamental in defining policy: 'The Thirteenth National Party Congress will explain what stage China is in: the primary stage of socialism. Socialism itself is the first stage of communism, and here in China we are still in the primary stage of socialism – that is, the underdeveloped stage. In everything we do we must proceed from this reality, and all planning must be consistent with it.' (Deng, 29 August 1987)

The fundamental characterisations by Deng have been maintained to the present – thus for example in July 2011 President Hu Jintao stressed that 'China is still in the primary stage of socialism and will remain so for a long time to come' (Xinhua, 2011), while speaking to the UN premier Wen Jiabao noted 'Taken as a whole, China is still in the primary stage of socialism' (Xinhua, 2010). The conclusion flowing from this as noted by Hsu, was that: 'From this perspective, a serious error in the past was the leftist belief that China could skip the primary stage and practice full socialism immediately.' (Hsu, 1991, p. 11)

The conclusion of such a contrast between a primary socialist stage of development and the principle of a communist society (which, as noted by Deng above, was regulated by 'from each according to their ability to each according to each according to his needs') was that in the present 'socialist' period the principle was 'to each according to their work': 'We must adhere to this socialist principle which calls for distribution according to the quantity and quality of an individual's work.' (Deng, 28 March 1978)

In Marxist theory, outlined by Marx in the opening chapter of Capital (Marx, 1867), economic distribution according to work/labour is the fundamental principle of commodity production – and a commodity necessarily implies a market. In this socialist period a market would therefore exist – hence the eventual Chinese terminology of a 'socialist market economy.' As presented by Deng Xiaoping and his successors above such Chinese analysis is highly compressed but clearly in line with Marx himself.

Marx's analysis

It is clear Marx envisaged that the transition from capitalism to communism would be a prolonged one, noting in The Communist Manifesto[45]: 'The proletariat will use its political supremacy to wrest, by degree, all capital from the bourgeoisie, to centralise all instruments of production in the hands of the State, i.e., of the proletariat organised as the ruling class; and to increase the total productive forces as rapidly as possible.' (Marx & Engels, 1848, p. 504)

The 'by degree' may be noted – Marx therefore clearly envisaged a period during which state-owned property and private property would exist. China's system, after Deng, of simultaneous existence of sectors of state and private ownership is therefore clearly more in line with Marx's conceptualisation than Stalin's introduction 'all at once' of essentially 100 per cent state ownership in 1929.

Regarding Deng's formulations on communist society being regulated by 'to each according to their need' versus the primary stage of socialism regulated by 'each according

to their work' Marx noted in the Critique of the Gotha Programme[46] of the post-capitalist transition to a communist
society: 'What we are dealing with here is a communist society, not as it has developed on its own foundations, but on
the contrary, just as it emerges from capitalist society, which
is thus in every respect, economically, morally, and intellectually, still stamped with the birth-marks of the old society
from whose womb it emerges.' (Marx, 1875, p. 85)

In such a transition Marx outlined payment in society,
and distribution of products and services, necessarily had
to be 'according to work' even within the state-owned sector of the economy: 'Accordingly, the individual producer
receives back from society – after the deductions have been
made – exactly what he gives to it. What he has given to it
is his individual quantum of labour. For example, the social
working day consists of the sum of the individual hours of
work; the individual labour time of the individual producer
is the part of the social working day contributed by him,
his share in it. He receives a certificate from society that
he has furnished such-and-such an amount of labour (after
deducting his labour for the common funds); and with this
certificate, he draws from the social stock of means of consumption as much as the same amount of labour cost. The
same amount of labour which he has given to society in one
form, he receives back in another.

'Here obviously the same principle prevails as that which
regulates the exchange of commodities, as far as this is
exchange of equal values.... as far as the distribution of the
latter among the individual producers is concerned, the same
principle prevails as in the exchange of commodity equivalents: a given amount of labour in one form is exchanged for
an equal amount of labour in another form.

'Hence, equal right here is still in principle – bourgeois
right... The right of the producers is proportional to the labour
they supply; the equality consists in the fact that measurement is made with an equal standard, labour.' (Marx, 1875,
p. 86)

In such a society inequality would necessarily still exist:
'one... is superior to another physically or mentally and so
supplies more labour in the same time, or can labour for
a longer time; and labour, to serve as a measure, must be
defined by its duration or intensity, otherwise it ceases to be

a standard of measurement. This equal right is an unequal right for unequal labour... it tacitly recognises the unequal individual endowment and thus the productive capacities of the workers as natural privileges. It is, therefore, a right of inequality in its content like every right. Right by its very nature can consist only as the application of an equal standard; but unequal individuals (and they would not be different individuals if they were not unequal) are measurable by an equal standard only insofar as they are made subject to an equal criterion, are taken from a certain side only, for instance, in the present case, are regarded only as workers and nothing more is seen in them, everything else being ignored. Besides, one worker is married, another not; one has more children than another, etc. etc.. Thus, given an equal amount of work done, and hence an equal share in the social consumption fund, one will in fact receive more than another, one will be richer than another, and so on. To avoid all these defects, right would have to be unequal rather than equal.' (Marx, 1875, pp. 86-87)

Marx considered only after a prolonged transition would payment according to work be replaced with the ultimately desired goal, distribution of products according to members of society's needs.

'Right can never be higher than the economic structure of society and its cultural development which this determines.

'In a higher phase of communist society... after the productive forces have also increased with the all-around development of the individual, and all the springs of common wealth flow more abundantly – only then can the narrow horizon of bourgeois right be crossed in its entirety and society inscribe on its banners: From each according to his abilities, to each according to his needs!' (Marx, 1875, p. 87)

It is therefore clear that post-Deng policies in China were more in line with Marx's prescriptions than post-1929 policies in the USSR. Given the essentially 100 per cent state ownership of industry in China in 1978 'Zhuada Fangxiao' (keep the large, let go the small) – maintaining the large enterprises within the state sector and releasing the small ones to the non-state sector – together with the creation of a new private sector created an economic structure clearly more in line with that envisaged by Marx than the essentially 100 per cent state ownership in the USSR after 1929.

Deng's insistence on the formula that in the transitional period reward would be 'according to work' and not 'according to need' was clearly in line with Marx's analyses. It is notable that in the USSR itself a number of economists discussed these issues – including Buhkarin (Bukharin,1925), Kondratiev (Kondratiev n.d.), and Preobrazhensky (Preobrazhensky, 1921-27). Their works were, however, almost unknown in China although several accounts have been published outside the USSR – see for example (Jasny, 1972) (Lewin, 1975). China's economic debates therefore preceded primarily with reference to China's conditions and Marx, and not any preceding debates in the USSR.

It is therefore clear that China's post-reform economic policy is in line with Marx's analysis of socialism and that, as stated in Chinese analysis, post-1929 Soviet policy departed from Marx's analysis – the argument that the converse is true, by Hsu and others, is invalid.

China's economic theory certainly differs from post-1929 Soviet policy – because it goes back to Marx.

Part 2: The triumph of Chinese Marxism - from 'reform and opening up' to the 19th Party Congress

24 March 2018

'Over the past 95 years, the CPC has accomplished so many tasks which were thought to be impossible by other political forces. The reason for this has been precisely attributed to our adoption of Marxism as our guide of action, while the theories of Marxism have then been further developed. This has allowed our Party to free itself from the limitations of all previous political forces, which focussed on pursuing their own special interests. This has enabled us to hold on to the materialist dialectic view and selflessly lead China's revolution, development and reform, while sticking to the truth and correcting mistakes we made. Our Party has never wavered in its belief in Marxism either in favourable or unfavourable circumstances...

'Marxism is the fundamental guiding thought for the establishment of our Party and our country. Departing from or abandoning Marxism, the Party would lose its soul and direction. On the issue of Marxism as the fundamental guiding thought, we shall not waver under any circumstances.'[47]

This statement by Xi Jinping on the 95th anniversary of the founding of the Communist Party of China (CPC) is particularly relevant as China celebrates the 40th anniversary of reform and opening up. A reason for this is because, despite this clear statement on the relation of China, the CPC and Marxism, attempts are made by some forces in the West, and even in China, to claim that China achieved its gigantic successes not 'because of' but 'despite' Marxism. Why this claim is made is simple. As this article will show in detail, systematic international and historic comparisons show that China's economic achievement during reform and opening up is by far the greatest in the whole of human history - from the viewpoint of speed of improvement in living standards, rapidity of economic growth, the proportion of the world's population benefitting from that growth, and the elimination of poverty. That is, in summary, under reform and opening up China's economic achievement was the greatest of any country in human history not only for itself but for the overall wellbeing of humanity. Which system created such unprecedented success is therefore of not merely Chinese but universal global significance. Because:

- If this success is due to Marxism and socialism then, as Chinese President Xi Jinping stated in his report to the 19th National Congress of the CPC in October 2017, socialism with Chinese characteristics, 'offers a new option for other countries and nations who want to speed up their development while preserving their independence.'[48] Indeed, the unprecedented achievements of reform and opening up show the superiority of the socialist path of development to capitalism.
- This latter admission is, of course, unacceptable to the West – if it acknowledged that the socialist path of development was proven to be superior to capitalism then the Western system would lose its legitimacy both internationally and domestically. Therefore, 'the West' necessarily has to claim that the unprecedented success of reform and opening up, of socialism with Chinese characteristics, occurred not because of Marxism but because China abandoned or deviated from Marxism.
- The aim of this article is therefore simple. It shows that China's analysis is correct and the claim of the West,

made to attempt to safeguard its capitalist legitimacy, is false. To do so four interrelated points will be established:

- ○ First, it will be demonstrated that the economic success of reform and opening up, as already stated, is indeed the greatest of any country in human history.
- ○ Second, that reform and opening up was entirely in line with Marx's concepts, and its success was therefore due to this. Indeed, reform and opening up was a 'return to Marx' after deviations from Marx which existed in the former USSR – this return to Marx's concepts, in turn, allowed the further development of Marxism up to the 19th Party Congress.
- ○ Third, it will be shown that Marx's economic concepts are proven correct not only as an issue of 'dogma', that is by analysis of Marx's writings, but also by factual studies of the Western capitalist economies. The success of reform and opening up, and the Marxism on which it was based, is therefore due to the method of 'seek truth from facts'.
- ○ Fourth, that because for ideological reasons the Western capitalism is forced to reject Marxism the West is itself caught in a trap of being forced to deny the facts of economic development - which weakens the West's ability to overcome its own economic problems. This is one of the key reasons why the last 40 years saw in parallel in China the greatest economic achievement in human history in reform and opening up, but in the West the same period witnessed the road to the 'new mediocre' and the international financial crisis.
- • In summary, analysing the Marxist foundations of the reform and opening up is of significance not only for understanding the success of China but for understanding the road to the present slow growth, the 'new mediocre' in the Western economies. The scale of China's success in reform and opening up is, therefore, of decisive importance to China and to the world both practically and theoretically – the two being necessarily interrelated.

In this article, following the method of 'seek truth from facts', first the full international and historical comparative scale of success of China's reform and opening up will be established, and then the theoretical reasons for this success will

be analysed in terms of both Marxist and 'Western' economics. Finally, some brief conclusions will be drawn on why
countries which do not accept a Marxist framework can still
benefit from the economic framework of China's reform and
opening up.

Part 1 – The factual results of reform and opening up

In such serious matters as China's economic development
there is no virtue in optimism, and no virtue in pessimism,
there is only a virtue in realism. It is therefore necessary
to be clear that China's economic achievement during the
40 years of reform and opening up is the greatest in the
whole of human history whether measured by speed of economic development, by the number of people whose lives
were improved by this development, by the proportion of
humanity which directly benefitted from this, by the sustained speed of increase in living standards achieved, and
by poverty reduction. These clear facts will be established
through a systematic series of historic and international
comparisons of China's reform and opening up with development in other countries.

It is, furthermore, crucial to establish these objective facts
as the starting point for analysis. First, because it relates
to the question of China's accurate judgement of its own
achievements and 'self-confidence'. US 'neo-con', 'economic
nationalist' and other enemies of China wish to factually hide
the scale of China's achievement because to admit it would
transform the world's understanding of China – including
changing the US population's judgement on China. Second,
because this determines how significant for economic theory
China's reform and opening up is. If the results of reform
and opening up were a minor or medium scale economic
event, then it would not be extremely significant to analyse
the reasons for its success. Because the success of reform
and opening up is a gigantic event it, in contrast, is absolutely necessary to theoretically explain it. More generally in
terms of the impact of reform and opening up:

•   For developing countries, that is the overwhelming
    majority of the world's population, to openly admit that
    China's economic achievement is the greatest in human

history would be to show that China's socialist 'economic model' is by far most effective practical way to achieve economic growth, to gigantically and rapidly improve the living standards of the average population, and to radically eliminate poverty.

- For the advanced economies China's socialist market economy, with its decisive role of the state sector, but combined with a private sector, shows a clear and more successful alternative to the failure of neo-liberalism in the 'Washington Consensus' and the neo-liberal 'austerity' policies pursued by advanced countries.
- Most seriously of all for US neo-cons and economic nationalists, China shows that the most successful economy in the world in producing economic growth and improving living standards is a socialist and not a capitalist one. Understanding of this situation by the US population would, of course, change the political situation in the US.
- Within China the 'comprador intelligentsia', that is those who are tied to foreign interests and not those of China, also wish to hide the true scale of China's development. This is because accurate understanding of the scale of China's achievement would destroy their claim that foreign models were superior to China.

Therefore, the first issue is to make a systematic international and historic comparison of China's economic achievements compared with other countries since reform and opening up was launched by Deng Xiaoping and Chen Yun.

The pre-reform and opening up period

To accurately judge the effects of reform and opening up it is necessary to put it in its historical and international context. However, to avoid making this article unnecessarily long, the period of China's period of development prior to reform and opening up, from 1949-1978, will not be analysed in detail here – this is dealt with in 一盘大棋? ——中国新命运解析. However, to put 'reform and opening up' in context certain key points regarding its starting point must be established.

First, it is necessary to accurately understand how extraordinarily poor China was in 1949 after a century of foreign interventions and invasions. The data accompanying

Maddison's classic work on long term economic development, *The World Economy*, shows that in 1950 only two Asian and eight African countries had lower per capita GDPs than China - Myanmar, Mongolia, Botswana, Burundi, Ethiopia, Guinea, Guinea Bissau, Lesotho, Malawi, and Tanzania while India's per capita GDP was 38% higher than China's. The Conference Board, analysing the same year, estimates that, for countries for which it gives data, Tanzania had a slightly higher per capita GDP than China, but Burkina Faso, Cambodia, and Mozambique had lower per capita GDP's than China – it also concludes that India's per capita GDP was only 27% higher than China's. It is evident such details make no significant difference – in 1949 China was not merely underdeveloped it was one of the poorest countries in the world.

Given China's extreme poverty and economic underdevelopment in 1949, some authors emphasise that in 1949-78 indispensable initial industrial bases were created from which reform and opening up could be launched. This is correct. But the most extraordinary achievement in China in 1949-78, a literal 'miracle', was in the social field. In the 27 years between the establishment of the People's Republic of China in 1949, and the death of Mao Zedong in 1976, life expectancy in China increased by 31 years – or over a year per chronological year. To understand the true scale of such an achievement in comparative terms, it need simply be noted that China's rate of increase of life expectancy in the three decades after 1949 was the fastest ever recorded in a major country in human history – detailed comparisons establishing this fact are given in 一盘大棋?——中国新命运解析. In comparison, in the most comparable country to China, in 27 years after India's independence average life expectancy increased by 19 years – this is shown in Figure 10. The theory of 'historical nihilism', denying the quite extraordinary social achievements of China prior to reform and opening up, is therefore simply false. As Xi Jinping noted regarding the two periods of China's post-1949 development:

'The two phases – at once related to and distinct from each other – are both pragmatic explorations in building socialism conducted by the people under the leadership of the Party. Chinese socialism was initiated after the launch of reform and opening up and based on more than 20 years of development

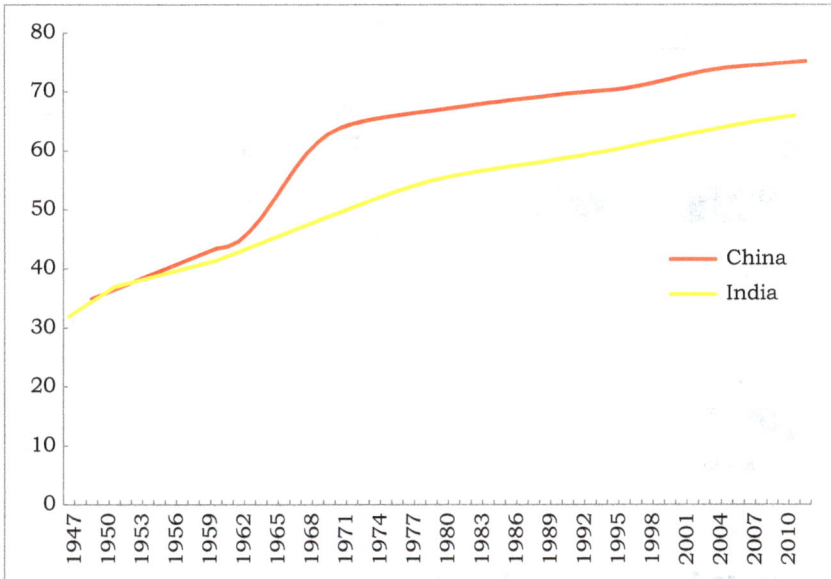

Figure 10: Life Expectancy – China and India in years
Sources: China 1949 Bergaglio 'Population Growth in China',
India 1947&1951 Kuruganti 'Healthcare achievements of
post-independent India', 1960 – 2011 World Bank World
Development Indicators

since the socialist system was established in the 1950s after
the People's Republic of China (PRC) was founded. Although
the two historical phases are very different in their guiding thoughts, principles, policies, and practical work, they
are by no means separated from or opposed to each other.
We should neither negate the pre- reform-and-opening-up
phase in comparison with the post-reform-and -opening-up
phase, nor the converse.'[49]

China's is the fastest sustained growth in a major economy in human history

Turning to the post-1978 period, the first point which may
be established is that China's economic growth under socialist reform and opening up is the fastest in a major economy
in human history. The comparison made here is systematic -
with all countries both after and before World War II. Taking
the most rapidly growing major economies, and also the largest economies, the following is the situation – see Figure 11.

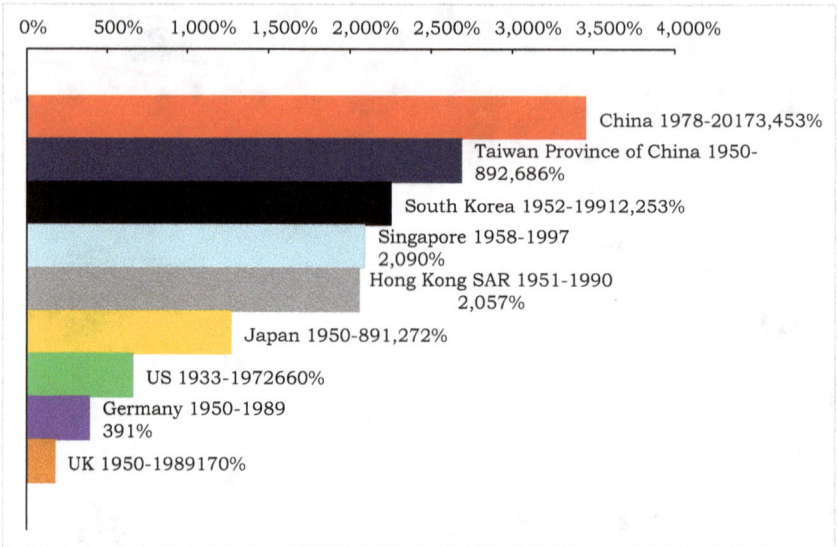

Figure 11: Maximum Economic Growth in a 39 Year Period
Inflation adjusted prices

Source: Calculated from The Conference Board Total Economy
Database 2017, World Bank World Development Indicators,
US Bureau of Economic Analysis NIPA Table 1.1.3, China National
Bureau of Statistics, Maddison

- Between 1978 and 2017 China's economy expanded at an annual average 9.5% growth rate, growing in size almost 35 times.

For comparison the fastest rates of growth of other major economies over a 39- year period were by the so called 'Asian Tigers'. These were:

- Taiwan Province of China, expanding at an average 8.8% and increasing in size almost 27 times in 1950-89;
- South Korea expanding at an annual average 8.3% or increasing in size almost 23 times in 1952-91;
- Hong Kong SAR growing at an average annual 8.1% or expanding almost 21 times in 1958-1997;
- Singapore growing at an annual average 8.1% or expanding almost 21 times in 1951-1990.
- But all the 'Asian Tiger' economies were very small compared to China. They comprised only 1.4% of the world's population compared to the 22.3% for China in 1978. Taking really large economies, which are therefore more

comparable to China, the fastest growth over a 39- year period ever recorded, outside recovery from almost total devastation of an economy by wartime defeat, was Japan in 1950-89 when it expanded at an annual average 6.7% or by almost 13 times.

It is also clear China far outperformed the advanced economies:

- As already noted, prior to China, the fastest prolonged growth recorded in a large economy, outside recovery from devastation by defeat in war, was Japan in 1950-89 when it expanded at an annual average 6.7%[50].
- The fastest growth recorded by the US over a 39-year period was 660% in 1933-1972 – an annual average 5.0%.
- The fastest growth ever recorded by Germany, outside recovery from devastation by defeat in war, was in 1950-89 when it expanded at an annual average 3.6% or by almost four times.[51]
- The UK's fastest ever growth was 170%, an annual average 2.6%, in 1950-1989.

This data therefore also shows clearly that it is misunderstanding to believe that at some point in the past the Western advanced economies grew as rapidly as China and that they have slowed. The advanced economies never grew in a sustained way remotely as rapidly as China.

The size of China's economic achievement

Although the fact that China's is the fastest sustained growth in a major economy in human history is by itself astonishing nevertheless, stated in that way, it greatly understates the scale of China's economic achievement. **This is because China is a far larger part of humanity than any other country which has ever undergone sustained very rapid economic growth.** The chart and the table below therefore show the percentage of the world's population at the time when major economies began sustained rapid economic growth. Analysing these historical examples in chronological order:

- The first country to experience sustained rapid economic growth was the UK in the Industrial Revolution, with 2.0% of the world's population.

- The US grew rapidly from soon after its creation in 1776, but at that time the United States was a small part of the world economy – in 1820 it is estimated it was only 1.8% of world GDP. The consolidation of the US as the world's largest economy came following its Civil War – by 1870, it was approximately 8.9% of world GDP compared to 9.0% for the UK and 17.0% for China. This post US Civil War growth was in a country with 3.2% of the world's population.
- After the unification of Germany in 1870 it immediately began rapid growth – in 1870 Germany was 3.1% of the world's population.
- When Soviet rapid industrialisation began at the end of the 1920s the USSR contained 8.4% of the world's population.
- Japan's rapid post-World War II growth was in a country with 3.3% of the world's people.
- The growth of the four 'Asian Tigers' (Hong Kong, Singapore, South Korea, and Taiwan Province of China) was in economies which together only comprised 1.4% of the world's population.
- No other economy commencing sustained rapid economic growth therefore even comes close to the 22.3% of the world's population in China in 1978 at the beginning of reform and opening up.

Therefore China, at the time of the beginning of reform and opening up:

- was more than ten times the percentage of the world population of the UK when it began rapid growth;
- was seven times the percentage of the world population of the US or Japan as they became major economies undergoing rapid growth,
- was almost three times the proportion of the world's population of the USSR when it began rapid growth.

The scale of China's rapid economic growth during its socialist 'reform and opening up', in terms of the proportion of the world's population experiencing that growth, therefore dwarfs that of any other country experiencing rapid growth in the whole of world history.

China's improvement in living standards

Despite the extraordinary reality that China's economic development under reform and opening up is both the fastest and by far the largest in scale of any major country in human history GDP growth is not the aim of economic policy - it is simply a necessary means to achieve other ends. The fundamental aim of economic policy is the improvement of the human conditions of the Chinese people and the all-round rejuvenation of the Chinese nation. Furthermore, it is practically important to understand which is the aim and which is the means. If GDP growth is set as the main aim, and not as the means to achieve other aims, then damage to the environment, pollution, dangerous working practices, failure to raise living standards of the mass of the population etc may be carried out in pursuit of GDP growth. Well known examples of this have occurred in China. Correction of any misunderstanding on this and placing the emphasis firmly on 'people centred' development was one of the most important emphases of the 19th Party Congress as analysed below.

Nevertheless, while it is extremely important to understand the correct relation of ends and means, it is also crucial not to 'throw the baby out with the bathwater'. Although economic growth is only the means to achieve other aims it is an indispensable means to do so. The close international correlation of average life expectancy, the best single indicator of overall human conditions, with per capita GDP confirms that while economic growth is not the aim of economic development nevertheless it is an indispensable means to achieve human well-being - international comparisons show that per capita GDP accounts for more than 70% of differences in life expectancy between countries. Consequently, as Xi Jinping noted: 'Development is the top priority of the Party and our country, and holds the key to solving all problems in China'.[52]

The same principle applies to consumption – the direct material basis of human living standards. The aim of economic development is the fastest possible sustainable increase in consumption – sustainability including that it protects and does not damage the environment, and that the rapid increase in consumption can be sustained over a long period of time. But while the goal in this area is the increase in consumption, not increase in GDP, the strong international

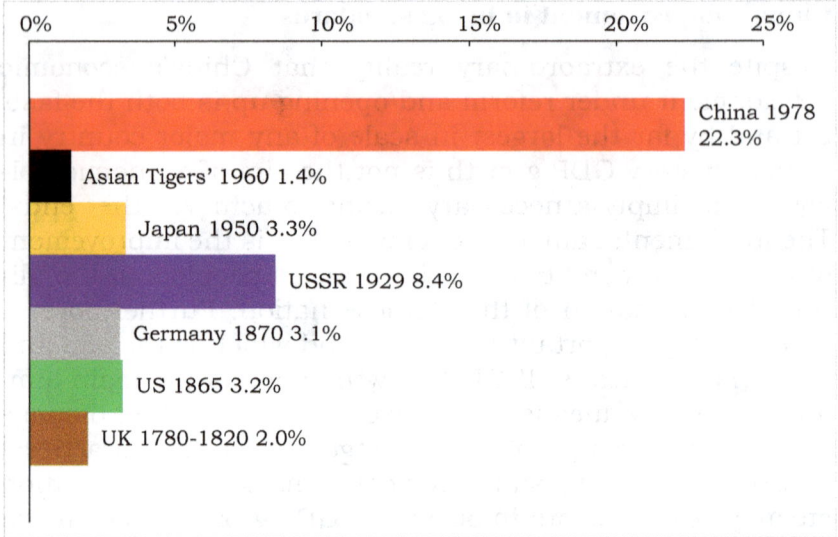

Figure 12: % of the World's Population at the Beginning of Sustained Very Rapid Economic Growth Date indicates year when very rapid growth began

Source: Calculated from Maddison Statistics on World Population, GDP and Per Capita GDP, 1-2008 AD

Table 6

% of World Population in Countries at Beginning of Sustained Rapid Economic Growth		
Country	Year	% of World Population
UK	1780-1820	2.0%
US	1865	3.2%
Germany	1870	3.1%
USSR[1]	1929	8.4%
Japan	1950	3.3%
Asian 'Tiger' economies[2]	1960	1.4%
China	1978	22.3%
1. Average of 1920 (8.3%) and 1940 (8.5%) 2. Total for South Korea (0.8%), Taiwan Province (0.4%), Hong Kong (0.1%) and Singapore (0.1%) Source: Calculated from Maddison Statistics on World Population, GDP and Per Capita GDP, 1-2008 AD		

correlation between increase in consumption and increase in GDP means GDP growth is a necessary means to achieve increases in consumption – internationally more than 80% of the increase in consumption over the medium/long term is accounted for by the increase in GDP growth.

Confusion over consumption

Regarding growth in consumption during reform and opening up some confusion has existed in both international and some sections of the media in China. Clarity on this issue is crucial because as Xi Jinping has stressed: 'Prosperity for the people is the basic political position of the CPC.'[53] It is sometimes stated that consumption has been 'underdeveloped' in China during reform and opening up. But this is based on a simple confusion between two different things - the percentage of consumption in GDP and rate of growth of consumption. As will be shown, the increase of consumption in China during reform and opening up has been the greatest of any country.

Comparison with developing countries

Data on the growth of household consumption is unfortunately only available for a smaller number of countries than data for GDP - and for a shorter period. World Bank internationally comparable data on household consumption is generally only available from 1960, and it does not include Taiwan Province of China. Fortunately, however, in practice this data limitation does not turn out to be a major problem in making an historical and international comparison of reform and opening up for two fundamental reasons:

- China's lead over other countries in the growth of household consumption turns out to be so large that inclusion of other data would not change the situation.
- The most rapid period of economic growth of developing countries took place not only after World War II but from the 1960s onwards. [54]

To analyse the growth of household consumption, first the comparison of China with other developing countries (defined as being a developing country at the beginning of the period of growth), will be taken and then a comparison of China with advanced economies will be made.

Figure 13 therefore shows the 10 major developing economies with the most rapid growth of household consumption over a 38-year period between 1960 and 2016 – a major economy is defined as one with a population of more than five million. China's 1,816% growth in household consumption in 1978-2016, an annual average 7.9%, is the fastest for any developing country. The second highest is Hong Kong SAR in 1961-1999 with a growth of 1,605%. However, Hong Kong SAR in 2017 had a population of only 7.4 million and therefore only just meets the population criteria for a major economy. The first really large economy after China, in terms of household consumption growth, is South Korea, with a population of 51.4 million in 2017, which saw growth of household consumption of 1,479% in 1964-2002. If really large countries, which are therefore most comparable to China, are considered then those with the most rapid household consumption

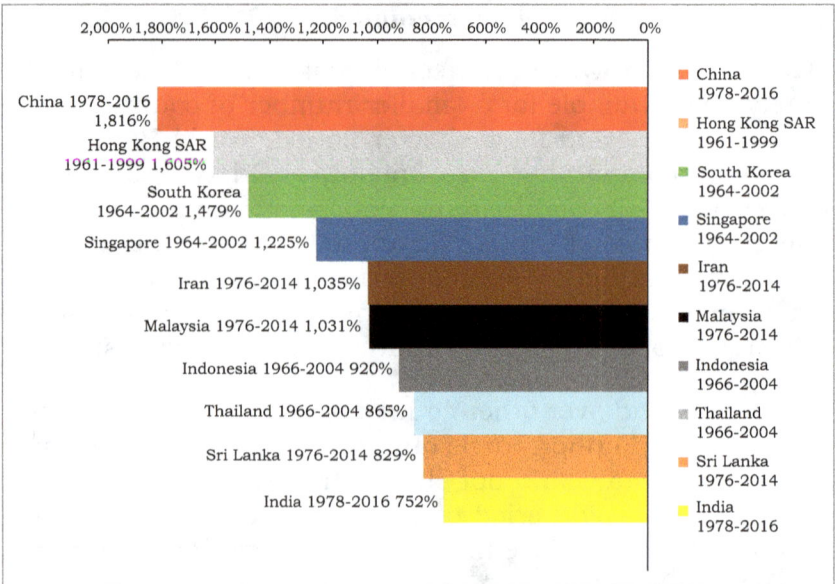

Figure 13: Maximum 38 Year Growth of Household Consumption During period 1960-2016, inflation adjusted prices

Source: Calculated from World Bank World Development Indicators, China Statistical Yearboook 2017 Table 3-16

growth are Indonesia with 920% growth in 1966-2000, an annual average increase of 6.0%, and India with 752% in 1978-2016, an annual average increase of 5.5%.

The situation is therefore clear. China's growth of household consumption was more rapid than for any other major developing country.

Comparison to advanced economies

Turning to the comparison of China with advanced economies, data is not available for all advanced countries for a long period which would take in growth prior to World War II. However, as will be seen it is certain no advanced economy has ever achieved household consumption growth as fast as China. This is clear for two reasons:

- The fastest growth ever experienced by a large, advanced economy was Japan after World War II, and long-term data is available for Japan and it shows clearly that its household consumption growth was not as fast as China.
- Advanced economies experienced more rapid long-term growth during or after World War II than before it and data is available for major economies for this post-World War II period.

Figure 14 therefore shows the data for three advanced economies for which long term data including before World War II is available – the US, Japan, and UK. It may be seen immediately that Japan's growth of household consumption far exceeded the US or UK. The household consumption growth figure of 1,554% for Japan in the period 1946-84 is boosted by the extremely low starting point constituted by Japan's economy in 1946 – Japan's consumption in that year was severely depressed by devastation of its economy by defeat in World War II. However, even if the exceptional situation of the extreme depression of Japan's economy after defeat in war is excluded, Japan's growth of household consumption still is much faster than any other major advanced economy – if the peacetime period 1950-1988 is taken, for example, Japan's total growth of household consumption is still 1,236%. The fact that China's growth of household consumption in 1978-2016, of 1,816%, exceeds even the artificially high figure

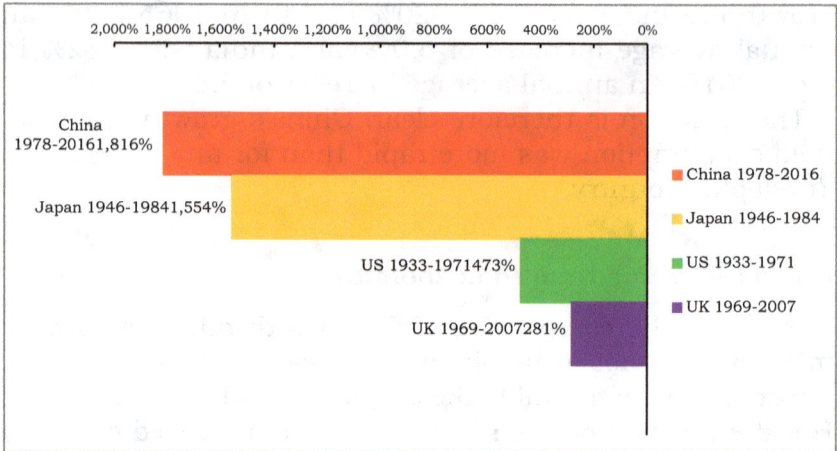

Figure 14: Maximum 38 Year Growth of Household Consumption
Inflation adjusted prices

Source: Calculated from World Bank World Development Indicators,
Leisner One Hundred Years of Economic Statistics. US Bureau of
Economic Analysis NIPA Table 1.1.3

for Japan starting in 1946 therefore shows just how much
faster China's growth of household consumption was than
any advanced economy. Taking other comparisons, US
household consumption growth of 473% in 1933-1971, and
the UK's 281% in 1969-2007, is clearly far behind China's –
China's total growth of household consumption was almost
four times that of the US and over six times that of the UK.

In summary, China's growth of household consumption
during reform and opening up was faster than any developing or advanced country, and therefore the fastest in a major
economy in human history.

Total consumption in developing economies

So far household consumption has been analysed. However,
although household consumption is by far the largest part
of consumption, a significant part of GDP is also consumption of government goods and services. Unfortunately, long
term data for total consumption, i.e. household consumption plus government consumption, is not available for most
countries. World Bank internationally comparable data for
total consumption is only available from 1990. Therefore, in
this case, it is not possible to make a comparison for China

to other countries during the whole period of reform and opening up but only since 1990. This comparison, however, shows the same pattern as for household consumption – i.e. China's growth of total consumption is far higher than for any other country.

To make this comparison Figure 15 shows the growth of total consumption in 1990-2016 for the developing economies already analysed, which had the most rapid growth of household consumption in the period since 1960. As can be seen China's 990% growth of total consumption in 1990-2016 far outperformed any other major economy – the next most rapid growth of total consumption in this period among these economies was 490% in Malaysia. China's growth of total consumption was more than twice as fast as any other major economy in this period.

To complete the comparison with developing economies, however, it may be noted that a number of economies in Africa and Latin America and the Caribbean showed particularly strong growth of total consumption after 1990, outperforming in this field some of the traditionally most rapidly growing Asian developing economies. Data including these countries, illustrated in Figure 16, shows that China's 990% increase in total consumption in 1999-2016

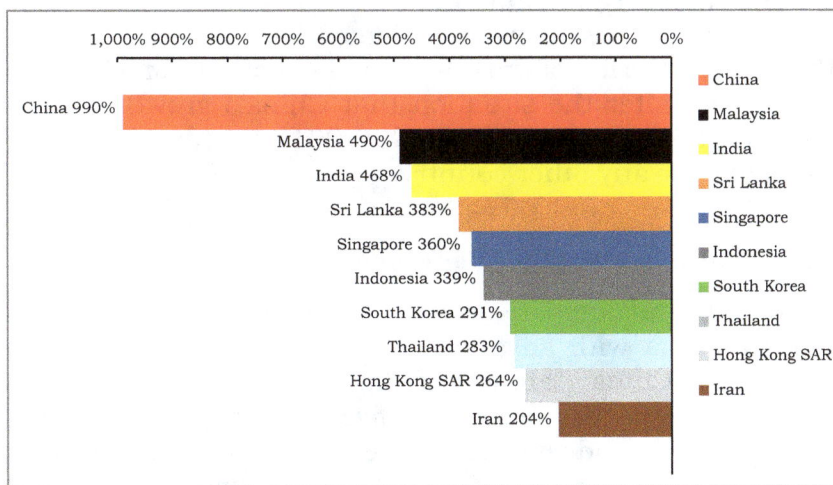

Figure 15: Growth of Total Consumption 1990-2016 Inflation adjusted prices

Source: Calculated from World Bank World Development Indicators

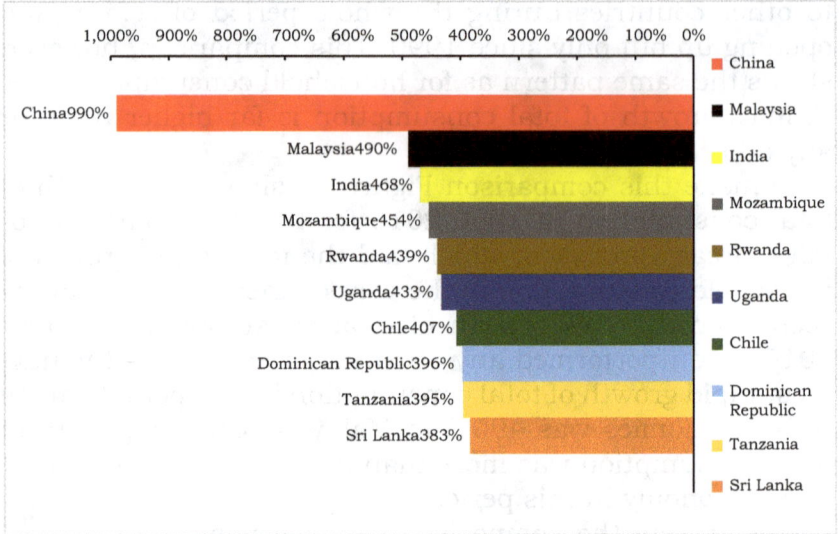

Figure 16: Growth of Total Consumption 1990-2016 Inflation adjusted prices

Source: Calculated from World Bank World Development Indicators

remains easily the fastest in the world. Malaysia and India retain their second and third positions respectively at 498% and 468%. However, Mozambique, Rwanda, Uganda, Chile and the Dominican Republic enter the top 10 economies for growth of total consumption.

Therefore, while the composition of the top 10 countries in the world in terms of growth of total consumption changes, it does not alter the situation that China's growth of total consumption over the period 1990-2016 is more than twice as fast as for any other country.

Growth of consumption in advanced economies

Turning to the comparison of the growth of total consumption in China with advanced economies, this is shown in Figure 17. China's growth of total consumption in 1990-2016, at 990%, was more than five times as fast as that of the US's 188% and was still further ahead of the UK, France, Germany and Japan Therefore China's growth in total consumption far outpaced the main advanced economies.

In summary China's growth of total consumption, as well as of household consumption, during reform and opening up

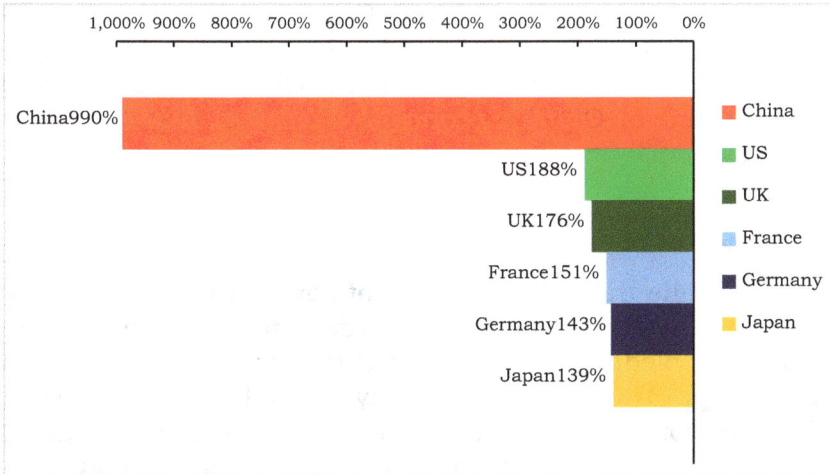

Figure 17: Total Growth of Total Consumption 1990-2016
Inflation adjusted prices

Source: Calculated from World Bank World Development Indicators

was the fastest of any major country. Reform and opening up therefore entirely fulfilled Xi Jinping's pledge that: 'Prosperity for the people is the basic political position of the CPC.'

Correction of some misunderstandings regarding Deng Xiaoping on GDP growth and living standards

It is evident from analysis here that the achievements of reform and opening up were astonishing. However, it is an indication of the fact that China's Marxism continuously develops that discussion around the 19th Party Congress further removed any ambiguities in understanding some formulas of Deng Xiaoping. Theoretically this particularly related to the issue of the relation of GDP growth and the aims of economic development. An example can be taken from Deng Xiaoping's 'Building a Socialism With a Specifically Chinese Character'. Here Deng states: 'the fundamental task... is to develop the productive forces... As they develop, the people's material and cultural life will constantly improve.' [55]

This formula was implicitly misinterpreted in some cases to mean that the goal is the development of the productive forces, which may be crudely interpreted as GDP growth, rather than that GDP growth was a means to the aim of improving the conditions of people and the comprehensive national rejuvenation of China. The emphasis placed by Xi Jinping on 'people centred development' prevents any such misunderstanding. This shows the further clarification and development of China's economic theory at the 19th Party Congress.

Reduction in poverty

Finally, while the overall growth of consumption is strongly related to average living standards, one of China's most important pledges is to complete the process of lifting its entire population out of nationally defined poverty by 2020. This will constitute one of the final results of the ongoing forty years of reform and opening up. But this issue, in turn, is of the greatest significance not only for China but for humanity as a whole - because the greatest problem facing the overwhelming majority of the people living in the world remains inadequate incomes and poverty.

This issue of low incomes and poverty is quite literally a life and death question in terms of its human consequences. As shown in Figure 18, which gives the latest internationally comparable data, a person living in a low-income country by standard World Bank classification lives only 62 years compared to 81 years in a high-income economy - a difference of

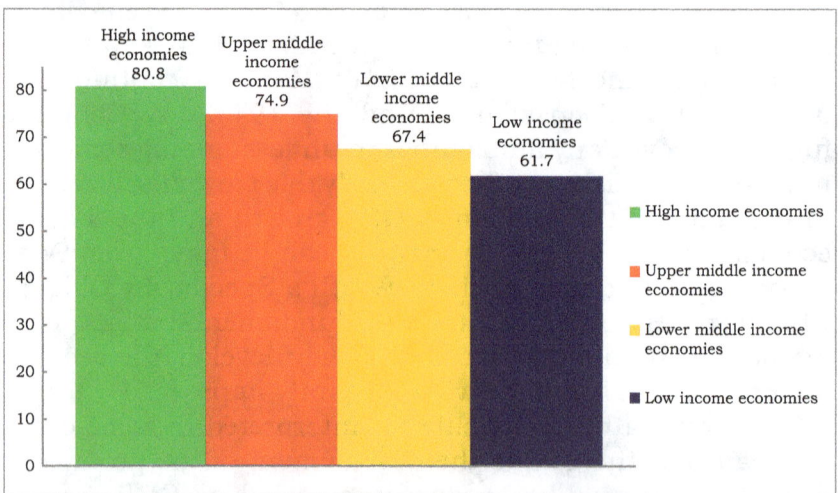

Figure 18: Average Life Expectancy in 2015 Years
Source: World Bank World Development Indicators

19 years. Therefore, not merely do those living in poverty, or indeed outside high income economies, have fewer real practical choices in life but they literally die many years younger than necessary.

It is therefore one of the very greatest achievements of China during reform and opening up that its contribution to the international reduction of the number of those living in poverty simply overwhelms that of every other country – China during reform and opening up accounts for three out of every four of the people taken out of poverty in the global economy!

World Bank international criterion for poverty

The World Bank periodically revises its international definition of poverty. Therefore, here data using the World Bank's latest internationally define definition of poverty will be used - expenditure of $1.90 a day at 2011 prices measured in internationally comparable prices (purchasing powers parities - PPPs). Using this criterion, the first available internationally comparable data for China is for 1981 and the most recent is for 2013. World data is also available for those years – making it easy to calculate the contribution of China to world poverty reduction. Data for other countries in what follows is taken for the nearest years for those totals for China and the world, or in cases where the number of those living in poverty continued to rise for a prolonged period, a comparison to the maximum number living in poverty is taken – in India, for example, the number of those living in poverty continued to rise until 2004.

The fundamental international data is shown in Figure 19 and Figure 20.

- China reduced the number of those living in internationally defined poverty by 853 million. This accounted for 75% of the reduction of those living in poverty in the world – an overwhelming contribution to world poverty reduction.
- It is also significant to note that socialist countries in Indochina (Vietnam, Laos and Cambodia) accounted for a further 3.0% of the reduction of those in the world living in poverty.

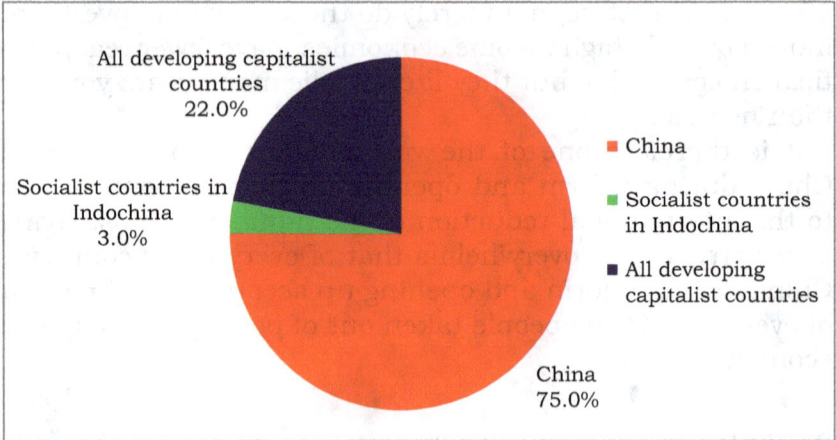

Figure 19: % of Reduction in World Poverty 1981-2013
Source: Calculated from World Bank World Development Indicators

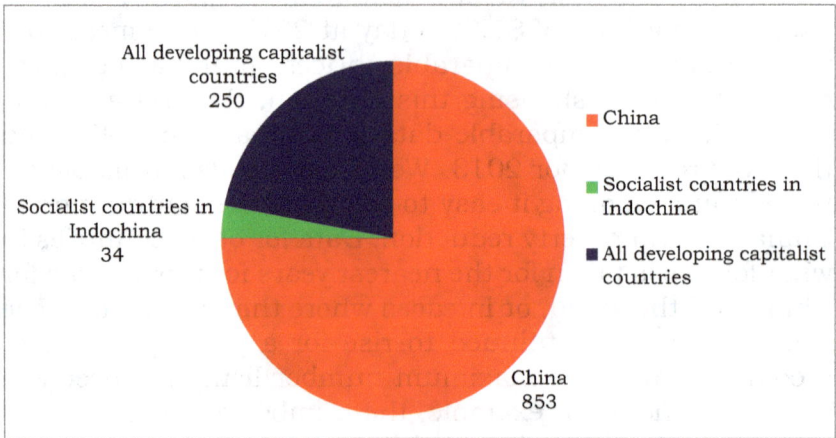

Figure 20: Reduction in Number Living in Poverty
1981-2013 million

Source: Calculated from World Bank World Development Indicators

- Capitalist developing countries accounted for only 22% of the reduction of the number of those living in poverty in the world.

This data, of course, shows the absolutely decisive role of China in the reduction of world poverty – China is responsible for three out of every four people taken out of poverty in the world. **But it also shows that socialism is overwhelmingly**

**responsible for poverty reduction, and capitalism is a
failure in comparison**. If capitalism were effective at eliminating poverty then the greatest reduction in the number
of those living in poverty would be in developing capitalist
countries – for example India, Indonesia, or sub-Saharan
Africa. But instead by far the greatest reduction is in socialist countries.

The latest data

To avoid any suggestion that the cut-off date of 2013 affected
the calculations above, Figure 21 shows the reduction in the
number of those living in poverty up to the latest available
data for the 10 countries or regions/continents which have
made the greatest contribution to the number of those living
in poverty internationally.[56]

From the point of view of the well-being of humanity it is,
of course, gratifying that India after 2004 at last began to
reduce the number of its citizens living in poverty. Nevertheless, India's reduction in the number living in poverty is less
than one fifth that of China. The reduction of the number
of those living in poverty in sub-Saharan Africa is also tiny
compared to the reduction in China.

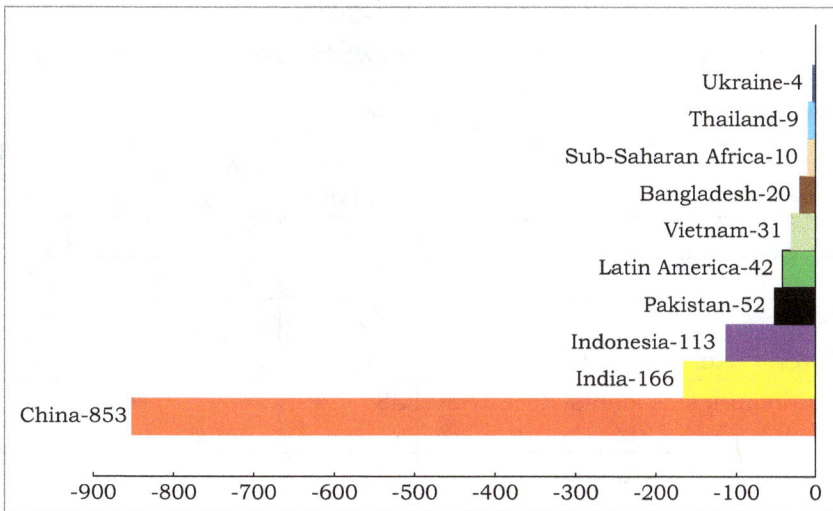

Figure 21: Reduction in Number Living in World Bank Defined
Poverty Reduction in millions since maximum level

Source: Calculated from World Bank World Development Indicators

Decisive role of socialism in reduction of world poverty

Finally, the decisive role of both China and socialism in eliminating poverty, and the inability of capitalism in comparison to do so, is entirely clear from the above data. It is summarised in Figure 22 and Table 7. This shows that:

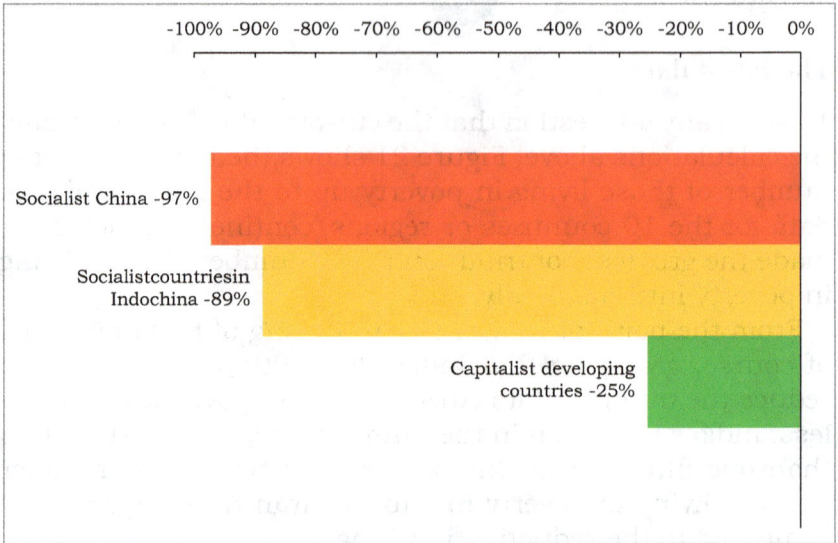

Figure 22: % Reduction of Those Living in World Bank Defined Poverty 1981-2013

Source: Calculated from World Bank World Development Indicators

Table 7

	Number in poverty (millions)		% Reduction
	1981	2013	
World	1,903	766	
China	878	25	-97%
World excluding China	1,025	741	-28%
Indochinese socialist countries 1992/94-2012[1]	38	4	-89%
Capitalist developing countries[1]	987	737	-25%
1. Assumes number in poverty in Indochina socialist countries in 1981 same as in 1992/94 Source: Calculated from World Bank World Development Indicators			

- In 1981, by the World Bank international criteria of poverty, 1,903 million people were living in poverty. From 1981 to 2013 China reduced the number living in internationally defined poverty from 878 million to 25 million – i.e. by 97%. The rest of the world, however, reduced the number living in poverty in the same period from 1,025 million to 741 million – i.e. by only 28%. The enormously greater success of socialist China in reducing poverty than the developing capitalist countries, which contained the vast majority of number of people in the rest of the world living in poverty, is therefore clear.
- But, even this data flatters the developing capitalist countries. This is because no detailed World Bank data exists for the number living in poverty in the Indochinese socialist countries in 1981 – the first data available is for Vietnam and Laos in 1992 and Cambodia in 1994. If it is assumed that there was no reduction in the number of those living in poverty in Indochinese socialist countries in 1981-1992/94 then the developing capitalist countries reduced the number of those living in poverty within them by only 25% - if it is assumed the Indochinese socialist countries did reduce the number of those living in poverty in 1981-1992/94 then the performance of the capitalist developing countries was even worse.
- Therefore, poverty reduction in socialist China was by 97%, poverty reduction in socialist Indochina was 89%, but poverty reduction in capitalist developing countries was only 25%. No greater demonstration of the superiority of socialism over capitalism in poverty reduction can be imagined!

This reality is, naturally, of the greatest significance for developing countries. It shows conclusively that it is socialism, not capitalism, which is the way to eliminate poverty. It also highlights the overwhelming contribution of socialist China to reduction in the number of those living in poverty in the world.

China's decisive role in the reduction of world poverty

To summarise the results regarding world reduction in poverty during reform and opening up:

- China accounts for three out of four people in the world lifted out of poverty. China accounts for over five times as many people lifted out of poverty as India, over seven times as many people lifted out of poverty as Indonesia, over 20 times as many people out of poverty as Latin America, and 85 times as many people out of poverty as sub-Saharan Africa.

- The lives of those 853 million people have been vastly improved and their real choices in life greatly widened. This has contributed far more to humanity's well-being than the ridiculous Western definition of 'human rights'. Ask a normal human in China or India to choose whether they would rather live in poverty but have the right to use Facebook (except if they are in real poverty they can't afford a computer or smartphone!), or they can be taken out of poverty but not be able to use Facebook, and you will soon find out why the West's definition of 'human rights' is entirely absurd.

- The same applies to the population of other developing countries. Ask someone whether it is more important to live 19 years longer, or be able to use Facebook, and you will again see why the Western definition of human rights is a farce.

China has lifted more people out of poverty than the entire population of the European Union and more people than the entire continent of Latin America. The poverty reduction in other countries is dwarfed by what has been achieved in China.

Conclusion on the unparalleled economic achievements of reform and opening up

To summarise the factual results, China's economic achievement during the 40 years of 'reform and opening up' is the greatest in the whole of human history as measured by:

- speed of development in a major economy;
- by the number of people whose lives were improved by this development;
- by the proportion of humanity which directly benefitted from this development;
- by the sustained speed of increase in living standards,
- by the reduction of the number of those living in poverty.

Given the scale of this development, China's reform and opening up is simply the greatest economic achievement in human history in terms not only of its consequences for China but in the improvement of the overall condition of humanity. Such a statement, is not made by an 'overheated' Chinese nationalist - obviously as the author is not even Chinese! Nor are they 'polite words' uttered for the Chinese media. The statement that China's economic development during reform and opening up is the greatest in the whole of human history is simply a statement of fact.

This is the fundamental reason that the 'Western media', and China's 'comprador intelligentsia', has to suppress knowledge of the fact that China's growth dwarfs that of any previous country in human history. **It is because this unmatched speed and scale of China's economic development was achieved by a socialist and not by a capitalist country and economy**. If that fact were widely understood it would change the world's perception of itself. Therefore the 'Western media' and China's comprador intelligentsia has to engage in one of its typical forms of 'fake news' - to suppress knowledge of the fact that China's speed and scale of economic development is quite literally without parallel in human history.

Part 2 – Reform and opening up and the foundations of Marxist economic theory

In Section 1 it was established factually that the economic achievements of reform and opening up is by far the greatest in any country in history from the point of view of its contribution to the wellbeing not only of China but of humanity. In this section the relation of reform and opening up to the foundations of Marxist economic theory will therefore be analysed, before in further sections considering in more detail issues of economic development.

Having established factually the unprecedented scale of the achievement of reform and opening up, however, this clearly has immediate decisive implications for economic theory. What created this unparalleled economic development? Why did China achieve economic results unequalled by any other country – in particular by any capitalist country? The idea that the greatest economic development in human history was created 'without ideas or theory' may immediately be discarded as entirely implausible. Furthermore, if it were in fact true that the greatest economic development in human history could be achieved without economic ideas or theory, or with false ones, then the study of economics should be immediately abandoned – if superior performance could be achieved without knowledge of economics then it is clearly a subject without practical value!

Instead, it will be demonstrated that China's historically unparalleled economic development during reform and opening up was achieved not despite lack of ideas and economic theory but because of economic theory. **To be precise China's extraordinary success during reform and opening up was based on adherence to Marxist theory and is the largest possible scale vindication of the Marxism in the framework of which reform and opening up was developed**. This, naturally, does not mean that China's ideas were merely a mechanical repetition of Marx. But as will be seen reform and opening up marked a return to Marx, from distortions of his ideas which had developed in the USSR and which affected China's economic policy in the immediate post-1949 period. Reform and opening up will therefore be seen to represent a return to Marx - in order to achieve a further development of Marxism.

Nor does the practical and theoretical achievements of the launching of reform and opening up mean that China's theory has not developed further. On the contrary it was already shown, taking the example of ends and means in economic development, that discussion around the 19th Party Congress improved further some formulations used in launching reform and opening up – thereby simultaneously achieving a 'return to Marx' and a further development in economic theory. It will also be shown how, around the 19th Party Congress, a further development of Marxist theory took place.

This section, therefore, deals with the relation of reform and opening up to the foundations of Marxist economic theory. Given that reform and opening up was launched against a background of China's earlier adoption of an economic system highly influenced by the post-1929 economy of the USSR, first a comparison of Marx's concepts to that Soviet system will he made. Then a contrast of Marx to 'Western economics', more strictly speaking to the 'marginalist' school of economics originated by Walras, Jevons and Marshall, will be given. To accurately understand these issues, however, it is useful to briefly recapitulate Marx's fundamental economic concepts.

Marx's analysis of the transition from capitalism

Marx's fundamental framework is well known. Marx analysed a transition from capitalism to a future society the principle of which would be 'from each according to his abilities, to each according to his needs'.[57] This latter was termed by Marx and or communist society. In economic terms this constituted a transition from a capitalist economy based on 'exchange values' to an economy/society based on 'use values'.

Regarding the human consequences of this, in capitalist society 'equality' consists of exchange of equal amounts of labour, and a corresponding purely formal definition of equality regardless of the different conditions or needs of people. In contrast a socialist/communist society would be based on meeting people's differing needs. Such an advanced socialist/communist society would therefore not be based on a purely formal equality but on differences in ability ('from each according to his abilities' - not everyone will be Einstein or Li Bai) and on differences in need ('to each according to their needs' – a person confined to a wheelchair has different needs to someone who is not handicapped, the needs of women and men during their lives are not identical). Formally defined these economic concepts are outlined in the first chapters of Marx's *Capital* - analysing the difference between use value and exchange value.

It is also entirely clear that Marx envisaged this transition from capitalism to advanced socialism/communism as taking place over a prolonged period of time. In *The Communist Manifesto* he noted: 'The proletariat will use its political supremacy to wrest, by degree, all capital from the bourgeoisie, to centralise all instruments of production in the hands of the State, i.e., of the proletariat organised as the ruling class; and to increase the total productive forces as rapidly as possible.'[58] The 'by degree' may be noted – Marx therefore clearly envisaged a period during which both state-owned property and private property would exist.

It may be easily established that Marx's more detailed analysis in his later works of this transition from capitalist to socialist/communist society, as involving a prolonged transition period, remained entirely consistent with that in *The Communist Manifesto.* He noted in one of his final works, the *Critique of the Gotha Programme,* of the post-capitalist transition to a communist society:

'What we are dealing with here is a communist society, not as it has *developed* on its own foundations, but on the contrary, just as it *emerges* from capitalist society, which is thus in every respect, economically, morally, and intellectually, still stamped with the birth-marks of the old society from whose womb it emerges.'[59]

At the beginning of such a transition Marx outlined that payment in society, and distribution of products and services, necessarily had to be according to work, that is on the basis of exchange values, even within the state-owned sector of the economy:

'Accordingly, the individual producer receives back from society - after the deductions have been made - exactly what he gives to it....

'Here obviously the same principle prevails as that which regulates the exchange of commodities, as far as this is exchange of equal values.... as far as the distribution of the latter among the individual producers is concerned, the same principle prevails as in the exchange of commodity equivalents: a given amount of labour in one form is exchanged for an equal amount of labour in another form.

'Hence, *equal right* here is still in principle - *bourgeois right...* The right of the producers is *proportional* to the labour they supply; the equality consists in the fact that measurement is made with an *equal standard*, labour.'[60]

In such a society economic inequality would necessarily still exist:

'one... is superior to another physically or mentally and so supplies more labour in the same time, or can labour for a longer time; and labour, to serve as a measure, must be defined by its duration or intensity, otherwise it ceases to be a standard of measurement. This *equal* right is an unequal right for unequal labour... it tacitly recognises the unequal individual endowment and thus the productive capacities of the workers as natural privileges. *It is, therefore, a right of inequality in its content like every right.* Right by its very nature can consist only as the application of an equal standard; but unequal individuals (and they would not be different individuals if they were not unequal) are measurable by an equal standard only insofar as they are made subject to an equal criterion, are taken from a *certain* side only, for instance, in the present case, are regarded *only as workers* and nothing more is seen in them, everything else being ignored. Besides, one worker is married, another not; one has more children than another, etc. etc.. Thus, given an equal amount of work done, and hence an equal share in the social consumption fund, one will in fact receive more than another, one will be richer than another, and so on. To avoid all these defects, right would have to be unequal rather than equal.'[61]

Marx noted that only after a prolonged transition would payment according to work be replaced with the ultimately desired goal, distribution of products according to members of society's needs.

'Right can never be higher than the economic structure of society and its cultural development which this determines.

'In a higher phase of communist society... after the productive forces have also increased with the all-around development of the individual, and all the springs of common wealth flow more abundantly - only then can the narrow horizon of bourgeois right be crossed in its entirety and society inscribe on its banners: From each according to his abilities, to each according to his needs!'[62]

Deng Xiaoping and Marx

These passages from Marx immediately make entirely clear that Deng Xiaoping formulated reform and opening up in strict Marxist terms. Indeed, as is well known, Deng asserted that the basis of China's policy was the integration of Marxism with China's specific conditions. [63]

Some authors in the West, have contended that Deng's economic policies were not in accord with those of Marx. However, as will be analysed below, while China's economic policies clearly differed from those of the USSR after the introduction of the First Five Year Plan in 1929, which introduced comprehensive planning and essentially total state ownership, it is clear that China's economic policies were in line with those indicated by Marx - i.e.it was China's policies under reform and opening up which were in line with Marx, not the economic policies of the USSR after 1929.

Regarding China's economic reform policies Deng noted, as stated in Marxist terms, that China was in the socialist and not the (higher) communist stage of development. Large scale development of the productive forces/output was the prerequisite before China could make the transition to a developed socialist/communist society. Indeed, it is quite clear that Deng Xiaoping was paraphrasing Marx in the *Critique of the Gotha Programme* noting:

'A Communist society is one in which there is no exploitation of man by man, there is great material abundance, and the principle of from each according to their ability, to each according to his needs is applied. It is impossible to apply that principle without overwhelming material wealth. In order to realise communism, we have to accomplish the tasks set in the socialist stage. They are legion, but the fundamental one is to develop the productive forces.'[64]

More precisely, in a characterisation maintained to the present, Deng noted, in line with Marx's concept of a prolonged transition, that China was in the 'primary stage' of socialism - which was fundamental in defining policy:

'The Thirteenth National Party Congress will explain what stage China is in: the primary stage of socialism. Socialism itself is the first stage of communism, and here in China we are still in the primary stage of socialism – that is, the underdeveloped stage. In everything we do we must proceed from this reality, and all planning must be consistent with it.' [65]

The conclusion of such a contrast between a primary socialist stage of development and the principle of a communist society ('from each according to their ability to each according to each according to his needs') was that, precisely in line with Marx in the *Critique of the Gotha Programme*, in the present socialist period the principle was 'to each according to their work'. Deng noted: 'We must adhere to this socialist principle which calls for distribution according to the quantity and quality of an individual's work.'[66] As already noted In Marxist theory, outlined by Marx in the opening chapter of *Capital,* economic distribution according to work/labour is the fundamental principle of commodity production – and a commodity necessarily implies a market. In this socialist period a market would therefore exist – hence the eventual Chinese terminology of a 'socialist market economy.'

As demonstrated here, therefore, the analysis of Deng Xiaoping with which reform and opening up was formulated was strictly in line with the analysis of Marx.

The post-1929 Soviet system

Returning to Marx's analysis clearly also allows an evaluation of the economic system introduced in the USSR with the First Five Year Plan of 1929 – the fundamental framework of which was taken over by China immediately after 1949. This Soviet post-1929 economic structure introduced in the USSR an economic system which had never been seen previously in history. In this system:

- Not merely all major but thousands of minor prices were fixed by the state – it was illegal to sell a small product at a different price in Moscow and in Vladivostock more than 6,000 kilometres away;
- Almost all significant urban economic units, down to the level of local shops and restaurants, were state-owned while in the countryside individual peasant tenure was almost eliminated and replaced by state-owned or large scale cooperative farms.
- Resources were allocated within this economy not by the market but by 'material balances'.
- As the international economy was difficult to predict international trade therefore introduced severe complications into this economic system and was reduced to a low level.

This system is sometimes called a 'planned economy' but a more accurate term is 'administered economy' - because a plan can deal merely with a few key variables, while allowing the market to determine most others, whereas in the Soviet system literally thousands of economic variables were strictly centrally controlled.

From a fundamental economic viewpoint this post-1929 system therefore constituted the abolition of a system based on allocation of resources via exchange values and a market and its replacement with one based on use values ('material balances'). However, instead of this transition being spread out over a long period of time, as envisaged by Marx, it was carried out 'at a stroke' with the introduction of the First Five Year Plan in 1929. Simultaneously, regarding property relations, instead of the concept of *The Communist Manifesto* 'to wrest, by degree, all capital from the bourgeoisie', that is a prolonged process of transition in which both state and private property would exist, in 1929 an essentially completely state-owned or dominated system was introduced immediately in an extremely short period of time.

It is therefore clear that such a system was not in line with Marx's concepts. In addition to the fundamental criteria already previously noted, Marx also made it clear in *Das Kapital* that socialism, the very name of which derives from 'socialised', was based on the development of large scale socialised production - Marx noting of the transition from capitalism:

'As soon as this process of transformation has sufficiently decomposed the old society from top to bottom... then the further socialisation of labour and further transformation of the land and other means of production into socially exploited and, therefore, common means of production, as well as the further expropriation of private proprietors, takes a new form... One capitalist always kills many. Hand in hand with this centralisation, or this expropriation of many capitalists by few, develop, on an ever-extending scale, the co-operative form of the labour process, the conscious technical application of science, the methodical cultivation of the soil, the transformation of the instruments of labour into instruments of labour only usable in common, the economising of all means of production by their use as the means of production of combined, socialised labour... The monopoly of capital becomes a fetter upon the mode of production, which has sprung up and flourished along with, and under it. Centralisation of the means of production and socialisation of labour at last reach a point where they become incompatible with their capitalist integument. Thus integument is burst asunder. The knell of capitalist private property sounds. The expropriators are expropriated.'[67]

In order to leave no doubt as to the consistency of this analysis with his earlier writing Marx specifically appended to this passage from *Das Kapital* a long quotation from *The Communist Manifesto*. But peasant production, or individual ownership of restaurants and local shops, all of which were transferred to de facto or de jure state ownership in the USSR after 1929, were not large scale 'socialised' production – they were small scale, frequently purely individual, forms of production. The expropriation of such property therefore did not correspond to the concepts put forward by Marx at any time, whether in the early formulas of *The Communist Manifesto*, his late writing in *The Critique of the Gotha Programme*, or in *Das Kapital.*

It is clear, therefore, that the system introduced in 1929 in the USSR *did not* correspond to Marx's concept of a long transition to developed socialism. The post-1929 USSR saw the abolition of market, and all major forms of private ownership, in a single step – not a process 'by degrees' as Marx put it. It was an attempt to impose full state ownership on almost all major sectors of the economy – in Marxist terminology an attempt to impose a superstructure (state legal forms of ownership) on the economic base in a single step. **Objectively in the economic field this post-1929 Soviet system was therefore not Marx's but an ultra-left adventure**.

An argument is sometimes put forward that the system introduced in 1929 in the USSR was necessary due to military/geopolitical considerations – this administered economy was used to create a priority for military and heavy industry and this military-industrial complex, in turn, allowed the USSR to win World War II against Nazi invasion. As issues of national defence and military considerations, when faced with the threat of war, must take priority over purely economic ones, this constitutes a serious argument that the Stalin system of 'administered economy' was necessary in the 1930s - Deng Xiaoping himself stated that a world war would necessarily take precedence over all other factors, stating of reform and opening up that this would be the one factor that would override it: 'Nothing short of a world war would tear us away from this line.'[68] Counter arguments can also be made to the argument that the administered economy of the 1929 First Five Year Plan was a necessary response to geopolitical considerations – it was introduced four years before Hitler came to power in 1933.

For present purposes, however, it is unnecessary to settle this issue of whether the Stalin ultra-left administered economy of the 1930s, which clearly was not in line with Marx's fundamental concepts of the transition to socialism, was necessary to win the war with German fascism or whether there were alternatives. For present purposes it is merely necessary to note that whatever the situation of the 1930s this system of an administered economy was continued after the victorious conclusion of World War II – indeed it existed in the USSR almost to its collapse in 1991. Whatever were the geopolitical considerations of the 1930s, this decades long continuation of an administered, essentially entirely state, economy after World War II was not in line with the concepts of Marx already outlined.

The system of the 'administered economy' was of course introduced into China in the years immediately following the creation of the People's Republic with the gradual transfer of all major economic units into the state sector and the creation of communes in agriculture. In summary, the economic course in China prior to reform and opening up constituted the same ultra-left deviation from Marx's concepts as had existed in the USSR.

A systematic comparison of Marx's concepts with those of the post-1929 Soviet Union therefore makes entirely clear that post-Deng policies in China under reform and opening up were far more in line with Marx's than were the USSR's. Given the essentially 100 per cent state ownership of industry in China "Zhuada Fangxiao" – maintaining the large enterprises within the state sector and releasing the small ones to the non-state sector – together with the creation of a new private sector created an economic structure clearly more in line with that envisaged by Marx than the essentially 100 per cent state ownership in the USSR after 1929. The same, of course, applies to the introduction of the household responsibility system in agriculture. Deng's insistence on the formula that in the transitional period reward would be 'according to work' and not 'according to need' was similarly strictly in line with Marx's analyses. Reform and opening up, with its creation of a 'socialist market economy', through a simultaneous 'return to Marx' in the creation of a new economic system, thereby laid the basis, as has already been seen, for the greatest economic development in world history.

Marx and 'marginalist' economics

Having shown above that China's economic policy under reform and opening up was more in line with Marx's concepts than the economic policy of the USSR a comparison with the capitalist economies and theories that dominated the West will now also be made.

In this field a terminological counterposition is sometimes made between Marx and 'Western economics'. But this way of formulating the issue is misleading. Not only was Marx self-evidently 'Western', he was a German who lived for the majority of his life in Britain, but his economic theories were developed from those of Adam Smith, the founder of modern economics, and David Ricardo. As will be shown the correct terminological counterposition is that of Marx and 'marginalist economics'.

To see the precise significance of this distinction it necessary to understand which issue Marx analysed. It is entirely untrue, a misunderstanding, to believe that Marx was not concerned with 'the market', and the balance of supply and demand. On the contrary Marx's entire analysis in *Das Kapital* was based on the assumption that the market was operating. To be precise, the analysis of value in *Das Kapital* assumes that the market operates and supply and demand balance. The issue Marx addressed was simply much more profound. **The question Marx analysed was: if it is assumed that supply and demand are in balance then what is the economy's dynamic?** In what way does the economy then develop? Therefore, Marx asked the question: 'assume supply and demand balance, then what happens to the economy?'

This fundamental question, naturally, did not mean that Marx assumed that at any particular point in time supply and demand were in balance – he knew perfectly well they were not. Marx simply assumed for purposes of analysis: (i) in competitive markets, market operation would over time on average iron out imbalances in supply and demand; (ii) in non-competitive markets, above average profits would be generated in the form of rent (not merely 'rent of land' but 'rent' in the technical economic sense of the long term ability to generate above average profits– a large section of the third volume of *Das Kapital* is of such economic rents generated by monopoly). Marx, therefore, did not at all ignore markets, or supply and demand, he simply wanted to analyse what were the dynamics of the economy when supply and demand were in balance.

Analysis of the interaction of supply and demand carried out in 'Western', or more correctly 'marginalist', economics is therefore not necessarily contrary to Marx – that depends on other features of its overall framework. Interesting developments may take place in this field of study, it is merely that Marx was analysing another, and as will be seen more important, question. If the root of Marx's analysis is to be seen, however, this is most clearly understood by going back to the works of Ricardo and of Adam Smith, the founder of modern economics, and understanding Marx's relation to them.

Adam Smith

It is a paradox that Adam Smith's *The Wealth of Nations* and Marx's *Das Kapital* are without doubt two of the most famous books on economics ever written, but Marx's *Das Kapital* is certainly far more read than Smith's *The Wealth of Nations.* The reason for this is that almost all Marxist economists read *Das Kapital* whereas few 'Western' economists have read Smith's *The Wealth of Nations* – they merely falsely assume they know what is says or read second hand commentaries on it.

But whereas most 'Western' economists don't read Adam Smith, Marx read *The Wealth of Nations* in great detail – Marx's notes and commentaries on it in run to hundreds of pages. Indeed, it will become clear to what a huge degree Smith's analysis formed one of the most fundamental sources of Marx's ideas. It is therefore necessary to analyse the relation between Marx and Adam Smith – doing so makes clear their close interrelation, and the way that Marx's views are far closer to Smith's than are those of marginalist economics.

Marx and Smith

Smith announced his fundamental conclusion in *The Wealth of Nations,* the founding work of modern economics, in its first sentence.

'The greatest improvement in the productive powers of labour, and the greater part of the skill, dexterity, and judgment with which it is directed, or applied, seem to have been the effect of the division of labour.'

The rest of the book follows logically from this sentence. Marx in turn in his initial works, for example *The German Ideology*, simply took over Smith's terminology of 'division of labour' - in later works Marx used the terminology of 'socialisation of labour'[69] or 'socialised production'[70] but this did not alter the content. Marx, of course, regarded socialised labour/division of labour as the most important productive force and increasing socialisation of labour as the most fundamental source of human progress - as Marx put it: 'Division of labour increases with civilisation.'[71]

As will be seen Marx shows that economic concepts are not eclectically separated from each other, but they form an integrated system each expressing the consequences of the increasing division/socialisation of labour. Realisation of this is made more difficult for 'Western', more accurately 'marginalist' economists, by the fact that the overwhelming majority of them have never actually read *The Wealth of Nations* and that Marx changed terminology from 'division of labour' to 'socialisation of labour' in his later works. However, as will be seen Marx developed his concepts originally using the vocabulary of 'division of labour' – making the process extremely clear for anyone who has actually read Adam Smith. Therefore, here a systematic study of the interrelation of Smith and Marx will be made.

Marx on the socialisation of labour

Smith was not the first person to note division of labour, his genius was that he was the first person to draw out its consequences – thereby creating modern economics. As will be seen, while Marx corrected certain specific errors in Smith he in no way altered Smith's fundamental conclusion that division of labour/socialisation of labour was the most powerful force in economic development – Marx's genius lay in understanding the implications of this even more clearly that Smith. Indeed, the attempt to counterpose Smith and Marx, to present Smith as the founder of 'Western' economics and Marx to have created something entirely different, is simply factually false. It can only be sustained by those who have never read Smith's magnum opus - which, as already noted, unfortunately means most 'Western economists'. As will become clear Marx's ideas on economic dynamics are much closer to those of Smith than are those of 'marginalist' economics.

The fundamental consequences of socialisation of labour

Before dealing with detailed working out of Marx's theories, and their development of Smith, it is essential to understand their most general consequence. This is that **increasing socialisation/division of labour means that each producer and therefore, as consumers of production each individual, becomes increasingly dependent on the production of others.** In more detail this means:

- Production by others contributes an increasingly large part of the inputs of each producer. Put in technical terms 'indirect' inputs, that is the output of others, into production increases relative to 'direct' ones – that is the work of a single producer. The various technical categories of economics – for example the role of circulating capital/ intermediate products, the rising organic composition of capital, the increasing role of skilled (i.e. educated and trained) labour, the increasing proportion of the economy devoted to technological research and R&D – are simply expression of this fundamental process of increasing socialisation/division of labour.
- Each country becomes more dependent on the production of other countries and on its interaction with other countries – this leads to Xi Jinping's analysis of a 'common future for humanity' analysed below.

The detailed working out of this process of increasing socialisation of labour will now be analysed. As Marx and Smith drew out in detail the numerous implications of increasing socialisation/division of labour, to avoid making this article excessively long all the necessary quotations from Marx and Smith will not be given here at full length but can be found in 一盘大棋?——中国新命运解析 and 为什么亚当·斯密的"古典经济理论"可以很好的诠释亚洲的增长？[72] Here, therefore, only a

summary and conclusions in relation to Chinese Marxism
will be given. In each case it demonstrates the superiority of
China's Marxism's analysis and its roots in the fundamental
concepts that drive reform and opening up.

Division of labour and trade - globalisation and scale of market

A first immediate conclusion that follows from the fact that
socialisation/division of labour is the most fundamental
force in developing productivity is that the bigger the market
the larger the possible division of labour. That is, as Smith
entitled the third chapter of *The Wealth of Nations*: 'That the
Division of Labour is limited by the Extent of the Market'. As
the largest market is the global one Smith was an unequivocal supporter of what is now known as 'globalisation' - as is
well known, Smith launched fierce attacks on protectionism.

Marx entirely supported Smith's analysis on this and it
constituted the clear foundation of his own concepts. Indeed,
in *The German Ideology*, in the passages which clearly prepared *The Communist Manifesto,* Marx made this entirely
clear using Smith's terminology of division of labour. For
this reason, it is worth quoting Marx's analysis at length
as it makes completely clear that Marx's concepts flowed
from those of Smith. More precisely, overall human progress
was conceptualised by Marx as flowing from the successive expansion of division of labour as envisaged by Smith.
Therefore:

'How far the productive forces of a nation are developed is
shown most manifestly by the degree to which the division
of labour has been carried. Each new productive force, insofar as it is not merely a quantitative extension of productive
forces already known (for instance, the bringing into cultivation of fresh land), causes a further development of the
division of labour.

At the very earliest stage:

'The division of labour inside a nation leads at first to the
separation of industrial and commercial from agricultural
labour, and hence to the separation of town and country
and to the conflict of their interests. Its further development
leads to the separation of commercial from industrial labour.
At the same time through the division of labour inside these

various branches there develop various divisions among the individuals co-operating in definite kinds of labour.' [73]

Marx then analysed how each progressive expansion of the division of labour (or in his later terminology socialisation of labour) created new productive and property relations, underlying his well known analysis of the development of successive modes of production:

'The various stages of development in the division of labour are just so many different forms of property, i.e., the existing stage in the division of labour determines also the relations of individuals to one another with reference to the material, instrument and product of labour. The first form of property is tribal property [Stammeigentum]. It corresponds to the undeveloped stage of production, at which a people lives by hunting and fishing, by cattle-raising or, at most, by agriculture...

'The second form is the ancient communal and state property, which proceeds especially from the union of several tribes into a city by agreement or by conquest, and which is still accompanied by slavery... The division of labour is already more developed... The class relations between citizens and slaves are now completely developed...

'The third form is feudal or estate property. If antiquity started out from the town and its small territory, the Middle Ages started out from the country. This different starting-point was determined by the sparseness of the population at that time, which was scattered over a large area and which received no large increases from the conquerors. In contrast to Greece and Rome, feudal development, therefore, begins over a much wider territory, prepared by the Roman conquests and the spread of agriculture at first associated with them.... As soon as feudalism is fully developed, there also arises antagonism to the towns.'[74]

This process in turn gave rise to capitalism and the rise of modern machine production – first developing in the textile industry which finally became the first core of the British Industrial Revolution and the creation of the first modern large-scale capital:

'The immediate consequence of the division of labour between the various towns was the rise of manufactures... Intercourse with foreign nations was the historical premise for the first flourishing of manufactures, in Italy and later in Flanders....

'The kind of labour which from the first presupposed machines, even of the crudest sort, soon showed itself the most capable of development. Weaving... was the first labour to receive an impetus and a further development through the extension of intercourse. Weaving was the first and remained the principal manufacture.... Alongside the peasants weaving for their own use... there emerged a new class of weavers in the towns, whose fabrics were destined for the whole home market and usually for foreign markets too. Weaving, an occupation demanding in most cases little skill and soon splitting up into countless branches, by its whole nature resisted the trammels of the guild. Weaving was, therefore, carried on mostly in villages and market centres, without guild organisation, which gradually became towns, and indeed the most flourishing towns in each land.

'With guild-free manufacture, property relations also quickly changed. The first advance beyond naturally derived estate capital was provided by the rise of merchants, whose capital was from the beginning movable, capital in the modern sense as far as one can speak of it, given the circumstances of those times. The second advance came with manufacture, which again mobilised a mass of natural capital, and altogether increased the mass of movable capital...

'Manufacture and the movement of production in general received an enormous impetus through the extension of intercourse which came with the discovery of America and the sea-route to the East Indies...

'The expansion of commerce and manufacture accelerated the accumulation of movable capital... Commerce and manufacture created the big bourgeoise.' [75]

From this analysis of increasing division of labour Marx drew the famous fundamental conclusions regarding the transition from one mode of production to another – from slavery, to feudalism, to capitalism, to socialism - which were reiterated throughout his later works:

'These different forms [of production] are just so many forms of the organisation of labour, and hence of property. In each period a unification of the existing productive forces takes place, insofar as this has been rendered necessary by needs.

'The contradiction between the productive forces and the form of intercourse, which, as we saw, has occurred several times in past history, without, however, endangering its basis, necessarily on each occasion burst out in a revolution, taking on at the same time various subsidiary forms, such as all-embracing collisions, collisions of various classes, contradictions of consciousness, battle of ideas, political struggle, etc....

'Thus all collisions in history have their origin, according to our view, in the contradiction between the productive forces and the form of intercourse.'[76]

These formulas of Marx, which as was seen were explicitly formulated on the basis of Smith's analysis of the division of labour, were carried over into, and formed the foundations, of Marx's later works – *The Communist Manifesto*, *The Critique of Political Economy*, and *Das Kapital.*

These formulas therefore make entirely clear that Marx did not form his concepts in opposition to Adam Smith's views on the division of labour, but that on contrary Adam Smith's analysis of division of labour was the original foundation on which Marx formed his own concepts - the same will be seen when more detailed technical issues in economics are analysed. Marx drew out conclusions from Smith that Smith had never realised, but Marx's ideas were created not in opposition to Adam Smith but on the foundations of and as a fundamental development of Adam Smith. Indeed, instead of 'Marx vs Adam Smith' it is far more correct to speak of 'Marx and Adam Smith'. The only reason most Western economists don't realise this is because they have never actually read Smith's *The Wealth of Nations.*

On the basis of such an analysis, of course, Marx was as strong as supporter of globalisation as Smith – for example, launching fierce attacks on Friedrich List, one of the principal founders of 19th century 'protectionist' economic policy.

This Marx/Smith analysis of the decisive role of international division of labour, as the most advanced expression of overall socialisation/division of labour, is of course fully confirmed in the present day by the numerous factual studies showing the strong positive correlation between openness of an economy to trade and its speed of economic development – this strong correlation is the international expression of the key role played by domestic vision of labour, and the role of intermediate products/circulating, capital analysed in Section 3 below. Furthermore, as already noted, the low level of international trade which was an integral part of the Soviet system after 1929, which meant cutting off of the USSR from broad participation in the international division of labour, was therefore in counterposition to Marx's concepts. In contrast to the Soviet deviation from Marx, support of globalisation is one of the most fundamental features of China's Marxist economic policy – being incorporated into the very name of 'reform and opening up'. This is, of course, continued and is further developed in discussion around the 19th Party Congress.

A common future for humanity

President Xi Jinping's support of globalisation, building on the framework of reform and opening up, is of course unambiguous and entirely in line with Marx: 'economic globalization is a result of growing social productivity, and a natural outcome of scientific and technological progress.' [77] The foundations of this analysis in Marx, in reform and opening up, and in contradiction to the post-1929 Soviet system is evident. But because division/socialisation of labour is the most fundamental process analysed by Marx/Smith, it necessarily has enormous implications reaching far beyond economics. Drawing out the implications of this, in further theoretical developments, clearly illustrates the way in which China has continued to develop the concepts of reform and opening up in discussion around the 19th Party Congress.

This is particularly clear in Xi Jinping's formulation of the concept of a 'common future for humanity' – one of the most important foundations of China's foreign policy. This concept, developed from the original basis of Marx's analysis, is the most coherent analysis of global affairs. Xi Jinping's concept has had a particularly strong impact internationally since his speech at the World Economic Forum in Davos in January 2017 – as recognised even by those strongly in disagreement with China.

As Steve Bannon, former Chief Strategist to President Trump, and a strong opponent of China, stated starkly 'I think it'd be good if people compare Xi's speech at Davos and President Trump's speech in his inaugural.'[78] Gideon Rachman, chief foreign affairs columnist for the *Financial Times*, recently noted: 'An important factor in persuading

Mr Trump to attend the WEF was that the star of last year's Davos was China's President Xi Jinping. Mr Xi took the opportunity to position China as the champion of free trade, telling a delighted audience that "pursuing protectionism is like locking yourself in a dark room".[79] US National Security Adviser McMaster, and Director of the US National Economic Council Cohn, jointly authored a *Wall Street Journal* article de facto attempting to set out an alternative to Xi Jinping's analysis.

In contrast to the self-declared 'economic nationalism' of Bannon, and what will be seen to be the 'marginalist' concepts of McMaster/Cohn, President Xi Jinping's support of globalisation, as already noted, is unambiguous. But support of globalisation in foreign policy is directly related to division/socialisation of labour. The advantage of division/socialisation of labour is that, as Marx/Smith show, by producers interacting in their production the resulting productivity and output is much greater than the sum of their individual efforts - as President Xi stated it in popular fashion in economics: 'one plus one can be greater than two.'[80] This concept, which follows directly from the analysis of socialisation/division of labour first made by Smith/Marx, necessarily destroys the concept that international relations are a 'zero sum game'. Instead of a 'zero-sum' situation, by engaging in division of labour both or many sides can gain.

Naturally this concept of 'a common future for humanity' does not mean that there are no conflicts between countries. But it means that they have a more fundamental common interest, in that the prosperity of each country depends on international division of labour – the prosperity of each country depends on other countries. This creates the reality of the international community – the 'shared future for humanity'.

Diversity and equality

This reality of mutual benefit from division/socialisation of labour, however, immediately poses another question. Division of labour produces its greatest benefits not because those participating in it are the same but because they are different – if they were the same there would be less benefit! However, division of labour in the modern world is necessarily international in scope – the age when even the largest national economies could be essentially self-contained is past. As President Xi Jinping puts it: 'In today's world, all countries are interdependent and share a common future.'[81]

This creates a further pillar of Xi Jinping's concept of the 'community of shared future'. Human and national diversity is not a disadvantage, something to be feared, but it contributes to human development. As Xi Jinping puts it, citing *History of the Three Kingdoms*:

'"Delicious soup is made by combining different ingredients." Diversity in human civilization not only defines our world, but also drives human progress.... Diversity in civilizations should not be a source of global conflict; rather it should be a driver for progress... Diverse civilisations should draw on each other to achieve common progress. Exchanges among civilizations should become a source of inspiration for advancing human society.'[82]

Therefore, instead of an attempt to impose uniformity, a single model which is considered 'superior' to all others, and which is attempted to be imposed on others, China's foreign policy precisely embraces the diversity of different countries.

The marginalist/neo-liberal analysis

In summary, the fundamental and interrelated concepts in Xi Jinping's analysis, developed on the basis of the analyses of Marx, which in turn was developed from Smith, are the mutual advantages of international division of labour on which modern prosperity is based, of a shared destiny of humanity, recognition of diversity, and equality of countries.

This contrasts clearly with the main alternative which is promoted internationally. In what was really an attempt to reply to Xi Jinping US National Security Adviser McMaster and the then Director of the US National Economic Council Cohn jointly authored a *Wall Street Journal* article – which could not have appeared without sanction from the highest US authorities. In this they proclaimed: 'the world is not a "global community" but an arena where nations, nongovernmental actors and businesses engage and compete for advantage.' Or as they put it, drawing the practical conclusion. 'America First signals the restoration of American leadership.'[83] This, therefore is a profoundly unequal concept of international relations – in its most grotesque form expressed in references to 'sh*thole countries'.[84]

This analysis that there is no 'global community' is directly based in marginalist/neo-liberal economics. In the marginalist concept the fundamental unit is not the division/ socialisation of labour analysed by Smith/Marx but the concept that economy and society is simply composed of individual units. McMaster and Cohn's starting point is a restatement, and an attempt to defend on the international field, exactly what the neo-liberal Margaret Thatcher declared on the national terrain: 'there is no such thing as society. There are individual men and women.'[85] This marginalist concept of economics, and its conclusions, is therefore fundamentally counterposed to the analysis of Smith/Marx.

This issue once again clearly shows Xi Jinping's, and Chinese Marxism's, concepts are therefore simultaneously entirely rooted in Marx's analysis and a development of them. They are for this reason the most advanced of any major political leader in the world – there is bluntly no work by a Western leader which is its equal. Because it is an integrated concept, ranging from economic foundations to direct conclusions on relations between countries, it is capable of providing a firm long-term basis to China's foreign policy in a way that corresponds to the interests of other countries. China's foreign policy, therefore, does not consist of a series of unconnected initiatives but has a coherent underlying approach and strategy set out in this volume. These concepts are precisely simultaneously fundamentally rooted in Marx, and show the development of these concepts in reform and opening up and the analysis around the 19th Party Congress.

Part 3 – The detailed working out of economic theory

Division/socialist of labour and the possibility of economic development

In Section 2, the consequences of Marx's analysis of socialisation of labour, and its development by China in reform and opening up, have been analysed in terms of the foundations of Marxist economic theory regarding the characteristics of the transition from capitalism to advanced socialism and in globalisation/geopolitics. This showed that China's reform

and opening up was fully in line with Marx's theories –
indeed it was a return to Marx's concepts after the economic
ultra-leftism of the post 1929 Soviet model. It also showed
that analyses such as 'a common future for humanity' build
on and further develop Marxist concepts. But while this
establishes that China's reform and opening up was in line
with Marx's economics this then poses a further question.
Is Marx's economics true? That is, like every analysis, Marx
must be subject to the test of being in line with the facts.
Certainly, the fact that reform and opening up produced the
greatest growth and increase in living standards in human
history is prima facie evidence of the correctness of Marxist
conceptions. But, nevertheless, it is also necessary to exam-
ine Marx's concepts in more detail and in the light of the
latest factual research. That is, like every scientific theory,
the predictions of Marx's analysis must be tested against the
facts.

In making this comparison to facts it is important to grasp,
as already noted, that the more detailed economic categories developed by Marx, and earlier Smith, are simply the
detailed analyses of the means by which the consequences of
division/socialisation of labour work themselves out. It will
be shown that these Marxist concepts are fully confirmed by
factual research - and therefore explain the practical success of the Marxist framework of reform and opening up.
These issues involve more technical economics than the earlier section, but it demonstrates that modern econometric
research confirms the analysis of Marx. Indeed, it is one of
the great strengths of Marx's analysis, and earlier Smith's,
that it follows the scientific principle that a theory must yield
testable predictions which are then confirmed by factual
studies – or, to use the famous Chinese saying, it must 'seek
truth from facts'. In fact, as will be seen below, it has taken
a long period for Western economics influenced by marginalism to catch up with Marx – it is finally being forced to do so
by the need to make a more accurate analysis of the causes
of economic growth.

Supply side analysis

It can immediately be seen from points made in Part 2, and as
will be confirmed in greater detail below, that China's focus

on the 'supply side' in discussion leading to the 19th Congress fully follows from Marx's analysis. It should be made clear that supply side analysis does not mean that the economy's demand side is ignored, but it means it is recognised that the supply side is the most powerful and therefore determinant. This discussion around the 19th Party Congress is therefore precisely in line with Marx's conclusion that:

'The result at which we arrive is, not that production, distribution, exchange and consumption are identical, but that they are all elements of a totality, differences within a unity. Production is the dominant moment, both with regard to itself in the contradictory determination of production and with regard to the other moments. The process always starts afresh with production... exchange and consumption cannot be the dominant moments... A definite [mode of] production thus determines a definite [mode of] consumption, distribution, exchange.'[86]

Shorter term demand changes can be significant, and can be utilised for shorter term economic management, but in the longer term it is supply side changes which are determinant.

Similarly, in analysing the most fundamental economic dynamics, Marx assumes that demand and supply are in balance not only at a micro-economic level but also a macroeconomic one. This, as with micro-economic balance of supply and demand, naturally does not mean that Marx believes that at any point of time macro-economic supply and demand are actually balanced. On the contrary Marx demonstrated the errors of Say's Law, the theory that supply creates its own demand, more than seven decades before Keynes launched his attack on it. It is merely that Marx analysed a more fundamental question: if macro-economic and micro-economic supply and demand balance what is the pattern of development of the economy? Put in technical terms, Marx's asked if it is assumed general equilibrium exists (the concern of Walras, Jevons and Marshall), and there is no deficit or surplus of effective demand (the concern of Keynes), then what is the economy's dynamic, what is its course of development? This concern reflected Marx's analysis that production was the most powerful aspect of the economy – Marx knew perfectly well that less powerful processes also operated but he wanted to focus on the development of the most fundamental.

It therefore follows that China's emphasis on the supply side of the economy is entirely in line with Marx.

Increasing division of labour and productivity

Turning to the detailed working out of economic processes, and the economic concepts that flow from them, the starting point may be taken that Smith in *The Wealth of Nations* first illustrated his analysis of the effects of division of labour through analysis of a pin-factory. In a famous passage:

'To take an example, therefore, from a very trifling manufacture, but one in which the division of labour has been very often taken notice of, the trade of a pin-maker: a workman not educated to this business (which the division of labour has rendered a distinct trade), nor acquainted with the use of the machinery employed in it (to the invention of which the same division of labour has probably given occasion), could scarce, perhaps, with his utmost industry, make one pin in a day, and certainly could not make twenty. But in the way in which this business is now carried on, not only the whole work is a peculiar trade, but it is divided into a number of branches, of which the greater part are likewise peculiar trades... I have seen a small manufactory of this kind, where ten men only were employed.... Those ten persons, therefore, could make among them upwards of forty-eight thousand pins in a day... But if they had all wrought separately and independently... they certainly could not each of them have made twenty, perhaps not one pin in a day; that is, certainly, not the two hundred and fortieth, perhaps not the four thousand eight hundredth, part of what they are at present capable of performing, in consequence of a proper division and combination of their different operations.'

Smith then derives is fundamental conclusion regarding the increasing division of labour with economic development:

'In every other art and manufacture, the effects of the division of labour are similar to what they are in this very trifling one... The division of labour, however, so far as it can be introduced, occasions, in every art, a proportionable increase of the productive powers of labour. The separation of different trades and employments from one another, seems to have taken place in consequence of this advantage. This separation, too, is generally carried furthest in those countries which enjoy the highest degree of industry and improvement.'[87]

Or as Marx summarised succinctly, as already noted: 'Division of labour increases with civilisation.'[88]

Marx developed Smith's analysis of Smith in this field in great detail, specifically devoting Chapters 13-15 of the first volume of *Das Kapital* to it. But this was a development of Smith's analysis, not a contradiction of it. Marx's conclusion was exactly the same as Smith's: 'the collective labourer, who constitutes the living mechanism of manufacture, is made up solely of such specialised detail labourers. Hence, in comparison with the independent handicraft, more if produced in a given time, of the productive power of labour is increased.'[89]

It was because of this understanding of the 'collective labourer' that Marx in his later works replaced Smith's terminology of 'division of labour' with 'socialisation of labour'. But as already noted, Marx's fundamental concepts were originally developed using Smith's own terminology of 'division of labour' and Marx's change in this area was terminological.

Market and non-market division of labour

Marx also noted, more clearly than Smith, that division/socialisation of labour could take place through two different mechanisms – through the market or within an individual productive unit:

'Division of labour in society is brought about by the purchase and sale of the products of different branches of industry, while the connexion between the detail operations in a workshop, is due to the sale of the labour power of several workmen to one capitalist, who applies it as combined labour power. The division of labour in the workshop implies concentration of the means of production in the hands of one capitalist; the division of labour in society implies. their dispersion among many independent producers of commodities.' [90]

However, if socialisation/division of labour was the fundamental force in raising productivity then, according to the analysis of Marx/Smith, both market and non-market division/socialisation of labour should therefore produce beneficial effects. Modern econometric studies fully confirm this analysis of Marx/Smith.

Intermediate products

Analysing first socialisation/division of labour taking place through the market, this illustrates with great clarity the way in which the apparently 'technical' economic categories of Marx, as earlier with Smith, are merely manifestations of socialisation/division of labour.

The simplest form of division/socialist of labour taking place through the market is the use and exchange of products which are entirely used up within a single production cycle - for example a steering wheel in a car, a hard disk in a computer, the electricity a factory uses in production etc. Such products were termed by Marx 'circulating capital' - the term used in current 'Western' economics is 'intermediate products' but this is merely a difference in name, not content. Therefore, the analysis that division of labour increases with economic growth/development, originating in Marx/Smith, should be shown in increasing use of intermediate products in production. This factual dynamic is fully confirmed by the modern econometric studies.

Regarding the most developed economy Jorgenson, Gollop and Fraumeni found in their comprehensive study of the US:

'the contribution of intermediate input is by far the most significant source of growth in output. The contribution of intermediate input alone exceeds the rate of productivity growth for thirty six of the forty five industries for which we have a measure of intermediate input.'[91]

Considering findings for the US economy in more detail, Jorgenson noted:

'Comparing the contribution of intermediate input with other sources of growth demonstrates that this input is by far the most significant source of growth. The contribution of intermediate input exceeds productivity growth and the contributions of capital and labour inputs....

The explanatory power of this perspective is overwhelming at the sectoral level. For 46 of the 51 industrial sectors... the contribution of intermediate, capital and labour inputs is the predominant source of output growth.'[92]

The same result as for the US is found for other economies - specifically including China. Regarding rapidly growing Asian economies:

- For South Korea, Hak K. Pyo, Keun-Hee Rhee and Bong-chan Ha found regarding material intermediate inputs: 'The relative magnitude of contribution to output growth is in the order of: material, capital, labour, TFP [Total Factor Productivity] then energy.'[93]
- For Taiwan Province of China, analysing 26 sectors in 1981-99, Chi-Yuan Liang found regarding intermediate material inputs: 'Material input is the biggest contributor to output growth in all sectors during 1981-99, except... seven.'[94]
- For mainland China, Ren and Sun found that in the period 1981-2000, subdivided into 1984-88, 1988-94 and 1994-2000: 'Intermediate input growth is the primary source of output growth in most industries.'[95]

In summary, the analysis of Marx/Smith of the role of socialisation/division of labour through market mechanisms, that is the role of circulating capital/intermediate products, is fully factually confirmed.

It should also be noted that these factual studies show Solow made a substantial error in formulating Western 'growth accounting' in the 1950s by not including intermediate products in analysis. That is, in Marx's terms, Solow made the error of not calculating circulating capital as well as fixed capital. This has now been corrected in studies of intermediate products and analyses such as KLEMs - capital (K), labor (L), energy (E), materials (M), and services (S). Such official systems of industry-level production accounts are now part of the national accounts in the US and other countries. But 'Western' analysis has taken almost 150 years to correct errors and move to Marx's position – as the phrase goes 'better late than never'. But it is disturbing that material continues to appear in sections of the Chinese media which repeats Solow's error and is therefore not in line either with Marx or with modern Western growth accounting.

Division of labour within a single productive unit

As already analysed, Marx noted that socialisation/division of labour can also take place through non-market mechanisms in a single productive unit - within a single company or single factory. If socialisation/division of labour is the most fundamental force in developing productivity, therefore, this should also lead to rising productivity. This leads to an easily testable conclusion – that units of production in which there is greater division of labour, that is which are larger in scale, should be more productive than smaller productive units. Modern econometric research again fully confirms this.

The comprehensive OECD studies on productivity indicators since 2012 finds clearly that productivity in large companies is substantially higher than in small companies. As the latest, 2017, OECD study notes: 'large firms can exploit increasing returns to scale, productivity tends to increase with firm size.'[96] Therefore: 'In most countries, labour productivity gaps between micro and, to a lesser extent small and medium-sized firms, and large firms are relatively high.'[97] And: 'Larger firms are on average more productive than smaller ones.'[98] As may be seen in Figure 23, the productivity of a firm will less than 10 employees is only 55% of that of a company with more than 250 employees, the productivity of a firm with 10-19 employees was only 64% of a firm with more than 250 employees.

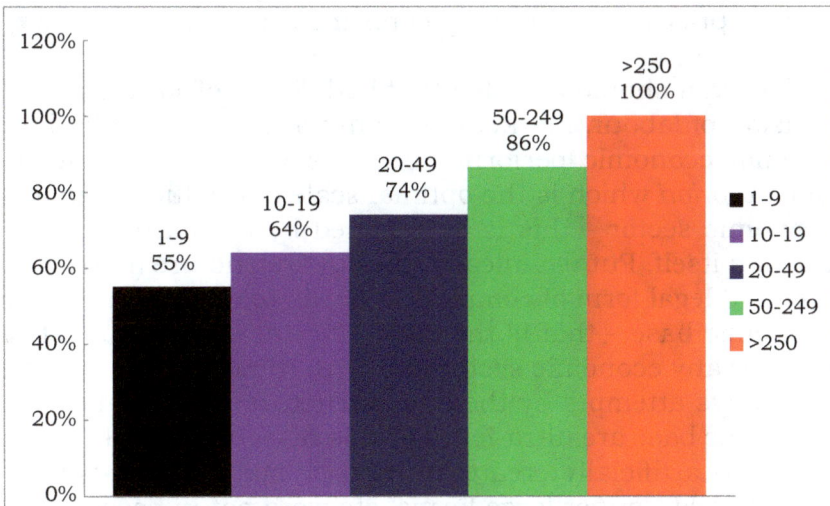

Figure 23: Productivity by Number of Company Employees
As % of firms with >250 employees

Source: Calculated from OECD Compendium of Productivity Indicators 2017

Global comparative data is therefore clear that large companies have higher productivity than small ones. In particular, the greater role played by large companies in the United States is one of the reasons for the US's superior productivity compared to its competitors. In the US 45% of employment is in companies with more than 250 employees, compared to only 33% in the EU. [99] In parallel, non-agricultural US self-employment is only just over half the average for the advanced economies – 7.5% of the workforce compared to 12.8%.[100] The same contrast as between the US and Europe is shown within Europe itself. In Europe, defining a small and medium enterprise (SME) as one with less than 250 employees, a small enterprise as having 0-49 employees, and a micro-enterprise as having under 10, the EU contained 20.4 million SMEs and only 43,000 large companies. Of the SMEs 92% were micro-enterprises.

The average productivity of labour in European small and medium enterprises is significantly lower than large enterprises. EU SMEs by 2005 accounted for 67% of jobs but only 58% of value added - EU SMEs had a productivity only 86% of the EU average. The country with the smallest ratio of SMEs to population was Germany – Europe's most successful economy.[101] This data on productivity of different sizes of enterprises therefore fully confirms the analysis of Marx/Smith.

Finally, it should be noted that both forms of socialisation/division of labour, market and non-market, are required for optimal economic performance. It is impossible to determine *a priori* which is the optimal scale of production in any economic sector – this is determined by the nature of production itself. Put technically, the superstructure (that it the size and legal form of companies) needs to correspond to the economic base – that is the most efficient size of productive unit for any economic sector at any particular point in time. As always attempts by the superstructure to determine the economic base are ultra-left. For this reason, attempts in the USSR to artificially create by legal or state means 'super-large hotels', 'super large farms' etc were not in accord with Marxist analysis. The development of the most efficient scale of economic unit must be decided by the practice of production itself, not by artificial state or legal interventions.

Lin Yifu and integrated development

At this point it is important to note a further implication of the Marx/Smith understanding that the most fundamental force in the development of production is the socialisation/division of labour which directly affects one the most recent fields of development of modern Chinese economic theory – Lin Yifu's 'New Structural Economics' (NSE).

The fact that socialisation/division of labour is the most fundamental force of production necessarily determines which economic development strategies will work and which will not. An immediate consequence is that a strategy of developing one sector of the economy without relation to others cannot achieve overall success - because an individual sector of production cannot be ripped out of the context of the vast division/socialisation of labour which determines its inputs and outputs.

At one time in the post-World War II period an erroneous type of development strategy of attempting to 'voluntaristically' develop individual industries or sectors of production was very popular in differing forms and therefore its errors were widely demonstrated. For example, following the international oil price increase in 1973, a number of Middle Eastern oil producers embarked on an attempt to diversify their economies by a strategy based on importing modern factories for producing petrochemicals and other oil related products. But although factory equipment they purchased was as modern as in Germany or the US the productivity of the new Middle Eastern factories failed to match Germany or the US. This was inevitably the result as production at such factories was part of a complex division of labour – which for efficiency required inputs and outputs including appropriate infrastructure, a skilled workforce, suitable power supplies, state of the art maintenance, logistics etc. These existed in the US or Germany but not in developing countries importing such factory equipment. Therefore, these production facilities could not achieve the same level of productivity as those using identical factory equipment in the US or Germany. This precisely expressed that efficient production relied on socialisation/division of labour - it was impossible to simply isolate one part of the productive chain.

Jones explains this consequence of the division/socialisation of labour more in more technical terms via the role of 'productivity multipliers':

'Low productivity in electric power generation reduces output in banking and construction. But this reduces the ease with which the electricity industry can build new dams and therefore further reduces output in electric power generation.'[102]

Consequently, 'intermediate goods provide links between sectors that create a productivity multiplier.'[103] Put non-technically, as advanced production is necessarily part of an integrated chain created by socialisation/division' of labour, productivity is held down by every weak link among the numerous ones which exist in the production chain.

Similarly, many developing countries in the 1950s and 1960s pursued an 'import substitution' strategy, attempting to develop manufacturing industries behind tariff barriers, while permitting the import of the capital equipment for such factories – the latter was necessary as developing countries could not produce such capital equipment themselves. This 'import substitution' strategy failed for three reasons related to division/socialisation of labour:

- As with the oil producers, isolated manufacturing plants could not function optimally without correspondingly efficient inputs and outputs.
- These manufacturing plants, often in heavy industry, were frequently not in line with these developing economies factor endowment (i.e. the abundance or scarcity of capital and labour) – developing economies have an advantage in labour intensive and not capital intensive industries, a fact stressed by Lin Yifu's NSE.
- the scale of market within a single developing economy is too small for the most efficient development of production.

A country can, of course, develop a particular economic sector if it is prepared to devote disproportionate resources to it – for example with military industry. But allocation of disproportionate resources to one part of the economy necessarily reduces resources available for other sectors - and it is in any case even in principle impossible to devote disproportionate resources to all economic sectors. For this reason, attempts to develop large economies which are not dominated by a single product (e.g. oil) on the basis of devoting disproportionate resources to individual sectors will not work – as numerous examples demonstrate.

Lin Yifu's NSE takes a different approach. It states that a country at a particular point in time needs to develop sectors in line with its factor endowment, that is its relative abundance of labour or capital. Then, over time, that country should aim to change its factor endowment – economic development being a progress from labour intensive to capital intensive growth.

Because NSE's strategy is based on changing the economy's overall factor endowment, which is spread across all sectors interconnected by division of labour, NSE's strategy does not violate the interconnected division of labour in an economy and does not suffer from problems of development strategies based on single sectors or import substitution. Furthermore, because NSE is based on comparative advantage in factor endowment at different stages of economic development it is entirely oriented to globalisation – the position supported by Marx/Smith.

While NSE can be stated in terms of marginalist neo-classical economics, which makes it more accessible to a Western audience, it is equally consistent with the Marx/Smith's analysis. Indeed, as will be seen, NSE's concept that development is a progression from labour intensive to capital intensive growth is in line with Marx's concept of the rising organic composition of capital analysed below. NSE is therefore a further clear example of the development of China's economic thinking based on the concepts underlying reform and opening up.

The organic composition of capital

As was noted above, increasing socialisation/division of labour has as an immediate consequence that indirect (socialised) inputs into production increase relative to direct ones. The first form of this, already analysed, is socialisation/division of labour in a single production cycle – whether in market or non-market forms.

However, not all indirect inputs are used up in single production cycle – for example machines, which produce over many cycles; buildings, also used over many production cycles; bridges, roads, railways and other infrastructure, which are involved in production over many years etc. Marx's terminology for productive assets whose use is spread over more than one production cycle, 'fixed investment', is the same as that of 'Western' economics. In the case of such products, therefore, increasing socialisation/division of labour will show itself in an increasing proportion of fixed investment in the economy.

Increasing socialisation/division of labour, that is the increase of indirect (socialised) inputs relative to direct labour, was therefore shown in two processes:

- In a single production cycle, by the increase in the proportion of circulating capital/intermediate products – the process just analysed.
- By the increase in the proportion of fixed investment relative to direct labour which operated not only over one production cycle but many – that is an increasing capital intensity of production.

This combined process, expressing the increasing socialisation/division of labour, was termed by Marx the rising 'organic composition of capital':

'it is a law of capitalist production that its development is attended by a relative decrease of variable in relation to constant capital... This is just another way of saying that owing to the distinctive methods of production developing in the capitalist system the same number of labourers, i.e., the same quantity of labour power set in motion by a variable capital of a given value, operate, work up and productively consume in the same time span an ever increasing quantity of means of labour, machinery and fixed capital of all sorts, raw and auxiliary materials — and consequently a constant capital of an ever-increasing value. This continual relative decrease of the variable capital vis-à-vis the constant, and consequently the total capital, is identical with the progressively higher organic composition of the social capital in its average. It is likewise just another expression for the progressive development of the social productive power of labour, which is demonstrated precisely by the fact that the same number of labourers, in the same time, i.e., with less labour, convert an ever-increasing quantity of raw and auxiliary materials into products, thanks to the growing application of machinery and fixed capital in general. To this growing quantity of value of the constant capital... corresponds a progressive cheapening of products... This mode of production produces a progressive relative decrease of the variable capital as compared to the constant capital, and consequently a continuously rising organic composition of the total capital.'[104]

This prediction that the percentage of fixed investment in the economy would increase with economic development was put forward by Smith, with Ricardo and Marx reaching the same conclusion. Once again modern econometric studies fully confirm Marx's analysis.

Lead economies in periods of economic development

To show this development of the increasing capital intensity of production, it is first useful to make a broad historic analysis of the lead economies in each period of economic development - as these show the most advanced production possibilities in each period. Analysing first the longest time-period, Figure 24 therefore shows the 'lead' economies in successive historical periods of economic development

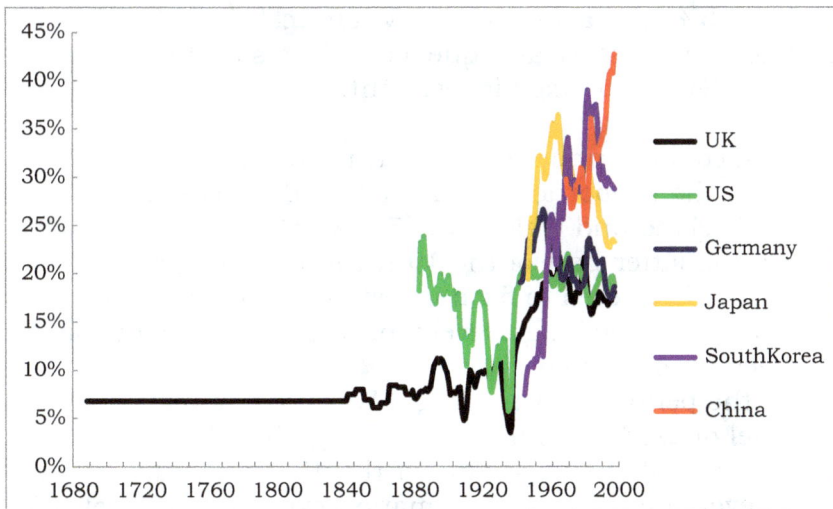

Figure 24: Fixed Investment % of GDP
Source: Deane and Cole, British Economic Growth 1688-1959, The Economist 100 Years of Economic Statistics, World Bank World Development

since the Industrial Revolution – i.e. the major economy which, in a given historical period, showed the most dynamic growth. As these major economies have been most studied, the longest term data exists for them.

The first economy for which estimates exist of the percentage of fixed investment in GDP is England in the period prior to the Industrial Revolution. The succeeding historical periods of growth and economic development were then, after the UK, in chronological order: the US from the second half of the 19th century; West Germany during its post-World War II 'economic miracle'; Japan in the 1960s and 1970s; the Asian 'Tiger' Economies in the 1980s, of which South Korea is taken as the example here; and finally, contemporary China. Figure 24 shows clearly that each lead economy in a period of economic development had a higher proportion of fixed investment in GDP than the one before and that these produced successively faster growth rates. Taking these countries in order in their period of emergence as international 'lead economy' in terms of growth rate then the UK achieved an average growth rate of 2%, the US a 3.5% average growth rate, West Germany after World War II a 6.8% growth rate, Japan an 8.6% growth rate, South Korea a growth rate of 8.3%/Singapore a 9.0% growth rate, and China 9.5% annual average growth from 1978-2016. The following is the historical sequence in terms of the percentage of GDP devoted to fixed investment.

- Immediately prior to and during the industrial revolution, the proportion of GDP devoted to fixed investment in England and Wales, was 5-7%.
- By the latter part of the 19th century, the proportion of US GDP devoted to fixed investment considerably exceed the UK's – reaching a level around 20% of GDP by the last decades of that century.
- In the period following World War II Germany achieved a level of fixed investment exceeding 25% of GDP.
- Starting at the beginning of the 1960s, Japan achieved a level of fixed capital formation exceeding 30% of GDP. This reached a peak in the early 1970s at 35% of GDP.
- During the 1980s South Korea achieved a level of fixed investment of above 35% of GDP and Singapore's was even higher.

- From the early 1990s China achieved sustained rates of fixed investment of 35% of GDP with, from the beginning of the 21st century, this rising to more than 40% of GDP. China's high level of fixed investment is therefore merely the logical culmination of a centuries long pattern of the rising proportion of fixed investment in GDP - each associated with faster growth rates.

Such data from lead economies in historical periods of economic development therefore fully confirms the rising contribution of investment to GDP foreseen by Smith, Ricardo, and Marx – as well as, later, by Keynes.

Contemporary measurement of the capital intensity of production

Turning to contemporary economic data, an increasing capital intensity of production, i.e. a rise in the ratio of fixed investment relative to direct labour inputs, may be measured by an economy's Incremental Capital Output Ratio (ICOR) - ICOR is the percentage of a country's GDP that must be invested to generate one percent growth of GDP. Stated formally:

ICOR = real GDP growth rate/percentage of fixed investment in GDP

The lower the ICOR number, provided it is positive, the less capital intensive is an economy's production, while the higher the ICOR the more capital intensive is an economy's production.

Figure 25 therefore shows ICOR for the world, for developing economies, and for advanced economies in 2015, the latest comprehensive internationally comparable World Bank data. This shows:

- Globally ICOR was 8.6 – i.e. 8.6% of GDP had to be invested for the world economy to grow by 1%.
- ICOR for developing economies was 7.7 – capital intensity of developing economies was therefore below the global average.
- ICOR for advanced economies was 9.7 – capital intensity of production in high income economies was above both the world average and even further above that for developing economies.

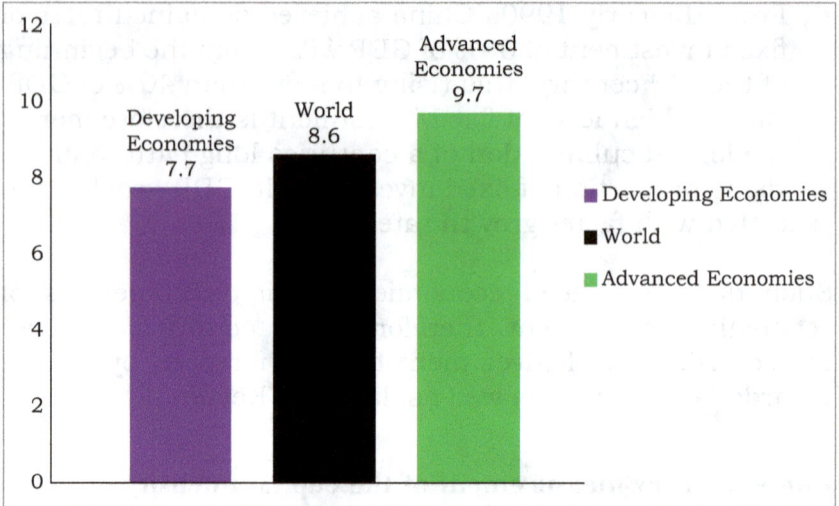

Figure 25: Incremental Capital Output Ratio -2015
Source: Calculated from World Bank World Development
Indicators

This comprehensive World Bank data for the latest internationally comparable year therefore fully confirms the analysis of Marx/Smith, and also Lin Yifu's NSE, that production in developed/high income economies is more capital intensive than in developing economies – i.e. that the capital intensity of production increases with economic development. This however, as already noted, is merely an expression of the increasing socialisation of labour.

It should be noted, however, that ICOR for a single year can be strongly affected by fluctuations in the business cycle, with its consequent accelerations or decelerations in GDP growth. As a cross check, to avoid suspicion that the latest data reflects simply an atypical situation for a single year, Figure 26 therefore shows a five-year average for ICOR calculated for the period 2010-2015 – an even longer term analysis is given below.

Taking a five-year moving average:

*   World ICOR was 8.5.
*   ICOR in developing economies was 6.1 - below the world average.
*   ICOR in high income economies was 12.1 – above the world average.

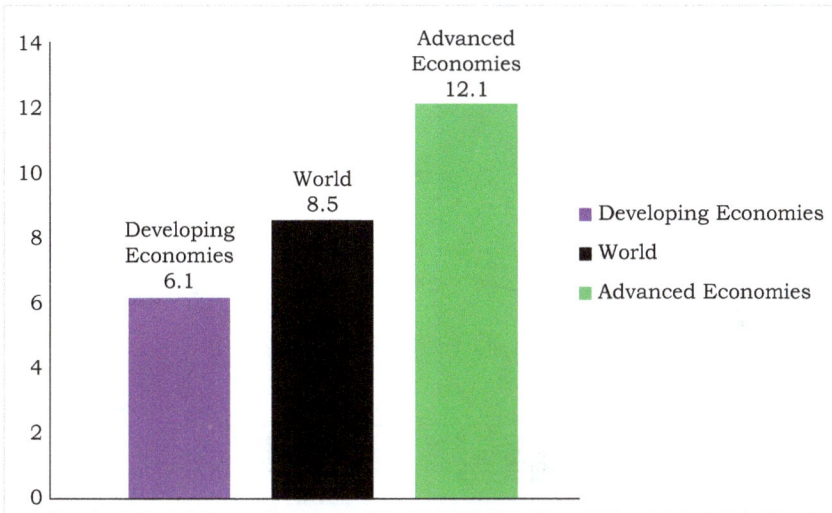

Figure 26: Incremental Capital Output Ratio 2010-2015
5 year average

Source: Calculated from World Bank World Development Indicators

- The analysis of Marx/Smith, and NSE, that advanced economies have more capital intensive production, was therefore again fully confirmed.

Finally, in order to consider a long-time frame, and bring out the structural features of the contemporary period, Figure 27 shows ICOR for the entire period for which internationally comparable World Bank data is available - a 10 year moving average is used to eliminate business cycle fluctuations. As may be seen, using this structural measure, over the entire period ICOR in high income economies is higher than in developing economies – precisely in line with the analysis of Marx/Smith (and NSE).

It is therefore clear from the global national accounts data that whatever time frame is taken the fundamental premise of Marx/Smith and New Structural Economics is confirmed – economic development sees a transition from less capital intensive to more capital-intensive development, which in turn reflects an increasing socialisation of labour.

Growth accounting analysis

Growth accounting data, as with national accounts data, also confirms that economic growth in advanced economies

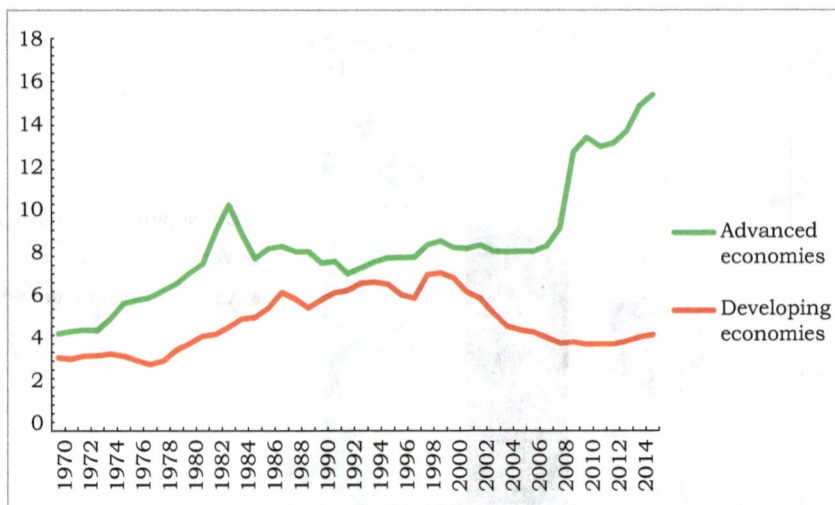

Figure 27: Incremental Capital Output Ratio 10 year moving average

Source: Calculated from World Bank World Development Indicators

is more capital intensive than in developing economies. To analyse these trends it is important to note the official improvements in the methods of measuring economic growth and its causes which have been formally adopted by the UN, OECD, and other statistical agencies The reasons for these changes in the official methods of calculating economic growth and its causes are analysed in detail in 为何联合国、经合组织与美国正式改变其经济增长成因测算方法？[105]. In this article data calculated according to the new and approved methods of calculation is used – that is, in the material here capital services not capital stock is used to measure capital inputs, and both labour quantity (hours worked) and labour quality (education, skills etc) are used in measuring labour inputs.

In order to factually assess the analysis of growth in developing and advanced economies, using growth accounting methods, the data used here is for the 30 largest advanced ('high income') economies and the 30 largest developing ('middle and low income') economies, as categorised by World Bank classification. These economies account for more than 91% of world GDP in purchasing power parities (PPPs) & more than 93% of world GDP at market exchange rates. This data may therefore be treated as conclusive - no results from small economies would be large enough to invalidate it.

The key factual data is set out in Figure 28 and Figure 29. This shows that in advanced economies an average 74% of GDP growth is accounted for by capital investment and in developing economies an average 62% of GDP growth is accounted for by capital investment – i.e. economic growth in advanced economies is more capital intensive than in developing economies.

The fact that both national accounts (ICOR) and growth accounting studies show the same result, that is they confirm that development in advanced economies is more capital intensive than growth in developing economies leaves no doubt as to the factual situation. **The analysis of Marx/ Smith of the rising capital intensity of production with economic development is fully factually confirmed**. Economic development is a process of transition from labour intensive to capital intensive growth. The analysis that economic development in advanced economies is more capital intensive than in developing economies is correct.

Finally, regarding this issue, the factual data on the increasing role played by intermediate products in production, and a rising capital intensity of production, therefore

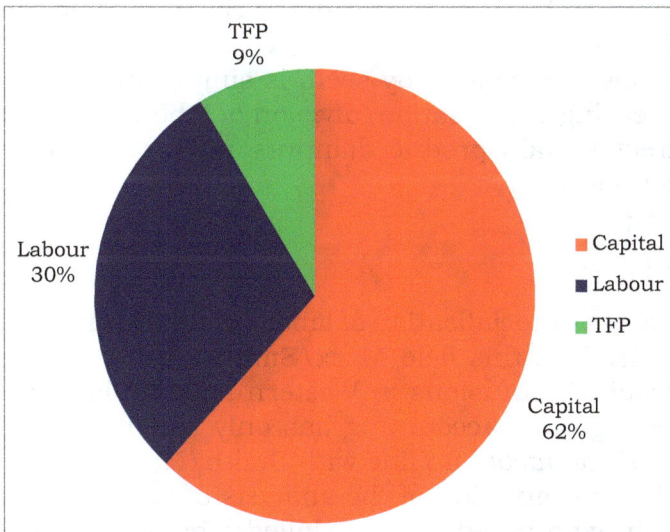

Figure 28: World's 30 Largest Developing Economies % average contribution to GDP growth 1990-2016

Source: Calculated from The Conference Board Total Economy Database 2017

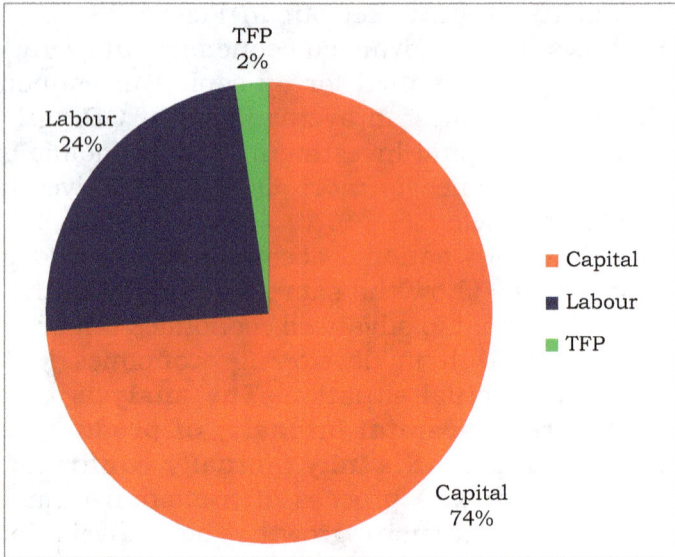

Figure 29: World's 30 Largest Advanced Economies % average
contribution to GDP growth 1990-2016
Source: Calculated from The Conference Board Total Economy
Database 2017

fully confirms Marx's analysis of the rising organic composition of capital.

This however, as already seen, is simply an expression of the increasing socialisation/division of labour – the increase in indirect (socially produced) inputs into production relative to direct ones.

Skilled labour

This process of socialisation of labour extends into the labour supply itself. In this field Marx/Smith were literally centuries ahead of confusions in Western marginalist economics – Western growth accounting has only recently adjusted to bring itself *de facto* into line with Smith/Marx.

The first formulation of the analysis of skilled labour was by Smith, who noted that unskilled labour became skilled through inputs of training and education – these inputs thereby allowing skilled labour to command higher pay than unskilled labour. Marx, similarly, noted that the starting point of every human was unskilled labour and that this labour became skilled through inputs of training and education. This training and education therefore expressed socialisation/division of labour – i.e. it was due to the input of educators, teachers, more skilled workers etc. For this reason, Marx/Smith therefore carefully distinguished skilled labour from unskilled labour.

However, unfortunately, when Solow formulated 'growth accounting' within Western marginalist economics in the 1950s, he did not incorporate this distinction between skilled and unskilled labour made by Marx/Smith and simply measured all labour by the number of hours worked. This necessarily leads to serious errors. It means, for example, that one hour of work by a South Korean former peasant in 1953, who may have been illiterate, is calculated as equivalent to one hour of work by a South Korean engineering PhD in 2018. The value of output created by a South Korean with an engineering PhD is obviously much greater than that of an illiterate former South Korean peasant in 1953. However, if their one hour of work is measured as the same then the greater value of output of the engineering PhD will be incorrectly categorised as due to increases in TFP, i.e. to increases in output not due to inputs of capital and labour, when that is not its cause – the increased output is due to the much greater skill and education of the engineering PhD, which in turn is created by the inputs from education into the teaching and training of the engineering PhD. The extra value of the output of the engineering PhD is therefore caused by socialisation of labour – the inputs from the education/training that PhD student received.

Fortunately, the official methods of calculation of the causes of economic growth adopted by the UN and OECD have now overturned Solow's error and *de facto* adopted the analysis of Marx/Smith of distinguishing between unskilled and skilled labour. This is done by separately measuring labour quantity (number of hours worked) and labour quality (the level of education, skill etc). This is analysed in detail in为何联合国、经合组织与美国正式改变其经济增长成因测算方法？It is therefore disturbing that various articles in China repeat the mistake of Solow and have not adopted the new official methods of calculation of the UN and OECD.

Once the correct methods of measurement are adopted it immediately becomes clear that Marx (and Smith's) analysis of the increasing socialisation of labour is fully factually confirmed. Figure 31 and Figure 30 therefore show the breakdown of total labour inputs between labour quantity and labour quality in the 30 largest advanced and 30 largest developing economies.[106] As already noted economic growth in developing countries is more labour intensive, and less capital intensive, than economic growth in advanced countries. In developing countries almost 30% of GDP growth is due to labour inputs whereas in advanced economies it is slightly under 24% - this is the obverse of the fact that growth in advanced economies is more capital intensive than in developing economies. However, examining these labour inputs in more detail it may be seen:

- In developing economies almost two thirds of labour inputs into GDP growth are simply due to increases in labour quantity (hours worked) and only one third due to improvements in labour quality.[107]
- In advanced economies the majority of labour inputs (51%) are due to increases in labour quality.

In summary, in advanced economies the majority of labour inputs are due to improvements in the education, skill etc of the workforce – the result of socialisation of labour. This

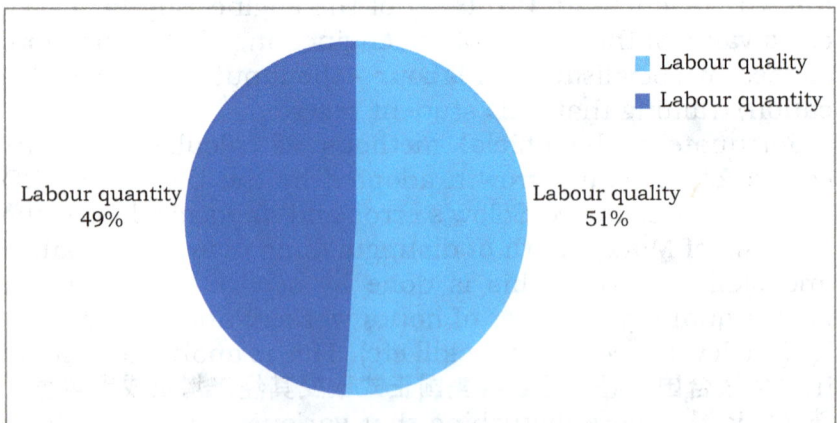

Figure 30: % of Labour Contribution to GDP Growth -30 Largest Advanced economies 1990-2016

Source: Calculated from The Conference Board Total Economy Database 2017

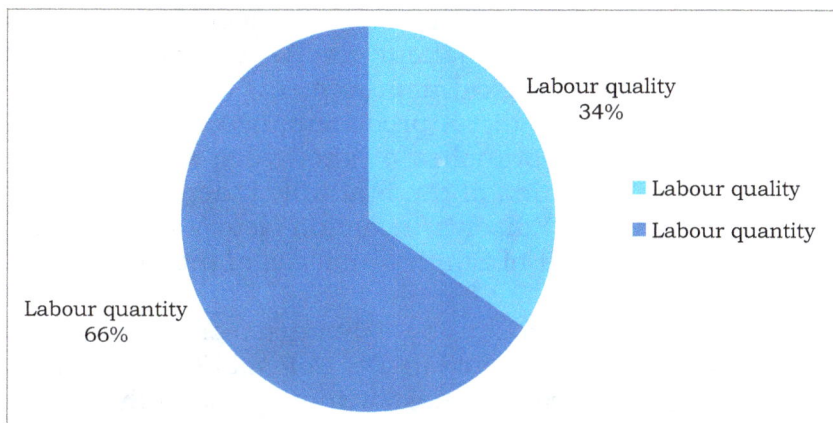

Figure 31: % of Labour Inputs to GDP Growth -30 Largest
Developing Economies 1990-2016

Source: Calculated from The Conference Board Total Economy
Database 2017

has in turn created enormous sectors of those engaged in education and training – lecturers, professors, teachers, kindergarten educators, vocational trainers etc. In all advanced economies these form a major part of the work force – itself a striking expression of the division/socialisation of labour. These layers form a very significant part of what are loosely referred to as 'middle income' groups, but which are most accurately termed very skilled workers (the term 'middle class', as used in the West, is entirely inaccurate as such groups do not form a class, and the term is used merely to try to hide the fact that the overwhelming majority of such groups are (skilled) workers).The analysis of Marx/Smith of the increasing socialisation of labour is therefore again fully confirmed – and the practical consequences of Solow's original error is clear. It has taken a long time for Western marginalist economics to correct its errors in this field and catch up with Smith/Marx.

Division of labour and technology

Finally, it is occasionally claimed that Smith, and even Marx, underestimated the role of technology in economic development. This is false and based on a misunderstanding. Smith's *The Wealth of Nations,* contains extremely detailed analysis of the development of technology which flows entirely from his analysis of the division of labour. Smith carefully notes the way in which technological improvement, which was originally primarily due to direct producers, becomes separated out into specialised branches of knowledge and research. The road to the creation of the first fully independent modern research centre, Edison's 'invention factory' of 1877, was a logical development of Smith's analysis of increasing division of labour.

As for Marx the claim he underestimated technology is even more false. He already noted in *The Communist Manifesto*:

'The bourgeoisie cannot exist without constantly revolutionising the instruments of production... The bourgeoisie, by the rapid improvement of all instruments of production, by the immensely facilitated means of communication, draws all, even the most barbarian, nations into civilisation. The cheap prices of its commodities are the heavy artillery with which it batters down all Chinese walls, with which it forces the barbarians' intensely obstinate hatred of foreigners to capitulate.'[108]

The enormous, more than 100-page, chapter on 'Machinery and Modern Industry' in the first Volume of *Das Kapital* is the longest in the entire work. Marx simply understood that technology, and scientific research, were expressions of socialisation/division of labour. Technology development does not consist of 'isolated geniuses' separated from society but of forces integrated into it. In particular in the modern economy technological development depends on the development of universities, themselves expressions of socialisation/ division of labour, vast expenditures on R&D which take up an increasing proportion of GDP, increasingly large research departments in companies etc. In the modern economy literally millions of researchers are involved in technological development. Factual research shows that progress in R&D is proportional to the inputs into it. This is why China, in line with other countries, is aiming to increase the percentage of its economy devoted to R&D – statistical details are given in 一盘大棋?——中国新命运解. 析In summary, technological development is a classic product of division/socialisation of labour.

Again, as with education, those engaged in such technological development – company R&D staff, university researchers, those employed in specialist research laboratories, state employees in technological development etc – now form a major part of the workforce – a striking expression of the socialisation/division of labour. Such highly educated/skilled researcher are themselves a product of the education system and overlap with it, and also form a large part of the 'middle income' layers/highly skilled workers. This huge R&D apparatus, not only in companies but in universities and state research institutions, forms the main engine of technological advance and confirms the analysis of both Marx and Xi Jinping, who noted:

'The working class is China's leading class; it represents China's advanced productive forces and relations of production; it is our Party's most steadfast and reliable class foundation; and it is the main force for realizing a moderately prosperous society in all respects... we must rely wholeheartedly on the working class, enhance its position as China's leading class, and give full play to its role as our main force.'[109]

A reason for this, which Western ideology tries to hide of course, is that the employees of such research facilities are highly skilled workers. It is too disturbing for Western ideology to admit that Einstein (university employee), Tu Youyou (research institute worker), Fleming (discoverer of the 1st antibiotic, university employee), Bardeen, Brattain, and Shockley (inventors of the transistor, workers at AT&T's laboratories);   Townes, Schawlow, Gould, and Maiman (investors of the laser, company and university employees), Kilby (creator of the first integrated circuit, a state and then company employee), and the others who have fundamentally propelled scientific and technological research, are from an economic viewpoint very highly skilled workers, and products of the division of labour analysed by Smith and Marx!

Summary on socialisation/division of labour

The conclusion of modern factual research on the causes of economic growth and development is therefore clear:

- The most powerful source of economic growth is division/socialisation of labour in the form of intermediate products/circulating capital – similarly division/socialisation of labour is also expressed in non-market forms in large productive units having higher productivity than smaller ones. This socialisation/division of labour develops domestically but is also clearly expressed in international trade – making globalisation indispensable for successful economic development.

- The second most powerful force in economic development is the increasing capital intensity of growth – economic development sees a transition from labour intensive to capital intensive growth.
- The third most powerful process in economic development is the increasing skill/education of labour, which itself expresses socialisation of labour. Economic development sees an increasing proportion of labour inputs being constituted by increasing skill/education of the workforce as opposed to simply increases in the number of hours worked by the workforce.
- Technology and science constitute an increasingly important part of economic development. Technological and scientific development itself increasingly relies on division/socialisation of labour in the creation of the huge private and state resources devoted to R&D.

Other forces in economic growth and development, as analysed below, are all less powerful than these fundamental factors which Marx, and earlier Smith, analysed. The precise role of these less powerful factors in economic development will be analysed below.

It is because Marx's analysis of economic development, building on the earlier foundations of Smith, is fully factually confirmed that China's reform and opening up, which corresponded to Marxism, is so successful.

Part 4 – The Western economies road to the 'new mediocre'

Western economic growth is now slower than after 1929

If 40 years of reform and opening up saw in China the greatest economic achievement in human history, in contrast in the West they were the road to the international financial crisis. The latter, in 2008, produced the greatest economic crisis since the Great Depression. Furthermore, the consequences of this international financial crisis have still not been fully overcome but instead they are continuing in the very slow growth in the Western economies. In 2007-2017 annual average GDP growth in the advanced Western economies was only 1.4% - a situation aptly termed by IMF Managing Director Christine Lagarde as 'the new mediocre'.

Even more serious cumulatively than the very slow rate of growth in individual years was the accumulating effect. As Figure 32 shows, by the end of 2017, 10 years after the last pre-crisis year, total growth in the major advanced Western economies, the G7, was even slower than during the decade after the beginning of the Great Depression after 1929 – total G7 growth in the decade after 1929 was 15.9% whereas in the decade after 2007 it was only 10.9%. This extremely slow growth in the Western economies necessarily turned itself into increasing political turmoil – election of Trump in 2016 against the wishes of the overwhelming majority of the US political establishment and the sharp US political clashes which have continued since, the economically irrational vote for Brexit in the UK, the rise of populist parties in France and other European countries, the difficulties even in such a traditionally stable country as Germany as forming government

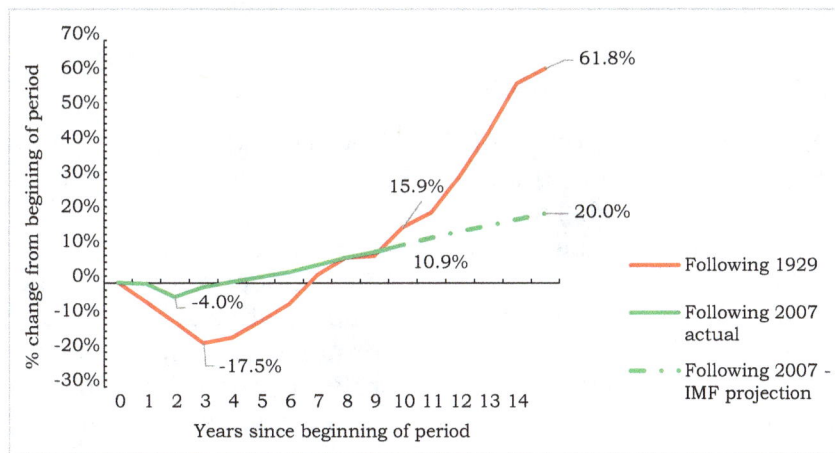

Figure 32: G7 GDP After 1929 and 2007 % change since beginning of the period

Source: Calculated from Maddison *Historical Statistics of the World Economy*: 1-2008 AD and IMF World Economic Outlook October 2017

etc. What, therefore, explains the totally contrasting outcomes in China and 'the West'?

This issue is indeed particularly crucial because, as already shown, the economics originally developed by Adam Smith was the foundation not only of Marxist but of 'Western' economics. Marx noted numerous implications Smith had not seen, and corrected individual points in Smith, but Marx took over, and did not overturn, implications Smith had drawn out of the fundamental framework established by the opening sentence of *The Wealth of Nations*. Furthermore, the data proving the correctness of Marx/Smith's analysis cited above is chiefly provided by Western econometricians. Why, therefore, did marginalist economics ignore not only Marx but the founder of economics, Adam Smith, as well as the factual evidence which Western specialists in this field had established?

The reason was that it was not in the interests of capitalism to know or tell the truth. Keynes concluded *The General Theory of Employment, Interest and Money* with the statement that: 'the power of vested interests is vastly exaggerated compared with the gradual encroachment of ideas.'[110] Marx, of course, held the exact opposite view – 'vested interest', more precisely class position, would mean that the truth would be ignored in favour of false ideology. Marx was proved right, Keynes wrong.

Individual entrepreneurship

The reason the findings of Smith, Marx and modern econometric studies were unacceptable to marginalist economics is easily explained. To legitimise itself capitalism necessarily has to claim that the decisive force in economic development is the capitalist class. As marginalist economics does not like to talk about class, the term the 'capitalist class' is typically re-termed the 'creative role of the individual entrepreneur', who allegedly plays the decisive role in promoting progress and ensuring that supply and demand balance, but that makes no difference to the content. The problem is that not merely does the theoretical framework stemming from Smith/ Marx, but also factual findings regarding economic growth, completely contradict this claim that the 'creative role of the individual entrepreneur' is the key force in economic growth.

On the contrary, the factual findings, as already analysed, are that the most powerful forces raising productivity and growth are, in descending order of importance: increasing socialisation of labour shown in the rising role of intermediate products/circulating capital; the role of globalisation; the increasing role of fixed investment/increasing capital intensity of growth; the rising skill of the labour force, and that the chief forces in scientific and technological advance are the inputs into R&D. In summary the findings of factual economic research lead to the conclusion established by Marx, and emphasised by Xi Jinping - that the working class is the most powerful force raising productivity and growth. As such a conclusion is evidently unacceptable to capitalism a 'theory' of economics instead has to be created which claims that it is the 'creative individual entrepreneur' (i.e. the capitalist) which is the decisive force in raising economic growth and productivity.

But the problem is that, as this theory is not in line with the facts, attempts to act on it become an obstacle to economic development. By concentrating purely on the shorter-term interaction of supply and demand and ignoring the more fundamental issue of how the economy develops when supply and demand are in balance, that is the issue analysed by Smith and Marx, marginalist economics deprived itself of the ability to accurately understand how the economy grew. The fact that marginalist economics creates an economic theory which is not in line with the facts helps explain, as will be seen, the inability of the Western economies to overcome the effects of the international financial crisis.

This theoretical issue may easily be stated formally and tested. If the 'creative role of the individual entrepreneur' were the decisive force in production, then this would be shown in a contribution to growth that was not due to inputs of capital and labour – formally stated the creative role of the individual entrepreneur would show up as part of TFP. However, as already seen, the percentage contribution of TFP to economic growth is a minority one – an average of only 2% in the world's 30 largest advanced economies and 9% in the world's 30 largest developing economies. Even if 'individual entrepreneurship' were held to contribute the whole of TFP growth – which is entirely unreasonable, as it would mean that technological advance, economies of scale and other factors played no role in TFP growth – then the contribution of creative individual entrepreneurship would be a minority, indeed a fairly small, contribution to economic growth.

The factual situation can be seen clearly even in US, which is normally held up as the home of 'creative individual entrepreneurs'. TFP growth does play a larger role in the US than the average for advanced economies – but it is still a far smaller role than growth of capital and labour inputs. Figure 33 shows that in the US in 1990-2016 capital inputs accounted for 48% of GDP growth, labour inputs for 31%, and TFP for 21%. This is in line with the findings for the entire post-World War II period, already analysed, which showed that the most powerful force raising US output was intermediate products, then fixed investment, then labour inputs and finally TFP.

Given that the US is the world's most technologically advanced economy there is no reason to suppose that all TFP growth is due to creative individual entrepreneurs, but even if that were the case it would mean that inputs of labour and capital were four times as important for economic development as 'individual entrepreneurship'. Even in the case of the US, therefore, the claim that 'creative individual entrepreneurs' are the decisive factor in economic growth will not withstand factual examination. Indeed, it may be noted

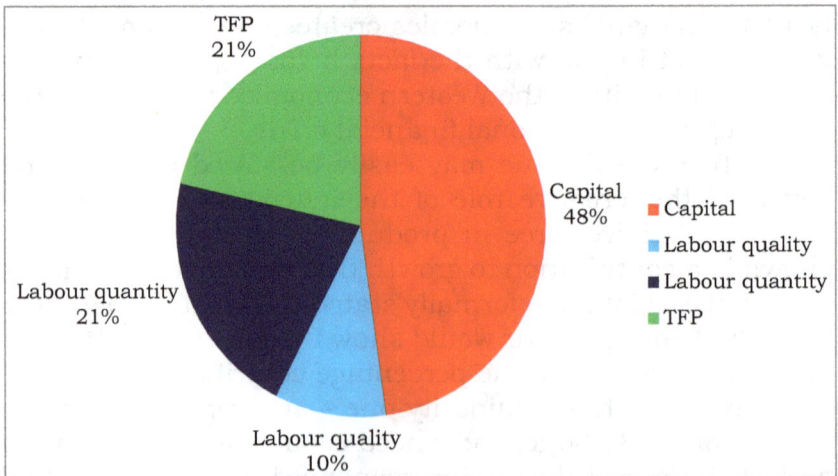

Figure 33: Sources of US Economic Growth Average 1990-2016

Source: Calculated from The Conference Board. 2015. The Conference Board Total Economy Database, 2017

that the role of capital investment in US economic development is over twice as important as the role of TFP and that the role of the inputs of labour quantity (hours worked) is as important as TFP – and the total role of labour inputs is significantly more important than TFP growth. Furthermore, the US has a high rate of TFP growth compared to most advanced economies - and therefore the role of individual entrepreneurs/capitalists will be even smaller in most advanced economies.

To summarize, marginalist economics, because of the vested interests/class interests it represents, is forced to suppress the facts regarding economic development. But this has an inevitable consequence: attempts to ensure economic growth, or overcome economic problems, based on this false economic theory will inevitably be unsuccessful – which, as will be seen below, is precisely what has occurred with the Western 'new mediocre'.

Correction of Solow's errors

It was already noted above that the original formulation of Western 'growth accounting' by Solow in the 1950s made a serious error in not making the distinction between skilled and unskilled labour drawn by Smith/Marx – that is between 'labour quantity' and 'labour quality' to use contemporary Western economic terminology.

Solow also made an error in measuring capital inputs by capital stock rather than the specific contribution made by capital to GDP growth during a given period - the latter being the analysis Marx used. Put in contemporary Western economic terminology, Solow therefore made the mistake of analysing capital inputs in terms of 'capital stock' rather than 'capital services'.

These mistakes by Solow have now been corrected by the new official methods of calculating the sources of economic growth adopted by the OECD, UN, and US statistical services in the period 1994-2001, and which are analysed in 为何联合国、经合组织与美国正式改变其经济增长成因测算方法？ It had taken marginalist economics over 150 years to catch up with Marx and Smith! It is, however, disturbing that articles continue to appear in parts of the Chinese media using methods derived from Solow which are in contradiction with

Marxism, which are no longer accepted even by Western statistical agencies, and which are simply wrong.

Milton Friedman

It is illustrative to note that, within the overall framework analysed above, however, the single most determined and explicit post-World War II attempt by marginalist economics to factually refute the theoretical framework deriving from Smith and Marx was by Milton Friedman. Friedman's own explicit target was Keynes but Friedman's point of attack, an attempt to refute the claim that the percentage of fixed investment in GDP rose with historical development, and that production was increasingly capital intensive, was also a direct attack on the framework of Marx/Smith for reasons already analysed. As this issue affected not only Smith, Ricardo, Marx and Keynes, but also China's reform and opening up and NSE, it is worth dealing with in detail.

The reason Friedman chose to specifically to centre his attack on this point of the increasing capital intensity of production was because of the implications for increasing economic instability which Keynes noted flowed from this tendency. As Friedman put it in his *A Theory of the Consumption Function*:

'The doubts about the adequacy of the Keynesian consumption function were reinforced by a theoretical controversy about Keynes's proposition that there is no automatic force in a monetary economy to assure the existence of a full-employment equilibrium position.'[111]

To attempt to refute the economic analysis flowing from Smith, through Ricardo and Marx up to Keynes of the increasing capital intensity of production, Friedman relied on data from the US - Friedman devoting an entire book to attempting to disprove this analysis which derived ultimately from Smith.[112]

Friedman's attempt to refute the Smith-Ricardo-Marx-Keynes analysis was accompanied by further factual analysis by Western econometricians. These modern econometric findings showed conclusively that Friedman made an error by relying on purely US and not international data, and that the analysis commenced by Smith and running via Ricardo and Marx up to Keynes of the increasing capital intensity of production with economic development was correct.

Friedman made a major factual error because he had not checked that the US represented an exception, not the overall trend, and internationally the percentage of fixed investment in GDP had clearly risen – it being an elementary factual error to rest a case on one example while failing to make a comprehensive international analysis. As even such a pillar of anti-Keynesian marginalism as Robert J Barro had to subsequently state, summarising the results of study of the major economies:

'For the United States, the striking observation... is the stability over time of the ratios for domestic investment and national savings... The United State is, however, an outlier with respect to the stability of its investment and saving ratios; the data for the other... countries show a clear increase in these ratios over time. In particular, the ratios... are in all cases, substantially greater than those from before World War II. The long-term data therefore suggests that the ratios to GDP of gross domestic investment and gross national saving tend to rise as an economy develops.'[113]

This, of course, simply confirms Marx/Smith and the most recent economic research on this, cited above, fully confirms that Friedman was simply actually wrong and Smith-Ricardo-Marx-Keynes were correct – the capital intensity of production increases with economic development.

Keynes

Friedman's attempt to mount an attack on Keynes, and by implication on Smith/Marx therefore backfired, as the research it generated merely showed Friedman was wrong and Smith/Ricardo/Marx/Keynes were correct. Nevertheless, Friedman was quite correct in understanding that this issue was and remains of decisive significance not merely from the point of view of economic theory but from the practical angle of why, following the international financial crisis, the Western economies remained in the 'new mediocre'.

The reason Friedman was so concerned to attack the concept of a rising capital intensity of production, and of a rising percentage of fixed investment in GDP, was because, as Keynes had noted, as investment's role in the economy increases a necessary consequence is that any instability or decline in investment has increasingly serious consequences. Put technically Keynes noted:

'the richer the community, the wider will tend to be the gap between its actual and its potential production... For a poor community will be prone to consume by far the greater part of its output, so that a very modest measure of investment will be sufficient to provide full employment; whereas a wealthy community will have to discover much ampler opportunities for investment if the saving propensities of its wealthier members are to be compatible with the employment of its poorer members. If in a potentially wealthy community the inducement to invest is weak... the working of the principle of effective demand will compel it to reduce its actual output, until, in spite of its potential wealth, it has become so poor that its surplus over its consumption is sufficiently diminished to correspond to the weakness of the inducement to invest.'[114]

As Keynes noted, therefore this meant that output and employment became increasingly dependent on the investment level:

'when aggregate real income is increased aggregate consumption is increased but not by as much as income... Thus to justify any given amount of employment there must be an amount of current investment sufficient to absorb the excess of total output over what the community chooses to consume when employment is at the given level... It follows... that given what we shall call the community's propensity to consume, the equilibrium level of employment, i.e. the level at which there is no inducement to employers as a whole either to expand or to contract employment, will depend on the amount of current investment.'[115]

However, as Keynes noted, in a capitalist economy no automatic mechanism ensures a necessary volume and level of investment to maintain effective demand. That is, the claim that supply creates its own demand, Says Law, is false – on this point Keynes arrived at the same conclusion Marx had over 70 years previously. Stated in his terminology Keynes concluded:

'the effective demand associated with full employment is a special case... It can only exist when, by accident or design, current investment provides an amount of demand just equal to the excess of the aggregate supply price of the output resulting from full employment over what the community will choose to spend on consumption when it is fully employed.'[116]

Put aphoristically:

'An act of individual saving means – so to speak – a decision not to have dinner today. But it does not necessitate a decision to have dinner or buy a pair of boots a week hence or a year hence.' [117]

In more technical terminology:

'The error lies in proceeding to the ... inference that, when an individual saves, he will increase aggregate investment by an equal amount.'[118]

Any investment shortfall would then be amplified by the well-known economic 'multiplier', that is the cumulative knock on effects through the economy of any initial investment or lack of investment, into much stronger cyclical fluctuations: 'It is... to the general principle of the multiplier to which we have to look for an explanation of how fluctuations in the amount of investment, which are a comparatively small proportion of the national income, are capable of generating fluctuations in aggregate employment and income so much greater in amplitude than themselves.'[119] Such fluctuations in investment, combined with consumption, in turn determined employment: 'The propensity to consume and the rate of new investment determine between them the volume of employment.'[120]

The road to the 'new mediocre'

Analysis of the facts show that this issue of regulation of investment, as follows from Marxist theory of the increasing capital intensity of production, and as Keynes had foreseen, became decisive in the road to the Western economies 'new mediocre'. To understand this, however, it is useful to be clear that the slowing of the Western economies was not a result purely of the international financial crisis - the advanced Western economies have been slowing for many decades. As this latter trend is obscured by analysing merely short-term business cycle fluctuations, Figure 35 shows a 20 year moving average for annual growth in the total GDP of the advanced Western economies – the use of a long term

moving average eliminates the effect of purely cyclical fluctuations and shows the underlying trend clearly. As many
be seen, annual growth in the advanced Western economies
fell from 4.5% in 1980, to 3.0% in 2002, to 2.0% in 2016. In
the last 36 years for which data is available, growth in the
Western economies has therefore fallen by more than half.
In countries for which there is longer term data, as with the
US, it may be seen clearly that their economies have been
slowing for an even longer period.

Using shorter time periods to analyse trends, naturally,
shows greater fluctuations but does not alter the trend in
the Western economies. Figure 34 therefore shows a five-
year moving average of growth in the Western advanced
capitalist economies as a whole. The sharply slowing growth
from 6.9% in 1966, to 4.0% in 1988, to 3.3% in 2000, to
1.7% in 2016 is clear. Taking a five-year moving average,
between 1966 and 2016 the growth rate of the advanced
Western economies fell by over 70%.

The US economy

Detailed analysis for all the major Western economies shows
the same trend as for the economic grouping as a whole –

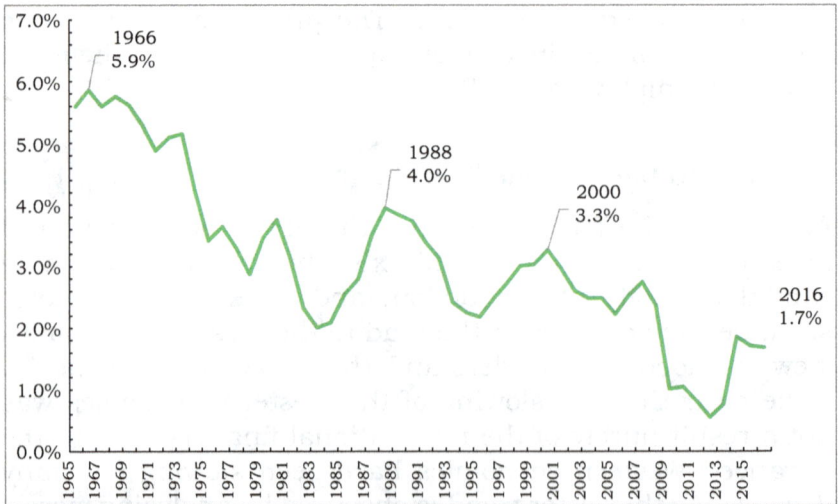

Figure 34: Total Annual GDP Growth in All OECD Economies 5
year moving average -inflation adjusted prices

Source: Calculated from World Bank World Development Indicators

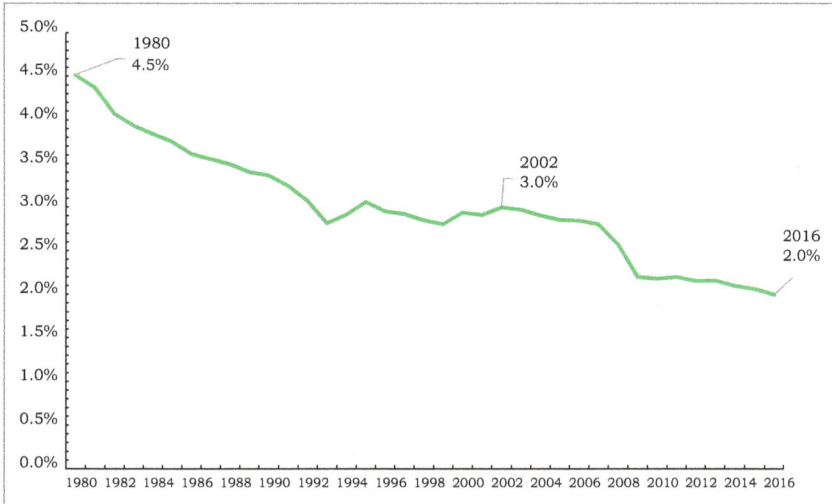

Figure 35: Total Annual GDP Growth in All OECD Economies 20
year moving average -inflation adjusted prices

Source: Calculated from World Bank World Development Indicators

that is it this severe slowing is a universal trend, without
exceptions. To avoid lengthening the article further, detailed
charts for all Western economies will not be given but as the
US is the most important capitalist economy it may be taken
as a representative example Figure 36 therefore shows that,
taking a 20-year moving average, US annual average GDP
growth fell from 4.4% in 1969, to 4.1% in 1978, to 3.5% in
2002, to 2,2% in 2017 – i.e. the US growth rate halved over
the last half century.

Why was Keynes not accepted?

Returning to consider the relative strength of the deter-
minants of economic growth given in the earlier sections
of this article, the reasons for the severe slowdown in the
Western economies in the last decades is clear. Theoretically
such a slowdown could have been produced by a decline
in the most powerful source of economic growth, intermediate products/division of labour in large productive units/
globalisation. This was indeed a key reason for the Great
Depression after 1929 – protectionism in that period, sym-
bolised by the US Smoot-Hawley tariff, severely broke up
the international division of labour. However, while there is

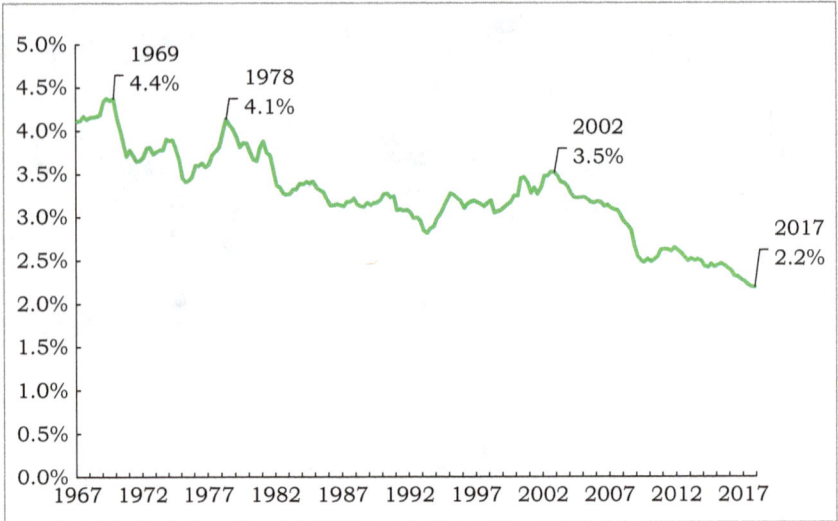

Figure 36: Annual US GDP Growth 20 Year Moving Average
Source: Calculated from Bureau of Economic Analysis Table 1.1.3

talk about protectionism in the present period, and some protectionist measures such as the US tariffs on solar panels, washing machines, steel and aluminium, this is small in scale compared to the full-blooded protectionism of the 1930s. Nor is there any evidence that the process of division of labour seen in the growth of intermediate products has gone into reverse. Therefore there is no evidence that such a substantial fall in growth as has occurred in the Western economies, unlike in the Great Depression of the 1930s, is fundamentally influenced by a collapse in globalisation or disruption in international division of labour.

However, the situation of fixed investment, the second most powerful factor in economic growth, is quite different to that of globalisation or intermediate products (that is division of labour within a single production cycle). Figure 37 shows net fixed capital investment, i.e. gross fixed capital investment minus depreciation, in the advanced Western economies. The severe decline in the investment level shown is clear. Net fixed capital investment fell from 13.4% of Gross National Income (GNI) in 1973, to 12.1% in 1979, to 9.9% in 1989, to 7.7% in 2000, to 6.9% in 2006, to 4.1% in 2015 – the latest available data. The proportion of net fixed investment in GNI in the advanced Western economies therefore

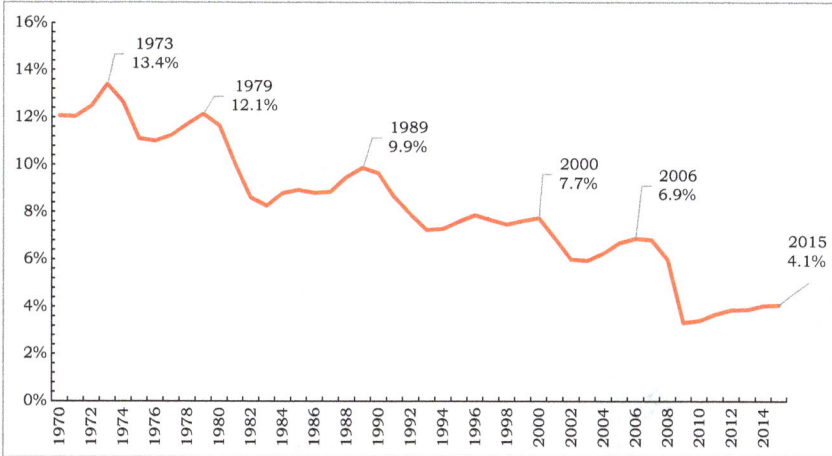

Figure 37: Net Fixed Capital Investment in OECD Economies %
of Gross National Income

Source: Calculated from World Bank World Development Indicators

has fallen by almost 70%. As capital investment is the second most powerful source of economic growth, such a very severe fall in fixed investment necessarily leads to a major slowdown in the Western economies.

Decline in US investment

This process which has taken place can be seen particularly clearly by analysing the case of the US - as US data for a longer period than simply post-World War II is available. Figure 38 therefore shows US net fixed investment from 1929 to 2016. The curve of development is clear. At the depth of the Great Depression, in 1933, US net capital investment was negative – the US was consuming more capital than it was investing, and the US capital stock was actually falling. World War II saw an unprecedented rise in US net fixed investment to 14.8% of GDP in 1943 - as would be expected from such a huge investment surge the US underwent dramatic growth, with, from the outbreak of World War II until 1945, the US experiencing 11.3% average annual GDP growth, or total growth of 91%, the fastest in US history. After a fall in the immediate post-World War II period, US net fixed investment then rose to a post-World War II peak of 10.9% of GDP in 1966 – coinciding with the peak of the post-World War II

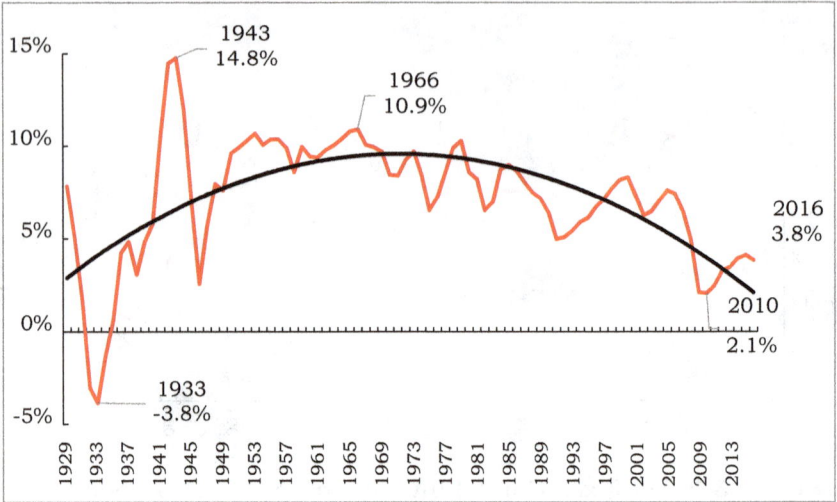

Figure 38: US -Net Fixed Investment
Source: Calculated from US Bureau of Economic Analysis
NIPA Tables 1.5.5 & 5.1

boom. After that US net fixed investment then fell relentlessly for five decades – reaching a low of 2.1% of GDP during the international financial crisis in 2010 and only increasing to 3.8% of GDP in 2016. **Between 1966 and 2016 US net fixed investment as a share of GDP therefore fell by almost two thirds.** Given that capital investment is the second most powerful source of economic growth a severe slowdown of the US economy was inevitable.

Why was Keynes rejected?

This severe fall in net fixed investment in the Western economies in the last decades therefore made a sharp fall in their growth, the road to the 'new mediocre', inevitable. But the question is why was nothing done to reverse this? This would appear even more curious as it was not even necessary to be a Marxist to understand the situation. It could be easily understood in terms of one of the greatest 'Western' economists of the 20th century – Keynes. However, for reasons that will be analysed, when faced with the severe situation created by the international financial crisis, the Western economies implemented part of Keynes analysis but refused to implement the decisive part – which then explains why the Western economies remained locked in a growth which is now actually slower than after 1929. Analysing this issue also clearly shows the superiority of China's economic structure under reform and opening up compared to the Western economies.

As was noted above, Keynes saw the key to economic fluctuations as lying in changes in investment. But from this analysis Keynes drew far more profound conclusions that simply the role of budget deficits – the issue to which his analysis is primarily reduced in marginalist economics. But, for reasons that will become clear, marginalist economics did not wish to acknowledge Keynes most fundamental conclusions.

In addition to use of budget deficits, one of Keynes conclusions which the Western economies were prepared to accept, was that Keynes considered it imperative, when serious economic problems existed, to achieve low interest rates. The decade long ultra-low interest rates of all major Western central banks following 2008, and the use of quantitative easing (QE) to drive down market interest rates, all directly flowed from Keynes analysis that: 'the succession of boom and slump can be described and analysed in terms of the fluctuations of the marginal efficiency of capital relatively to the rate of interest.'[121] More precisely, as Keynes understood that in a modern economy large scale investment is not financed out of cashflow, but from borrowing which is repaid from future profits, the aim of very low interest rates was to make borrowing cheaper and therefore make investment more profitable and attractive.

In turn, the necessity for QE flowed from the fact that Keynes believed that left to purely market forces interest rates would not fall to sufficiently low levels. Or as Keynes put it:

'Not only is the marginal propensity to consume weaker in a wealthy community, but owing to its accumulation of capital being already larger, the opportunities for further investment are less attractive unless the rate of interest falls at a sufficiently rapid rate; which brings us to the theory of the rate of interest and... reasons why it does not automatically fall to the appropriate levels.'[122]

QE was pursued by all major Western central banks (US, Japan, EU) after the international financial crisis and

therefore this part of Keynes diagnosis and policies was comprehensively implemented.

A somewhat comprehensive socialisation of investment

But nevertheless, despite his support for low interest rates,
Keynes did not judge these would be likely by themselves to
overcome the effects of an investment decline. Keynes therefore concluded it would be necessary for the state, which in
Marxist terms is the most socialised representative of production as it is based on the totality of society, to play a
greater role:

'Only experience... can show how far management of the
rate of interest is capable of continuously stimulating the
appropriate volume of investment... I am now somewhat
sceptical of the success of a merely monetary policy directed
towards influencing the rate of interest... I expect to see
the State... taking an ever greater responsibility for directly
organising investment.'[123]

Consequently, Keynes believed that regulating the level of
investment would have to be undertaken by the state and
not by the private sector: 'I conclude that the duty of ordering the current volume of investment cannot safely be left
in private hands.[124] It was necessary, therefore, to aim at 'a
socially controlled rate of investment.' [125]

If, however, the state were to determine 'the current volume of investment' then this led Keynes to the conclusion
it would be necessary to undertake a certain 'socialisation',
that is state control, of investment:

'It seems unlikely that the influence of banking policy on the
rate of interest will be sufficient by itself to determine an optimum rate of investment. I conceive, therefore, that a somewhat
comprehensive socialisation of investment will prove the only
means of securing an approximation to full employment.' [126]

Keynes noted that this 'somewhat comprehensive socialisation of investment' did not mean the elimination of the
private sector, but socialised investment operating together
with a private sector:

'This need not exclude all manner of compromises and
devices by which public authority will co-operate with private initiative... apart from the necessity of central controls
to bring about an adjustment between the propensity to

consume and the inducement to invest there is no more need to socialise economic life than there was before.... The central controls necessary to ensure full employment will, of course, involve a large extension of the traditional functions of government.'[127]

It is therefore clear that the economic structure Keynes envisaged was not one in which the state-owned all the productive apparatus (i.e. not the post-1929 Soviet model) but it was one in which the extension of the role of the state would allow it to set the overall level of investment which 'cannot safely be left in private hands.'

But such an economic structure as Keynes envisaged does not exist in the capitalist West, where, by definition the level of investment is set by private capital. It was for this reason that the Western economies after the international financial crisis were prepared to accept Keynes's budget deficits and QE policies but would not accept his 'somewhat comprehensive socialisation of investment.' Because if control of investment were taken out of the control of private capital it would no longer be a capitalist economy!

But it is clear by this argument that one has now arrived at a 'Chinese' economic structure - although approaching it via a Keynesian and not a Marxist framework. 'Zhuada Fangxiao', grasping large state firms and releasing small ones to the non-state/private sector, coupled with abandonment of quantitative planning, means that China's economy is not being regulated via administrative means but by general macro-economic control, including centrally of the level of investment – as Keynes advocated.

Macro-economic regulation and investment

Given the above facts the economic structure created in China by reform and opening up, and a decisive advantage of China's socialist economic system compared to the capitalist West, was accurately described by the *Wall Street Journal*:

'Most economies can pull two levers to bolster growth: fiscal and monetary. China has a third option. The National Development and Reform Commission can accelerate the flow of investment projects.'[128]

The operation and advantage of this economic structure can be clearly seen. For example, in early 2016 China's economy was judged to be slowing too much – it will be recalled from data given above that international context was that 2016 was a year of extremely weak growth in the Western and particularly US economies. China launched a state investment programme, with the year on year increase of state investment reaching 23.7% in April 2016. This helped ensure adequate economic growth. As a knock-on effect, this growth began to stimulate private investment, which started to accelerate from a low level in November 2016. This demonstrated that instead of state investment 'crowding out' private investment, which is the claim by neo-liberalism, arguing that state sector and private sector interests are counterposed, in China state investment by aiding economic growth stimulated private investment – that is, in China's economic system the state and private sectors were complimentary not counterposed.

It is therefore clear that although this economic structure created by reform and opening up expresses 'socialism with Chinese characteristics', it also approximated to the structure envisaged by Keynes. In such a structure China does not administer' its economy – the market plays a decisive role in allocating resources. But China can use the state to avoid the severe fall in investment which, as has been seen, explains the West's 'new mediocre' (and China can also cut back state investment in order to avoid overheating). But why, therefore, does the West not use such means to avoid its own severe investment fall and resulting 'new mediocre'?

The reason is political and directly follows from the fact that the Western economies are capitalist and not socialist in nature. The economic structure envisaged by Keynes, or the one which exists in socialism with Chinese characteristics, is not acceptable to the Western capitalist class. The state is an expression of society as a whole, and furthermore the state is far more under the pressure of mass social layers, the people, than are individual privatively owned enterprises. In summary, the existence of a large state sector creates far more control by society than does a purely private economic structure. Furthermore, a situation in which the state, not private capital, regulates the overall level of investment is not acceptable to the Western capitalism – which insists that private economic interests must predominate. Therefore, although the means which would permit overcoming the 'new mediocre' are intellectually clear the Western capitalist economies are not prepared to implement them.

It is therefore an irony that, although Keynes was a 'Western' economist, the structure and ideology of the US and European economies made it impossible to implement Keynes's policies even in 2008 when confronted with the most severe recession since the Great Depression – the idea of large scale state investment, a 'somewhat comprehensive socialisation of investment', was unacceptable in a capitalist economy. In contrast, the anti-crisis measures of China's 'socialist market economy' are far closer to those Keynes foresaw that are those in any capitalist economy.

China's socialist economic structure, because it allowed 'a socially controlled rate of investment' and a 'somewhat comprehensive socialisation of investment', therefore could if required utilise policy tools analysed by Keynes which the US and European economies could not. Ironically again, although Keynes explicitly wished to save capitalism it turned out that Western capitalism could not use the tools he suggested but China's 'socialism with Chinese characteristics' could. Deng Xiaoping and Chen Yun could not fit in the framework of Keynes, but Keynes could fit rather neatly when required within the framework of Deng Xiaoping and Chen Yun.

The visible hand and the invisible hand

These points therefore also make clear that the structure of China's socialist economy is entirely different to a Western capitalist economy – the claims made in the Western media that China is 'capitalist' are simply untrue as there is no Western capitalist economy in which almost 40% of investment is carried out by the state as in China. As analysed in detail above, in line with Marx's analysis, China rejects an administered economy of the post-1929 Soviet type but, as a socialist country, China is not worried about use of the state sector of the economy as well as the private one. As was reaffirmed in the last major CPC Central Committee Plenum focussed on the economy, in November 2013 at the 3rd Plenum of the Central Committee of 18th Congress of the CPC:

'We must unswervingly consolidate and develop the public economy, persist in the dominant position of public ownership, give full play to the leading role of the state-owned sector.'[129]

Or as Xi Jinping put it:

'Our market economy is socialist, of course. We need to give leverage to the superiority of our socialist system, and let the Party and government perform their positive functions.' [130]

In detail:

'The market plays a decisive role in allocating resources but is not the sole actor in this regard. To develop the socialist market economy, leverage should be given to both the market and the government, with differentiated functions. The Decision [of the Central Committee of the Communist Party of China on Some Major Issues Concerning Comprehensively Continuing the Reform] put forth clear requirements for improving the functions of the government, emphasizing that scientific macro control and effective governance are the intrinsic requirements for giving more leverage to the advantages of the socialist market economy... It stresses that the main responsibility and role of the government is to maintain the stability of the macro economy, strengthen and improve public services, ensure fair competition, strengthen market oversight, maintain market order, promote sustainable development and common prosperity, and intervene in situations where market failure occurs. Second, adhering to and improving the basic economic system.

Regarding this latter point Xi Jinping noted:

The basic economic system with public ownership playing a leading role and all forms of ownership growing side by side is an important pillar of the socialist system with Chinese characteristics...

'It is emphasized in the Decision that we must unswervingly consolidate and develop the public economy, persist in the leading role of public ownership, give full play to the leading role of the state-owned economy, and incessantly increase its vitality, leveraging power and impact.'[131]

Phrased in more popular terms, as Xi Jinping put it in his interview with the *Wall Street Journal* in September 2015, before his first visit to the US as President: 'we need to make good use of both the invisible hand and the visible hand'[132] China can and will, because of its economic structure, use both the 'invisible hand' of the market and the 'visible hand' of the state. No Western capitalist economy has such a structure.

The practical consequences of this using 'both hands', as opposed to the West's reliance purely on the private sector hand, can be seen both in the unprecedented economic achievements of China during the 40 years of reform and opening up and in the far superior performance of China compared to the Western economies since the beginning of the financial crisis. To adapt the famous phrase of Deng Xiaoping, China, depending on which is best, is prepared to use both the state sector cat and the private sector cat. The West, by insisting only the private sector cat is good, has left itself mired in the 'new mediocre'.

In summary, if the China's reform and opening up proves the correctness of its economic approach and theories 'from the positive' the 'new mediocre' of the Western economies therefore proves them 'from the negative.'

International implications

It is now possible to see clearly the reasons for the triumph of Chinese Marxism in reform and opening up. Deng Xiaoping and Chen Yun created, in the socialist market economy, that is the foundation of socialism with Chinese characteristics, only the third fundamental type of economy to have existed in the last five centuries – after the capitalist economy, first analysed by Smith and Marx, and then the 'administered economy' created by Stalin in 1929. Deng Xiaoping and Chen Yun created this economic system not by overturning Marx but by a 'return to Marx'. That return to the actual ideas of Marx, however, created the basis for a further development of Marxism which has continued up the 19th Party Congress. Furthermore, not only China's Marxist analysis but factual studies confirm the correctness of Marx's analysis.

This certainly does not mean that the gigantic success of reform and opening up ensures that there are no problems and dangers. The most fundamental danger of all, which US neo-cons seek to achieve, is to overturn the socialist system in China. If that were achieved the mechanisms that have made reform and opening up the greatest economic success in world history, not only for China but for the overall well-being of humanity, would be destroyed and China would suffer national catastrophe – precisely as occurred in the former USSR. This would be disastrous not only for China but for humanity.

It is for this reason that all the steps taken to further reinforce China's socialism system at the 19th Party Congress and since are of such importance. As Xi Jinping stressed in his speech on the 95th anniversary of the founding of the CPC: 'what we build is socialism with Chinese characteristics, and nothing else.'[133] This is also a political meaning of the amendment to the constitution adopted at the 2018 NPC that: 'The leadership of the Communist Party of China (CPC) is the defining feature of socialism with Chinese characteristics.'

But it should also be noted that, in addition to the implications for China itself, at the 19th National Congress of the CPC in October 2017 Xi Jinping stressed that the culture of socialism with Chinese characteristics 'offers a new option for other countries and nations who want to speed up their development while preserving their independence.'[134] But how is this possible when most countries are not Marxist, and no other country can mechanically apply the lessons of China?

There two parts to the answer.

- First, of course, is the practical success of China – this is what encourages other countries not to mechanically copy but to learn from China.
- But the second feature is that while reform and opening up was developed and formulated within a Marxist framework it is possible to understand it in different economic frameworks.

To illustrate this, it was already shown that:

- Marx based his analysis on Smith – greatly extending it but not contradicting its most fundamental conclusions.
- It was also shown that reform and opening up, and socialism with Chinese characteristics, can be easily understood within the framework of Keynes.
- New Structural Economics, which is consistent with China's reform and opening up, can also be understood within the framework of Western neo-classical economics –

indeed Justin Yifu Lin has noted that this makes NSE more widely understandable in the West.

Therefore, although reform and opening up can be understood most coherently in the Marxist framework in which it was developed it is possible to understand it within other theoretical systems. It is therefore indeed likely, and is already occurring, that other countries will understand reform and opening up before they adopt a Marxist framework.

This international situation may be rather easily understood in terms of China's own experience. The CPC, a Marxist party, was the core of the creation of the People's Republic of China and the rejuvenation of the Chinese nations. But the CPC never claimed that it was the only force fighting for China's rejuvenation - it appealed to and worked with all patriotic forces in China. Today, in addition to state-to-state relations, the CPC organises large scale dialogues with numerous political parties of other countries. The last of these, the 'CPC in Dialogue with World Political Parties', in December 2017, was addressed by Xi Jinping and involved nearly 300 political parties from 120 countries.

Because, as has been shown above, Marx's economic analysis is confirmed by factual studies, that is it fulfils the criteria of 'seek truth from facts', other serious economic and political currents will begin to de facto approximate to the ideas of China's reform and opening up even before they are prepared to accept a full Marxist analysis of the type developed by the CPC. As in the case of its cooperation with all patriotic forces in the rejuvenation of China, the CPC can cooperate with other currents and economic frameworks in other countries, provided these base themselves on factual analysis. Indeed, this latter process is rather clear:

- In developing countries, the increasingly evident failure of the neo-liberal Washington Consensus has led to increasing interest in China's economic framework. In a number of countries, for example in Africa, this interest is quite explicit. Rapidly growing African countries, such as Ethiopia, admit quite openly that they are learning from China. This follows on from the very rapid economic growth generated in Vietnam, Laos and Cambodia by de facto learning decisively from China. In other cases, such as India, learning from China is not acknowledged but in reality, exists – it is not by accident that the chief economist of India appointed by Prime Minister Modi, Arvind Subramanian, is a specialist on China's economy!

- In advanced economies, as already analysed, the cumulative effects of the very slow growth under the 'new mediocre' has led to increasing political instability and also polarisation. This reached a recent peak in 2016, with extremely slow growth, only 1.4%, in the G7 region as a whole. This extremely slow growth was reflected in the political instability in that year – the election of Trump in the US and the Brexit vote in the UK. An inevitable cyclical recovery is taking place in 2017-2018 after 2016's extremely slow growth in 2016, with 2.0% growth in the G7 in 2017, but this has insufficient to restabilise the political situation – with ongoing political clashes around the Trump presidency in the US, continuing turmoil in Britain around Brexit and the spread of instability into Germany, with the difficulty in forming a government, and into Italy - with no party able to command a parliamentary majority. This situation necessarily leads to increasing interest both in practical economic cooperation with China and interest in China's economic policies – most sharply seen, for example, in Poland, one of Europe's most rapidly growing economies, adopting NSE as its official development strategy. As the advanced Western economies, for reasons analysed in this article, remain trapped within the 'new mediocre' this increase in China's economic policies will increase.

China's Marxism, therefore, remains the most coherent economic framework, but others can begin to approximate to it.

Conclusion

Finally, to return to the starting point, Xi Jinping has stressed: 'The theory of socialism with Chinese characteristics is the latest achievement in adapting Marxism to China's conditions... In contemporary China upholding the theory of socialism with Chinese characteristics means upholding Marxism in its true sense.'[135] And: 'We should not abandon Marxism- Leninism and Mao Zedong Thought; otherwise, we would be deprived of our foundation.' [136] The facts of the last 40 years of reform and opening up fully confirm this. As shown:

- Reform and opening up was carried out entirely in line with Marxism – indeed it was a 'return to Marx'.
- This Marxist analysis created the great economic success in human history in terms of its impact in improving the conditions not only of China but the wellbeing of humanity.
- This Marxist analysis corresponded to the facts of economic development – which is why, of course, reform and opening up produced such success.
- The Marxist analysis which created reform and opening itself became the basis for a further development of Marxism.
- This Marxist analysis does not cut China off from other economic analyses and currents which attempt to seek 'truth from facts' - China's Marxism is simply the most coherent and developed theoretical framework for understanding reality.

In short, the 40 years of reform and opening up saw the inseparable integration of both economic results and economic theory. Those 40 years were a triumph not only of China's practical achievement but of China's Marxism.

Part 3: Deng Xiaoping – the world's greatest economist

14 August 2014

22nd August 2014 is the 110th anniversary of the birth of Deng Xiaoping. Numerous achievements would ensure Deng Xiaoping a major position in China's history – his role in creating the People's Republic of China, his steadfastness during persecution in the Cultural Revolution, his extraordinarily balanced attitude even after return to power towards the development and recent history of China, his all-round role after 1978 in leading his country. But one ensures him a position among a tiny handful of people at the peak not only of Chinese but of world history. This was China's extraordinary economic achievement after reforms began in 1978, and the decisive role this played not only in the improvement of the living standards of China's people but the country's national rejuvenation. So great was the impact of this that it may objectively be said to have altered the situation not only of China but of the world.

China's economic performance after the beginning of its 1978 reforms simply exceeded the experience of any other country in human history. To give only a partial list:

- China achieved the most rapid growth in a major economy in world history.
- China experienced the fastest growth of living standards of any major economy.
- China lifted 620 million people out of internationally defined poverty.
- Measured in internationally comparable prices, adjusted for inflation, the greatest increase in economic output in a single year in any country outside China was the US in 1999, when it added $567 billion, whereas in 2010 China added $1,126 billion - twice as much.
- During the beginning of China's rapid growth 22% of the world's population was within its borders – seven times that of the US at the beginning of its own fast economic development.

Nevertheless, wholly implausibly, it is sometimes argued that this success was merely due to "pragmatism" and achieved without overall economic theories, concepts, or a leadership really understanding the subject (particularly with no knowledge of US academic economics!). If true, then the study of economics should immediately be abandoned – if the greatest economic success in world history can be achieved without any understanding of the subject it is evidently of no practical value whatever.

In reality this argument is false. Deng Xiaoping's approach to economic policy was certainly highly practical regarding application – his famous "it doesn't matter if a cat is black or white provided it catches mice". But it was extremely theoretical as regards the foundations of economic policy – shown clearly in works such as "We Are Undertaking An Entirely New Endeavour", "Adhere to the Principle 'to Each According to his Work'" and "In Everything We Do We Must Proceed From The Realities of the Primary Stage of Socialism." Outstanding practical success was therefore guided by a very well-defined theoretical underpinning, which can be understood particularly clearly in its historical context.

As is well known, after 1949 the newly created People's Republic of China embarked on constructing of an economy fundamental elements of which were drawn from the experience of the Soviet Union. There was nothing irrational in this at all – the USSR, up to that time, had the world's most rapidly growing economy.

The immediate post-1929 success of the USSR was extraordinary. During 1929-39 the USSR achieved 6% annual GDP growth – until then by far the fastest ever achieved by a major economy. Despite the colossal destruction of World War II, by 1949 the USSR had already regained its prewar production level. The 8.4% of the world's population in the USSR, which benefited from this economic development, was more than two and a half times the population of the US when the latter had commenced its rapid growth.

The elements which had produced this extraordinary economic growth were clear. From 1929, with the First Five Year Plan, the USSR launched an economic policy never previously attempted in any country - construction of a largely nationally self-enclosed administered economy. In these resources were not allocated by price but by material quantities – a steel factory did not buy coal or iron ore on the market but had them allocated by administrative decisions. Foreign trade was reduced to a low level. State ownership was applied even to small scale private enterprises such as restaurants. Farmers' small holdings were eliminated and agriculture organized into giant collective farms.

However, despite its verbal claims to the contrary, this policy was radically at variance with that of Marx – to which the USSR claimed verbal adherence. To use the Marxist terminology common to both China and the USSR, Soviet economic policy had in 1929, in a single step, replaced the economic mechanism of regulation by prices (exchange value) by allocation by material use (use value).

Marx, in the Communist Manifesto, had written a socialist state would: 'wrest, by degree, all capital from the bourgeoisie, to centralise all instruments of production in the hands of the State... and to increase the total productive forces as rapidly as possible.' In writing 'by degree' Marx evidently envisaged a period during which state-owned property and private property would both exist - whereas in the USSR in 1929 essentially all property had been taken over by the state.

Furthermore, the very word 'socialism' is derived from 'socialised', i.e. large scale, production – not small scale peasant production. However in the USSR, after 1929, small scale peasant plots were taken into state ownership - prior to their administrative suppression. But, simultaneously with the suppression of small scale private production, the advantages of very large scale production were eliminated by the nationally self- enclosed character of the USSR's economy – a US aircraft manufacturer such as Boeing sold into the world market, but a Soviet manufacturer such as Ilyushin could produce aircraft only for the far smaller Soviet economy.

Some Soviet economists pointed out these issues, but such criticism appeared 'theoretical quibbles' compared to proven Soviet economic success.

But after 1945 this situation began to change. In 1929, when Soviet economic policy was launched, the global economy was collapsing into relatively autarchic states or empires. The US, the British Empire, Japan, Nazi Germany, were cut from each other by tariff and other economic walls. The international monetary system, the Gold Standard, collapsed without any replacement. Amid global economic chaos the autarchic socialist USSR far outperformed autarchic capitalist economies.

But, following World War II, the integrated world economy was gradually rebuilt. A new international payments system, the dollar standard, was created. Tariff barriers were reduced. The Soviet economy was now small compared to this new world market, and could not be integrated into the world economy without a relaxation of its planning system - as global economic fluctuations could not be planned for. Collectivized Soviet agriculture was unproductive and the USSR's consumer goods of low quality, due to insistence on overwhelming priority to heavy industry. By the 1970s Soviet economic growth, while more rapid than the US, was far slower than Japan or South Korea - which were selling into the world market.

But, if the Soviet economy was heading to crisis, the free market system, its only existing alternative, was by the 1970s showing its own difficulties. After the 1973 'oil price crisis' most advanced capitalist economies slowed dramatically. The US both slowed and from the early 1980s began the huge debt accumulation which finally culminated in the 2008 international financial crisis. When the free-market model was applied to the former USSR from 1992 onwards, it led to the greatest economic collapse ever seen in history in a major economy in peacetime – Russia's GDP fell by 30%, while male life expectancy fell by four years.

Confronted with decisive problems in both dominant economic models, instead of being trapped into one or the other, Deng Xiaoping embarked on a policy never previously seen – the creation of what is now referred to in China as a 'socialist market economy.'

In constructing this in one sense Deng Xiaoping went from the USSR's post-1929 model 'back to Marx'. Underlying Deng Xiaoping's analysis from 1978, frequently in its literal wording, was Marx's famous "Critique of the Gotha Programme" – his extensive commentary on the construction of a socialist society.

This, for example, is Marx: "'What we are dealing with here is a communist society, not as it has developed on its own foundations, but... just as it emerges from capitalist society." For a person in such a society: "The same amount of labour which he has given to society in one form, he receives back in another...In a higher phase of communist society... after the productive forces have also increased... society inscribe on its banners: From each according to his abilities, to each according to his needs!'"

Comparing Deng Xiaoping's post-1978 formulation is to see almost word for word Marx: "A Communist society is one in which... there is great material abundance, and the principle of from each according to their ability, to each according to his needs is applied. It is impossible to apply that principle without overwhelming material wealth." But in the present period, before the accumulation of such wealth, the principle was to each according to their labour/work: "We must adhere to this socialist principle which calls for distribution according to the quantity and quality of an individual's work." Deng's fundamental characterization was: "China is in the primary stage of socialism. Socialism itself is the first stage of communism, and here in China we are still in the primary stage of socialism – that is, the underdeveloped stage. In everything we do we must proceed from this reality, and all planning must be consistent with it."

But while in one sense Deng Xiaoping staged 'a return to Marx', he simultaneously had to solve many problems Marx never envisaged. Purely theoretically a number of such issues had been analysed by Keynes in the 1930s. Keynes fundamental conclusions was that investment played the determining role in the economy, "the fluctuations of output... depend almost entirely on the amount of current investment" – a finding confirmed by statistics since. As, in a modern economy, investment is financed by borrowing, Keynes advocated very low interest rates – to incentivize investment. Nevertheless, Keynes judged these would not be sufficient to stably maintain a sufficient level of investment decline and it was therefore necessary for the state to play a direct role in this: "I am... skeptical of the success of a merely monetary policy directed towards influencing the rate of interest... I expect to see the State... taking an ever-greater responsibility for directly organising investment." Keynes noted: "I conclude that the duty of ordering the current volume of investment cannot safely be left in private hands"

If, however, the state were to determine 'the current volume of investment' then Keynes realized this meant large state role in investment: 'I conceive... that a somewhat comprehensive socialisation of investment will prove the only means of securing an approximation to full employment.'

Keynes noted that 'somewhat comprehensive socialisation of investment' did not mean the entirely eliminating the private sector, but socialised investment operating together with a private sector: "This need not exclude all manner of compromises and devices by which public authority will co-operate with private initiative... The central controls necessary to ensure full employment will, of course, involve a large extension of the traditional functions of government."

Keynes therefore envisaged an economy an economy in which a private sector existed but in which the state sector was sufficiently dominant to set the overall investment level.

But Keynes's theoretical solutions could not be implemented in the West for an insurmountable reason. Investment is 'the means of production'. If the most basic investment decisions were not taken by private capital it was not a capitalist society! Keynes' had developed an incisive theoretical analysis which unfortunately could not be implemented in the society in which he lived.

The problems which were insurmountable for Keynes were, however, no problem for Deng Xiaoping as he did not intend to create a capitalist society anyway. To be clear, there is no evidence Deng Xiaoping's economic concepts were directly influenced by Keynes. But the ideas Deng Xiaoping was entirely familiar with from Marx led to the same structure. The state would retain large scale (i.e socialized) economic sectors, thereby giving it the ability to regulate the investment level, while small scale economic sectors (non-socialised production) could be released to the non-state sector. The state did not at all need to own the overall economy, just to own enough to set the overall investment level.

This concept was applied from 1978 in the decollectivization of Chinese agriculture - a radical break from the Soviet model. This in China meant the replacement of large scale rural Peoples Communes, created in the 1950s, with small scale based agriculture – the 'household responsibility system'. Then the policy known as Zhuada Fangxiao ('keep the large, let go the small') could be embarked on – maintaining large state firms and releasing small ones to the non-state/private sector.

But although a private sector was created, the state sector was still large enough to set the overall investment level – i.e. the state sector remained dominant. As the Wall Street Journal put it: "Most economies can pull two levers to bolster growth – fiscal and monetary. China has a third option ... accelerate the flow of investment projects."

Deng Xiaoping's structure simultaneously solved the problem of how to divert resources away from heavy industry and create an abundant supply of consumer products. As the state-owned heavy industry prices in this sector could be controlled in this while simultaneously liberalizing them in agriculture and light consumer industry. As prices consequently rose in consumer industries and agriculture, resources flowed into them and their production soared. Simultaneously, initially the urban population was protected against the negative effects on living standards of these price rises by subsidies which were financed by reducing China's armaments expenditure. The extraordinarily rapid growth this structure produced created large scale savings which, in a virtuous circle, could then finance the building of heavy industry on a new basis.

Simultaneously with this reintroduction of small scale 'non-socialised' production, China's economy pursued international 'opening up', allowing it to participate in the largest scale production of all – for the global market.

Far from being purely pragmatic, therefore, Deng Xiaoping's economic reform, flowed in an integration fashion from underlying theoretical economic principles through to the solving of eminently practical issues of economic policy. It was this which produced by far the greatest economic growth and social advancement seen in any country in history.

This integrated system also explains why any diversion from Deng Xiaoping's path necessarily leads to economic difficulties. Any return to an administered economy leads to the inability to take advantage of small-scale production and in practice to the ability to integrate with a world economic market. Any system which create a system in which private enterprise is dominant, however, loses the ability of the state to regulate the level of investment and thereby recreating the problems which both Keynes and Deng Xiaoping had successfully solved.

In short, no one in history has ever combined such deep economic thinking with such successful economic policy as Deng Xiaoping

Deng Xiaoping was above all a greater leader of the Chinese people. Through pursuit of his countries national revival, which lifter 620 million people out of poverty, he also made an unparalleled contribution to humanity's overall well-being.

But if that were not enough Deng Xiaoping had another achievement. By far the greatest economist of the 20th century was not Keynes, Hayek or Friedman but Deng Xiaoping - and those who followed him in making China's economic reform.

Section *4*

Theoretical Bases of China's Foreign Policy

Xi Jinping's analysis of 'a common future for humanity' – its relation to Marx's Das Kapital

18 July 2017

Introduction

President Xi Jinping's analysis of 'a common future for humanity' is one of the most important and original features of China's foreign policy and of 'Xi Jinping's Thought on Socialism with Chinese Characteristics for a New Era'. It is a genuinely new concept, not to be found in classical Marxist authors. But, it will be shown, it directly builds on Marx's concepts. It is therefore a genuine creative application of Marxism.

As he is president of China, concerned with clear understanding by others of China's foreign policy, and not an academic speaking to students, Xi Jinping's main speeches naturally do not consist of quotations from Marx and he makes extensive references to classical Chinese authors. The aim of this paper is to show how the concept of 'a common future for humanity' also logically develops Marx's concepts. It similarly shows this concept is comprehensible not only in classical Chinese but in Western philosophical thought. 'A common future for humanity' is therefore shown to be a creative development of Marxism which is grounded in both classical Chinese and classical Western thought.

Such firm establishment of the concept of 'a common future for humanity' in Marxism, as well as in classical Chinese and Western thought, and its accurate relation to economic

reality, provides an exceptionally firm basis for China's foreign policy – and that of other countries.

A brief contrast to the chief alternative concept, that
derived from marginalist economics, which underlies Western 'neo-con' thinking is also given.

First the key concepts of Xi Jinping's 'common future for
humanity' are outlined and then its relation to classical
Western thought shown.

The philosophical features of 'a common future for humanity'

The economic foundation of the concept of 'a common future
for humanity' is Xi Jinping's unequivocal support for globalisation - building on the framework of 'reform and opening
up'. Xi Jinping notes: 'economic globalization is a result of
growing social productivity, and a natural outcome of scientific and technological progress.'[137] This analysis is, of
course, in line with Marx, who saw the most fundamental
force of human progress as socialisation of labour - fully
international socialisation of labour, that is globalisation, is
the greatest, and therefore most advanced, scope of socialisation of labour.

This analysis of Marx is in turn his development of the
fundamental conclusion of Adam Smith, announced in the
first sentence of the first chapter of *The Wealth of Nations,*
the founding work of modern economics, from which the
whole of the rest of that work flows:

'The greatest improvement in the productive powers of
labour, and the greater part of the skill, dexterity, and judgment with which it is directed, or applied, seem to have been
the effect of the division of labour.'

The building on Smith by Marx can be seen clearly in his
initial works, for example *The German Ideology,* in which the
fundamental concepts of *The Communist Manifesto* and later
analyses were developed. These simply took over Smith's
terminology of 'division of labour'. In later works Marx used
the terminology of 'socialisation of labour'[138] or 'socialised
production'[139], rather than division of labour, but this did
not alter the content.

Marx, of course, regarded socialised labour/division of
labour as the most important productive force and increasing

socialisation of labour as the most fundamental source of human progress - as Marx summarised: 'Division of labour increases with civilisation.'[140]

As globalisation is therefore the logical and most advanced expression of division/socialisation of labour it therefore forms the starting point of Xi Jinping's analysis.

Interdependence of countries

The crucial aspect of division/socialisation of labour is that, as Marx, developing Smith, shows is that by producers interacting in their production the resulting productivity and output is much greater than the sum of their individual efforts. - as President Xi stated it in popular fashion in economics: 'one plus one can be greater than two.'[141]

This concept, which follows directly from the analysis of socialisation/division of labour first made by Smith/Marx, however necessarily and immediately destroys the concept that international relations are a 'zero sum game'. Instead of a 'zero-sum' situation, by engaging in division of labour both or many sides can gain – that is, international interaction is mutually beneficial. International cooperation is therefore not merely necessarily required to deal with inherently international problems (climate change, terrorism etc.) but its mutual advantages in the highest possible high living standards are rooted in, and only achievable by, international division/socialisation of labour. That such benefits can only be achieved by interaction of states is therefore precisely expressed in Xi Jinping's concept of a 'community of common destiny' or 'a common future for humanity.'

Naturally this concept of 'a common future for humanity' does not mean that there are no conflicts between countries. But it means that they have a more fundamental common interest, in that the prosperity of each country depends on international division of labour – the prosperity of each country depends on other countries. This creates the reality of the international community – the 'shared future for humanity'.

Diversity and equality

This reality of mutual benefit from division/socialisation of labour, however, immediately poses another question within the overall concept of 'a common future for humanity'. Division of labour produces its greatest benefits not because those participating in it are the same but because they are different – if they were the same there would be less benefit! However, division of labour in the modern world is necessarily international in scope – the age when even the largest national economies could be essentially self-contained is past. As President Xi Jinping puts it: 'In today's world, all countries are interdependent and share a common future.'[142]

This creates a further pillar of Xi Jinping's concept of the 'community of shared future'. Human and national diversity is not a disadvantage, something to be feared, but it contributes to human development. To express this formally President Xi Jinping quoted the Chinese philosopher Mencius: 'As early as over 2,000 years ago, the Chinese people came to recognize that "it is natural for things to be different."'[143] Or as Xi Jinping put it in more popular idiom, citing *History of the Three Kingdoms*:

'"Delicious soup is made by combining different ingredients." Diversity in human civilization not only defines our world, but also drives human progress.... Diversity in civilizations should not be a source of global conflict; rather it should be a driver for progress... Diverse civilisations should draw on each other to achieve common progress. Exchanges among civilizations should become a source of inspiration for advancing human society.' [144]

This diversity of countries, and therefore of civilizations, in the concept of 'a common future for humanity', does not however imply their inequality. As Xi Jinping notes:

'civilizations are equal, and such equality has made exchanges and mutual learning among civilizations possible. All human civilizations... have their respective strengths and weaknesses. No civilization is perfect on the planet. Nor is it devoid of merit. No single civilization can be judged superior to another.... as a Chinese saying goes, "Radish or cabbage, each to his own delight."'[145]

Therefore, instead of an attempt to impose uniformity, a single model which is considered 'superior' to all others, and which is attempted to be imposed on others, in the concept of 'a common future for humanity', China's foreign policy precisely embraces the diversity of different countries.

The Western philosophical framework

While Xi Jinping's analysis explicitly refers, as already seen, to classical Chinese thought it may be equally seen it is equally comprehensible in terms of Western philosophical thought.

To summarise, the fundamental concepts of Xi Jinping's 'a common future for humanity' includes the following key points:

- Humanity, and therefore countries, are interdependent.
- All countries are equal.
- All countries are different.

Considering first the issue that all countries are different the idea of Mencius cited by Xi Jinping was, of course, also expressed by the ancient Greek philosopher Heraclitus, also over 2,000 years ago, in his famous aphorism 'No man ever steps in the same river twice' – that is, everything which exists is unique both in time and place. Within Western thought the philosophers Spinoza and Leibniz formally proved the same principle – its classic formulation being Leibniz's 'identity of indiscernibles'.

As Leibniz's noted: 'there are never two beings in nature that are perfectly alike.'[146] Or: 'no two substances are completely similar.' Therefore: 'nowhere are there things perfectly similar.'[147] And: 'it is not true that two substances can resemble each other completely.'[148] Therefore: 'There is no such thing as two things indiscernible from each other... To suppose two things indiscernible is to suppose the same thing under two names.'[149] Or as Leibniz summarised it: 'A consideration which is of the greatest importance in all philosophy... [is] that it is not possible for two things to differ from one another in respect of place and time alone.'[150]

Turning to this combination of inevitable and necessary difference with equality, which are foundations of Xi Jinping's 'common future for humanity', it is clear that these combined concepts are precisely in line with the opening chapters, and fundamental framework, of Marx's *Das Kapital*. In this, as is well known, Marx analyses that:

- Commodities can be measured against each other because they are the expression of (socialised) human labour.

- Equal quantities of (socially necessary) human labour exchange equally, that is they have equal exchange values, and the only feature they have in common in this exchange is the equal quantity of human labour – that is they are reduced to abstract labour. 'Let us take two commodities, e. g., corn and iron. The proportions in which they are exchangeable, whatever those proportions may be, can always be represented by an equation in which a given quantity of corn is equated to some quantity of iron: e. g., 1 quarter corn = x cwt. iron. What does this equation tell us? It tells us that in two different things — in 1 quarter of corn and x cwt. of iron, there exists in equal quantities something common to both... If then we leave out of consideration the use value of commodities, they have only one common property left, that of being products of labour.'[151]
- Commodities also possess use values, which unlike exchange values, are entirely concrete differing in an infinite number of features.

In summary, two, or more, commodities which exchange therefore simultaneously:

- Have entirely equal exchange values,
- Have entirely different/diverse use values

This conceptual structure of the first chapters of Marx's *Das Kapital* is, in turn, based on the structure of Hegel's *The Science of Logic*. In this:

- Everything is the same, and therefore equal, in the most abstract category 'Being'.
- Everything is differentiated in the more concrete categories which start with Determinate Being – including Quantity, Measure etc.

This specific combination of equality and diversity at the beginning of Marx's *Das Kapital*, which in turn is derived from Hegel, is of course the same structure as Xi Jinping's 'a common future for humanity'. Therefore, as may be seen, the concept of 'a common future for humanity', simultaneously is a creative development of Marx's concepts and is entirely comprehensible in terms of both Chinese and Western classical thought.

The marginalist/neo-liberal analysis

Finally, the fundamental and interrelated concepts in Xi Jinping's analysis, developed on the basis of Marx's analyses, contrasts clearly with the main alternative which is promoted internationally – that is that of US 'neo-cons'/neo-liberals which is, in turn, is based in marginalist non-Marxist economics.

In what was really an attempt to reply to Xi Jinping's speech at the 2017 Davos World Economic Forum, the then US National Security Adviser McMaster and the then Director of the US National Economic Council Cohn jointly authored a *Wall Street Journal* article – which could not have appeared without sanction from the highest US authorities. In this they proclaimed: 'the world is not a "global community" but an arena where nations, nongovernmental actors and businesses engage and compete for advantage.' Or as they put it, drawing the practical conclusion. 'America First signals the restoration of American leadership.'[152] This, therefore is a profoundly unequal concept of international relations – in its most grotesque form expressed in references to 'sh*thole countries'.[153]

This analysis that there is no 'global community' is directly based in marginalist/neo-liberal economics. In the marginalist concept the fundamental unit is not the division/ socialisation of labour analysed by Smith/Marx but the concept that economy and society is simply composed of individual units. McMaster and Cohn's starting point is a restatement, and an attempt to defend on the international field, exactly what the neo-liberal Margaret Thatcher declared on the national terrain: 'there is no such thing as society. There are individual men and women.'[154] This marginalist concept of economics, and its conclusions, is therefore fundamentally counterposed to the analysis of Smith/Marx.

As this marginalist analysis fails to identify the mutual advantages of division/socialisation of labour it is led not to the correct concept of 'a common future for humanity', creating the mutual interest of an international community, but to the concept of international relations as a zero-sum

game and therefore that: 'the world is not a "global community" but an arena where nations, nongovernmental actors
and businesses engage and compete for advantage.'

Conclusion

The conclusion is clear. Xi Jinping's analysis of 'a common future for humanity' is an outstanding example of the
creative development of Marxism - being firmly rooted in
fundamental Marxist concepts, and classical Chinese and
Western thought, but developing this in striking new ways
that directly relate to and reflect contemporary realities.

China and South-South Cooperation in the present global situation

14 January 2021

The increasing alignment of China and the 'Global South'

Biden becoming US president and the dramatic events at the end of the Trump presidency – the 6 January storming of the US Congress by rioters, Trump's loss of the Presidential election itself, the loss of control of the Senate by the Republican Party due to its defeats in Georgia – inevitably focussed attention on analysis of the prospects for the US's global position. It has led some respected analysts in China and the West to make claims such as that China's comprehensive national strength has already overtaken the US and to dramatic predictions such as that 'the West faces a perfect storm', 'that 2020 will be seen as the year of the Great Transition, when the majority of the world's population come to view China as the new global leader,' and that 'America is destined to become much less important. It is rapidly being replaced as the world's No 1 power by China.' [155]

Certainly, few subjects are more important for China, indeed for the whole of humanity, than correctly estimating the present global situation, China's place within it, and the effects of this on US attempts to block China's national rejuvenation. In a shorter timescale, within this framework, it is extremely important to analyse the fundamental dynamics of the Biden presidency. While the present author would indeed be extremely pleased if the US was rapidly replaced by China as the new global leader, and that 2020 will be when the majority of the world's population come to view China as the new global leader, and that this would be in the interests not only of China but humanity, he does not believe this is accurate for reasons which are analysed below.

The US is undoubtedly in its deepest political crisis since at least the Vietnam War but it's still not possible for the US to fall behind China in terms of comprehensive strength in the short term. Instead, what is created by US aggression against China is global competition and a situation within which the US still has considerable resources and in which it can maintain international allies - for reasons which will be analysed. A more correct framework for understanding the global situation than a rapid/sudden shift is the concept of a 'protracted' competition. It is indeed fitting that Mao Zedong's 'On Protracted War' has currently become one of his most widely read works in China - Guancha, for example, emphasising this by choosing to republish it to mark the anniversary of Mao Zedong's birth.

There are at least two reasons for taking 'On Protracted War' as a key aid to understanding the present situation. One is that it precisely provides a framework for understanding a 'prolonged' struggle to resist US attempts to prevent China's national rejuvenation – a struggle which, because of its huge global scale, cannot be over quickly. But a further, even more general, reason for such study is that it shows the importance of Mao Zedong Thought as a method for studying contemporary problems. The method of analysis displayed in 'On Protracted War' can be studied by everyone analysing the present situation with enormous benefit – even if, naturally, they cannot apply it with the same level of genius.

Certainly, there are further developments which develop and build on Mao's analysis. In particular Xi Jinping's concept of a common destiny of humanity shows clearly why the national rejuvenation of China and the progress of humanity are interlinked – which is why all references below to the progress of China apply to humanity and not only to China. But these concepts build on and do not contradict Mao Zedong Thought.

The aim of this article is therefore twofold. First, it is a humble effort to illustrate the way in which Mao Zedong's method of analysis in 'On Protracted War', as in all his works, is directly relevant to studying the present situation. Second, to analysing some of the conclusions which flow from key methodological points made by Mao for understanding present global dynamics, the real situation of the US, and for US-China dynamics.

Those who wish to proceed directly to the analysis of the present situation, without looking at the points on 'On Protracted War', may proceed directly to Part 2 of the article 'The global economic situation after Covid19.'

Part 1 – Some Lessons from Mao Zedong's 'On Protracted War'

Some points on the method of 'On Protracted War'

First a few methodological points from 'On Protracted War' may be emphasised which are directly relevant to the study of the present situation. The first, insisted on by Mao, is that that a subject of study, in the case of 'On Protracted War' the struggle against Japan, must be analysed as totally specific in both time and space - it must not be analysed in 'general' terms. 'Our war is not just any war, it is specifically a war between China and Japan fought in the Nineteen Thirties.'[156] And: 'The war between China and Japan is not just any war, it is specifically a war of life and death between semi-colonial and semi-feudal China and imperialist Japan, fought in the Nineteen Thirties. Herein lies the basis of the whole problem.'[157]

Methodologically, in order to understand the specific character of the war, Mao insists that all factors, not merely one or two, must be taken into account: 'Our perseverance in the War of Resistance and in the united front has been possible because of many factors.'[158] He noted: 'Internally, they comprise all the political parties in the country from the Communist Party to the Kuomintang, all the people from the workers and peasants to the bourgeoisie, and all the armed forces from the regular forces to the guerrillas; internationally, they range from the land of socialism [the USSR] to justice-loving people in all countries.'[159]

Therefore, as Mao notes in the most general terms: 'A correct answer to the question "Why a protracted war?" can be arrived at only on the basis of all the fundamental contrasts between China and Japan.... Therefore when we say that the War of Resistance Against Japan is a protracted war, our conclusion is derived from the interrelations of all the factors.' [160]

The section of 'On Protracted War' which particularly emphasises the importance of analysing all factors in the situation (the 'whole') is a further development of the lectures delivered by Mao in December 1936, 'Problems of Strategy in China's Revolutionary War' - in the section with the self-explanatory title 'Strategy is the Study of the Laws of a War Situation as a Whole'. 'Wherever there is war, there is a war situation as a whole.... Any war situation which acquires a comprehensive consideration of its various aspects and stages forms a war situation as a whole.

'The task of the science of strategy is to study those laws for directing a war that govern a war situation as a whole... The task of the science of campaigns and the science of tactics is to study those laws for directing a war that govern a partial situation.

'Why is it necessary for the commander of a campaign or a tactical operation to understand the laws of strategy to some degree? Because an understanding of the whole facilitates the handling of the part, and because the part is subordinate to the whole. The view that strategic victory is determined by tactical successes alone is wrong because it overlooks the fact that victory or defeat in a war is first and foremost a question of whether the situation as a whole and its various stages are properly taken into account...'

'All this explains the importance of taking into account the situation as a whole. What is most important for the person in over-all command is to concentrate on attending to the war situation as a whole.'[161]

Analysing the international as well as the domestic situation

As all factors must be taken into account Mao insists therefore necessarily the war against Japan had to be studied in not merely a domestic but in its international dimension: 'Japan has undertaken this war at a time when many countries have been or are about to be embroiled in war, when we are all fighting or preparing to fight against barbarous aggression, and China's fortunes are linked with those of most of the countries and peoples of the world. This is the root cause of the opposition Japan has aroused and will increasingly arouse among those countries and peoples.' [162]

The conclusion from this analysis of the international as well as the domestic situation was: 'In the existing international situation, China is not isolated in the war, and this fact too is without precedent in history. In the past, China's wars, and India's too, were wars fought in isolation. It is only today that we meet with world-wide popular movements, extraordinary in breadth and depth, which have arisen or are arising and which are supporting China. The Russian Revolution of 1917 also received international support, and thus the Russian workers and peasants won; but that support was not so broad in scale and deep in nature as ours today. The popular movements in the world today are developing on a scale and with a depth that are unprecedented. The existence of the Soviet Union is a particularly vital factor in present-day international politics, and the Soviet Union will certainly support China with the greatest enthusiasm; there was nothing like this twenty years ago. All these factors have created and are creating important conditions indispensable to China's final victory. Large-scale direct assistance is as yet lacking and will come only in the future, but China is progressive and is a big country, and these are the factors enabling her to protract the war and to promote as well as await international help.' [163]

Reject one sidedness

As a result of this necessity to analyse all elements of the situation Mao emphasises that it is a fundamental error to analyse only individual factors, or to exaggerate the weight and importance of individual aspects of the situation: 'Epistemologically speaking, the source of all erroneous views on war lies in idealist and mechanistic tendencies on the question. People with such tendencies are subjective and one-sided in their approach to problems. They either indulge in groundless and purely subjective talk, or, basing themselves upon a single aspect or a temporary manifestation, magnify it with similar subjectivity into the whole of the problem.... Therefore, only by opposing idealist and mechanistic tendencies and taking an objective and all-sided view in making a study of war can we draw correct conclusions on the question of war.' [164]

Mao emphatically noted, therefore, that not taking into account all the main aspects of the situation, and concentrating on only one or two of them, was unscientific: 'All the experience of the ten months of war proves the error both of the theory of China's inevitable subjugation and of the theory of China's quick victory. The former gives rise to the tendency to compromise and the latter to the tendency to underestimate the enemy. Both approaches to the problem are subjective and one-sided, or, in a word, unscientific.' [165]

In rejecting any method of simply ripping one feature of the situation out of is connection with all others it may be noted Mao took exactly the same position as Lenin who had noted: "The most widely used, and most fallacious, method in the realm of social phenomena is to tear out individual minor facts and juggle with examples. Selecting chance examples presents no difficulty at all, but is of no value, or of purely negative value, for in each individual case everything hinges on the historically concrete situation. Facts, if we take them in their entirety, in their interconnection, are not only stubborn things, but undoubtedly proof-bearing things. Minor facts, if taken out of their entirety, out of their interconnection, if they are arbitrarily selected and torn out of context, are merely things for juggling, or even worse.'[166]

Not all elements of the situation are of equal weight

But while stressing all factors had to be taken into account Mao emphasised that it was crucial to note that they are not of equal weight or importance in the situation – as Mao noted by saying the importance of different elements was of 'varying degrees': 'In short, all these forces have contributed in varying degrees to our War of Resistance.'[167] That is, with the framework of analysis of the whole, Mao analysed elements all elements in the situation in terms of their precise and different weights and importance.

Thus, for example, Mao noted his own reply to questions regarding which was the most important feature of the situation: 'Question: Under what conditions do you think China can defeat and destroy the forces of Japan?

'Answer: Three conditions are required: first, the establishment of an anti-Japanese united front in China; second, the formation of an international anti-Japanese united front; third, the rise of the revolutionary movement of the people in Japan and the Japanese colonies. From the standpoint of the Chinese people, the unity of the people of China is the most important of the three conditions.'[168]

Similarly, regarding analysis of this most important of these three conditions:

'Question: How long do you think such a war would last?

'Answer: That depends on the strength of China's anti-Japanese united front and many other conditioning factors involving China and Japan. That is to say, apart from China's own strength, which is the main thing'. [169]

Detailed analysis of different quantitative weights

Within the analysis of these different, and contradictory, features of the situation Mao insisted on examining in precise detail the weight of different forces. For example, he noted the existence in China of trends wanting to capitulate to or compromise with Japan but analysed that forces opposing this were more powerful – that is he established the relative strength of the two forces: 'Hence we may conclude that the danger of compromise exists but can be overcome... In China the social roots of compromise are present, but the opponents of compromise are in the majority. Internationally, also, some forces favour compromise but the main forces favour resistance. The combination of these three factors makes it possible to overcome the danger of compromise and persist to the end in the War of Resistance.' [170]

Wrong estimates of the situation arose from the error, already noted, of considering only one feature of the situation and not all elements within the whole and their relative weights: 'In our comparative study of the enemy and ourselves with respect to the basic contradictory characteristics, such as relative strength, relative size, progress or reaction, and the relative extent of support, we have already refuted the theory of national subjugation, and we have explained why compromise is unlikely and why political progress is possible. The subjugationists stress the contradiction between

strength and weakness and puff it up until it becomes the
basis of their whole argument on the question, neglecting
all the other contradictions. Their preoccupation with the
contrast in strength shows their one-sidedness, and their
exaggeration of this one side of the matter into the whole
shows their subjectivism. Thus, if one looks at the matter as
a whole, it will be seen that they have no ground to stand on
and are wrong.' [171]

A similar one sidedness, that is not analysing all features of
the situation, or incorrectly exaggerating the weight of some
factors in it, was shown by those who believed quick victory
over Japan was possible: 'The exponents of quick victory are
likewise wrong. Either they completely forget the contradiction between strength and weakness, remembering only the
other contradictions, or they exaggerate China's advantages
beyond all semblance of reality and beyond recognition, or
they presumptuously take the balance of forces at one time
and place for the whole situation, as in the old saying, "A
leaf before the eye shuts out Mount Tail" In a word, they
lack the courage to admit that the enemy is strong while we
are weak. They often deny this point and consequently deny
one aspect of the truth. Nor do they have the courage to
admit the limitations of our advantages, and thus they deny
another aspect of the truth. The result is that they make
mistakes, big and small, and here again it is subjectivism
and one-sidedness that are doing the mischief. These friends
have their hearts in the right place, and they, too, are patri-
ots. But while "the gentlemen aspirations are indeed lofty",
their views are wrong, and to act according to them would
certainly be to run into a brick wall.' [172]

If any analysis is not strictly objective, including in analysing the weight of different factors, it was not possible for
China to secure the best conditions for victory: 'if appraisal
does not conform to reality, action cannot attain its objective'[173] That is, for example: 'quick victory is something that
exists only in one's mind and not in objective reality, and
that it is a mere illusion, a false theory.' [174]

Development of the situation

The examination of this interrelation and precise weight of
all the different contradictory elements means Mao arrives

at a not a static view of the situation but at an analysis of its dynamic – precisely of the 'protracted' character of the struggle. He notes: 'In comparison with the original situation, the enemy is still strong, but unfavourable factors have reduced his strength, although not yet to a degree sufficient to destroy his superiority, and similarly we are still weak, but favourable factors have compensated for our weakness, although not yet to a degree sufficient to transform our inferiority. Thus it turns out that the enemy is relatively strong and we are relatively weak, that the enemy is in a relatively superior and we are in a relatively inferior position. On both sides, strength and weakness, superiority and inferiority, have never been absolute, and besides, our efforts in persevering in resistance to Japan and in the united front during the war have brought about further changes in the original balance of forces between us and the enemy. Therefore, in this stage the enemy's victory and our defeat are definitely restricted in degree, and hence the war becomes protracted.' [175]

This analysis of the dynamics of the situation is then considered in more precise detail. The lectures 'On Protracted War' were delivered in May 1938. At that time Mao could analyse: 'The first stage has not yet ended. The enemy's design is to occupy Canton, Wuhan and Lanchow and link up these three points. To accomplish this aim the enemy will have to use at least fifty divisions, or about one and a half million men, spend from one and a half to two years, and expend more than ten thousand million yen.' [176]

Then: 'The second stage may be termed one of strategic stalemate. At the tail end of the first stage, the enemy will be forced to fix certain terminal points to his strategic offensive owing to his shortage of troops and our firm resistance, and upon reaching them he will stop his strategic offensive and enter the stage of safeguarding his occupied areas. In the second stage, the enemy will attempt to safeguard the occupied areas and to make them his own by the fraudulent method of setting up puppet governments, while plundering the Chinese people to the limit; but again he will be confronted with stubborn guerrilla warfare.' [177]

In the end, and noting the interrelation of domestic and international factors already analysed: 'The third stage will be the stage of the counter-offensive to recover our lost territories. Their recovery will depend mainly upon the strength which China has built up in the preceding stage and which will continue to grow in the third stage. But China's strength alone will not be sufficient, and we shall also have to rely on the support of international forces... or otherwise we shall not be able to win; this adds to China's tasks in international propaganda and diplomacy.'[178]

It was this analysis of dynamics which led to the decisive conclusion on the protracted character of the war: 'Will China be subjugated? The answer is, No, she will not be subjugated, but will win final victory. Can China win quickly? The answer is, No, she cannot win quickly, and the war must be a protracted one.' [179]

These dynamics could then be compared to the unfolding of the situation. History, of course, confirmed the correctness of Mao's analysis that China would emerge victorious from its struggle against Japan in a 'Protracted War.'

The 'generally correct direction'

Finally, within this fundamental framework, Mao insisted it was impossible to foresee all precise details and interrelations of the struggle. However, by analysing the most powerful factors it was possible to foresee the fundamental trend, and what he termed the 'generally correct direction': 'We admit that the phenomenon of war is more elusive and is characterized by greater uncertainty than any other social phenomenon, in other words, that it is more a matter of "probability"... But whatever the situation and the moves in a war, one can know their general aspects and essential points. It is possible for a commander to reduce errors and give generally correct direction, first through all kinds of reconnaissance and then through intelligent inference and judgement. Armed with the weapon of "generally correct direction"'[180]

Finally, it should be noted, that while 'On Protracted War' is one of the most famous examples of application of Mao's methodology the same principles run through all his work.

The scientific basis of analysis

A comparison may make the scientific basis of the superiority of Mao's study of social phenomenon clear compared to Western non-Marxist ideas. At school in the West we are taught what might be termed the 'billiard ball' theory of causality. It says that a billiard ball goes across the table and strikes another ball and this determines the trajectory of the other ball. This might be termed a monocausal (or in Mao's terms 'one sided') theory of causality. Actually, the trajectory of the other ball is determined not by one but by numerous factors – the speed and direction of the first ball, the slope of the table, how rough or smooth the cloth on the table is etc. If sensitive enough equipment were available it would also be found that the trajectory of the ball was determined by the altitude of the table and air resistance, the gravity of the moon etc. In short, the trajectory of the second ball is not determined 'monocausally' (in a oneside way) at all but by numerous factors in the situation.

In the case of the billiard ball, the trajectory of the second ball only appears to be determined by one or a very few factors, such as the direction of the first ball, because this is overwhelmingly the most powerful factor in the situation. But in other more complex situations causality is not 'monocausal' at all. For example, in sending a long-distance rocket through the solar system numerous factors have to be taken into account and each given an appropriate weight – the initial speed of the rocket, the gravity of the Earth, the gravity of the Moon, the gravity of the Sun, the gravity of different planets etc. The study of social phenomena in general finds not one but numerous elements of the situation at work. In summary Mao's insistence of analysis of all contradictions in the situation, of precise analysis of their relative importance and weight, and of the dynamics of the situation is the only scientific method.

It may be superficially objected to this emphasis on the need to judge the weight of each element in the situation that 'On Protracted War' contains only a few numbers and statistical statements, unlike some other great works of Marxism which are full of statistics - most famously, of course, Marx's 'Capital', or Lenin's 'The Development of Capitalism in Russia'. But that is a misunderstanding. Language, not simply numbers, in fact contains its own mathematics and arithmetic. Mao's 'On Prolonged War' is full of expressions which have entirely precise mathematical/arithmetic/statistical meanings - 'main' (which means no other factor is important), 'all' (which means 100%), 'majority' (that is more than 50%), 'subsidiary' (which means not the most important), 'relative' (which means more important or less important) etc. In summary Mao wrote this work in language, not in statistics, but it contains numerous quantitative statements. Mao shows in these an extreme precision, precisely opposing any exaggeration.

Taking this into account now let us attempt to analyse the development of the present global situation. Naturally this cannot be done in any way remotely resembling the genius of 'On Protracted War' but the more accurately its method can be applied the more it will be possible to analyse the 'generally correct direction' of understanding the present situation.

Part2 - 'The global economic situation after Covid19.'

Economic situation

Starting with 'the whole' that is the global situation, it is well understood that the effect of Covid19 will be to produce the deepest global economic downturn since the Great Depression. To analyse in detail this situation the latest projections of the IMF will be taken - this data is not taken because the IMF projections will be correct in detail but because:

- the IMF cannot be considered a source under the control of China and therefore to be exaggerating China's growth.
- the differences shown between growth in different parts of the world economy are so large that even with considerable inaccuracies no doubt is left as to the key trends in the world economy.

Starting with the overall global trend, the IMF's latest projection for global growth is shown in Figure 39. This confirms the unprecedented character, since the Great Depression, of the global economic crisis following Covid19. It estimates that in 2020 the world economy will shrink by 4.4% - a hugely greater impact than the international financial crisis of 2008 which produced a global contraction of only 0.1%. It is equally widely understood in this context that China's economy at present is recovering much more rapidly than any other major economy. Specifically, in comparison

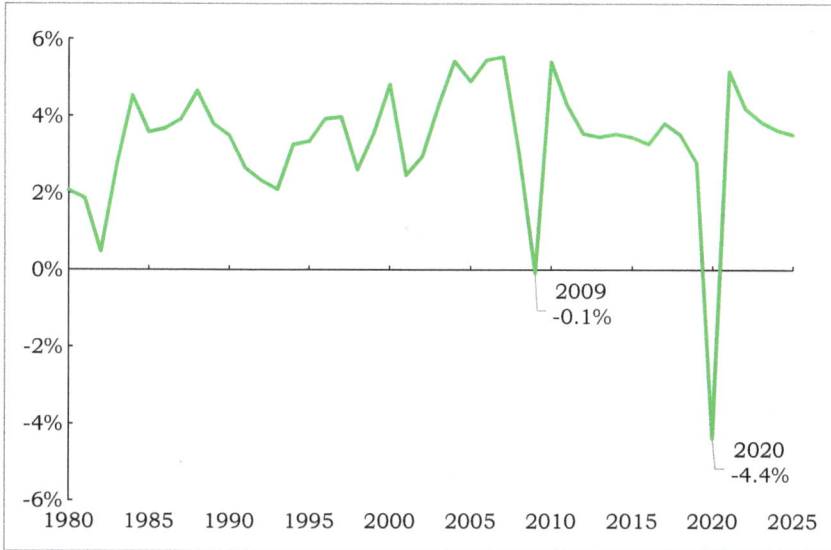

Figure 39: World GDP - Annual % Growth Inflation
adjusted prices
Source: IMF World Economic Outlook October 2020

to the US, in the third quarter of 2020, the latest available data, China's GDP was 4.9% higher than a year previously whereas US GDP was 2.9% lower than a year previously.

In terms of the geopolitical and social tension that will be produced this this will probably be even more serious than the one-year impact of the Covid19 recession because it will reduce average economic growth over a longer period – which will have a steadily mounting cumulative effect. This is shown in Figure 40 which gives 5 year and 10 year moving averages for global growth. Taking a 10-year moving annual average, global GDP growth will be reduced from 3.7% in 2019 to 2.9% by 2025, while taking a 10 year moving average the decline will be from 3.5% to 2.4%.

The slowing of the US economy

Within this overall global context, the US suffered a severe fall in GDP in 2020 due to Covid. But it is crucial for understanding global dynamics to grasp that this decline in 2020 simply exaggerated a slowing of the US economy which has been taking place for over 50 years. This can be clearly seen

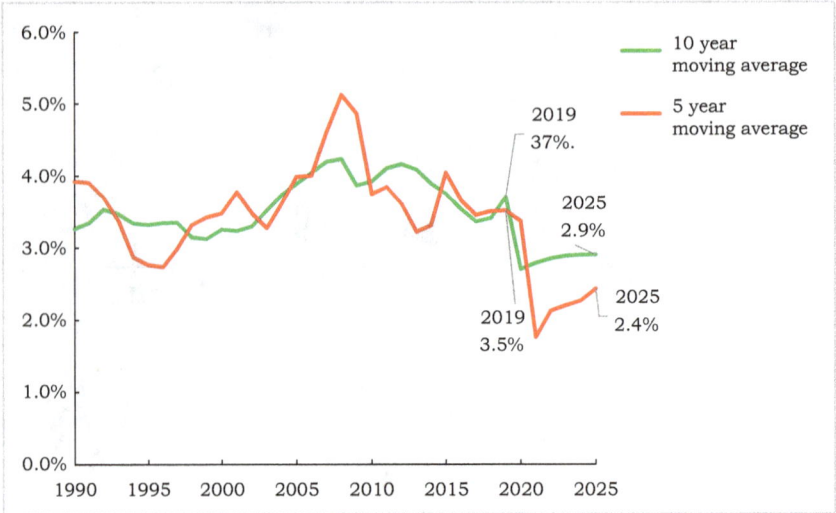

Figure 40: Annual % GDP Growth 5 year and 10 year moving averages - inflation adjusted prices

Source: Calculated from IMF World Economic Outlook October 2020

in Figure 41, which shows that, taking a long-term moving average to eliminate the effect of short-term business cycles, the annual average rate of growth of US GDP has fallen from 4.4% in 1969, to 4.1% in 1978, to 3.5% in 2002, to 2.0% in 2019 - before the outbreak of Covid19. That is, over a fifty-year period, annual average US GDP growth had fallen by over 50% before the impact of Covid19 began.

The long-term US average annual growth rate of 1.7% rate in the 3rd quarter of 2020 is, therefore, depressed by the impact of Covid19, and the US may be expected to recover from this extremely low level to somewhere closer to its long-term average of 2.0%. But nevertheless, while the US recession of 2020 is a continuation of a long-term slowing of the US economy it is also clear that US failure to deal adequately with the Covid19 crisis has dealt a severe blow to the US economy which has affected its relative global position – and, as will be seen, not only with China. It is clear that such a more than half century long slowing of the US economy must be rooted in extremely powerful social processes which can therefore only be reversed by strong changes in policy – which, as will be seen, the Biden administration has no possibility to undertake. The conclusion is therefore clear - US economic growth will continue to be slow.

Figure 41: Annual US GDP Growth 20 Year Moving Average
Source: Calculated from Bureau of Economic Analysis
Table 1.1.3

The consequences of the slowing of the US economy

This slow growth of the US economy is key to understanding the impact of the global situation facing the US and also greatly affects US-China relations.

- The slow growth of the US economy forces those in the US committed to maintaining US hegemony, who also see economic development as a 'zero sum game', to adopt
- a policy of attempting to slow other economies. This has been termed the US 'Tonya Harding' strategy – named after those around the US Olympic ice skater Tonya Harding who, as she was unable to get as high scores as her rival Nancy Kerrigan, arranged for an attack to injure Kerrigan aiming to lower her performance – i.e. the US, unable to speed up its own economy, aims to slow its competitors. The US used this approach to slow its competitor Germany in the 1960s, to slow Germany and Japan in the 1980s, and to slow the 'Asian Tiger' economies in the late 1990s - the methods used for slowing the German, Japanese and Asian Tiger economies were analysed in my book 《一盘大棋？——中国新命运解析. Now, of course, the US is seeking to win in competition by slowing China's economic development.

- But to grasp the international situation it is also necessary to note that simultaneously this slow growth of the US makes it on the economic field less attractive as a partner for other countries – the consequences of which are analysed below.

These fundamental features therefore determine the global position of the US.

Major shift of the world economy into developing economies

Analysing within this global framework, a key structural feature of the world economy is how much more rapidly developing countries are growing than advanced countries - as shown in Figure 42. Taking a 10-year moving average, to remove the effect of short term business cycles, the IMF projects that by 2025 developing countries will have an annual average growth rate of 3.9% compared to only 1.5% in advanced economies. That is, developing countries will be growing more than twice as fast as advanced economies.

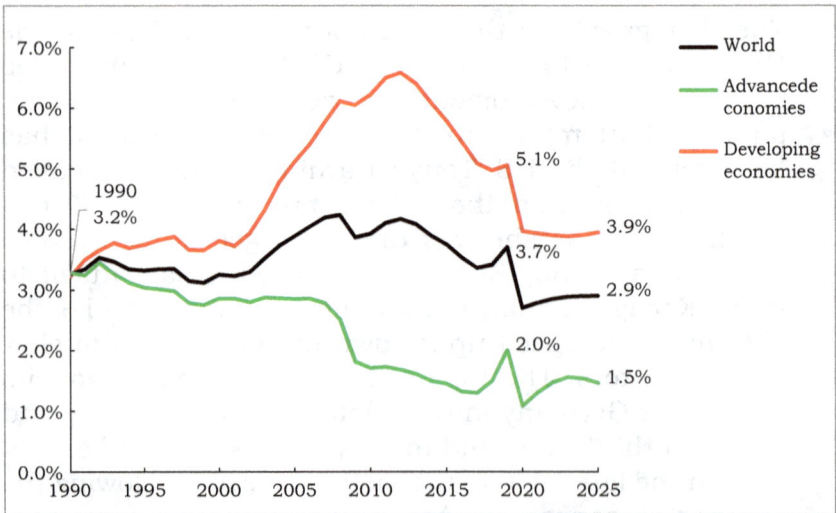

Figure 42: Annual % GDP Growth 10 year moving average
-inflation adjusted prices

Source: Calculated from IMF World Economic Outlook October 2020

Contributions to world growth

The result of the fact that developing economies will grow much faster than advanced economies is that they will contribute much more to world growth. This can be seen most clearly by analysing this in terms of the purchasing power parity (PPP) measures preferred by the IMF for analysing the real weight of national economies within the world economy. The reason for this preference is that the price levels for most products in almost all developing countries are lower than in advanced economies if measured at current market exchange rates. This means that increases in the volumes of markets are understated if measured at current exchange rates whereas measurements in terms of PPPs correct for this.

Taking the IMF's PPP measures the difference in growth of GDP between developing economies and advanced economies is shown in Figure 43. As may be seen the IMF projects that in the period up to 2025 the increase in GDP/market by

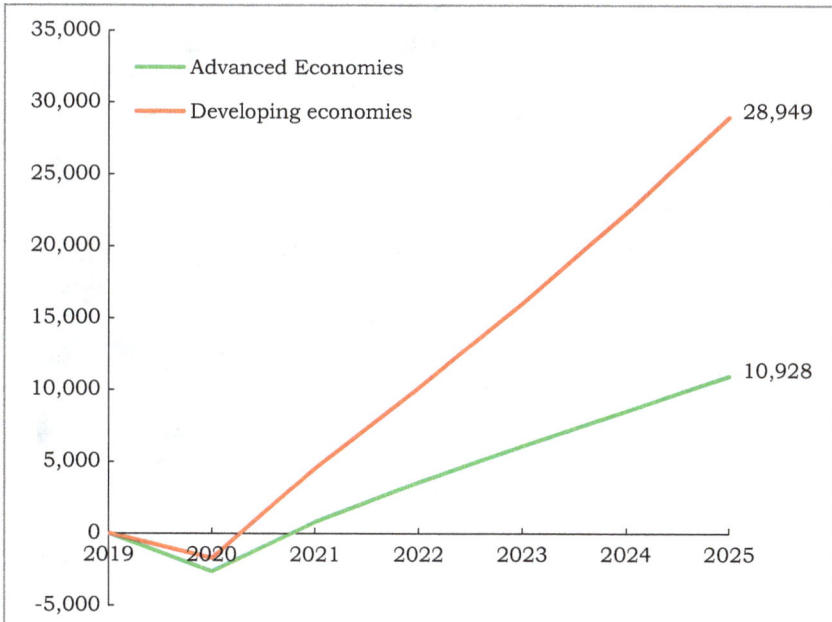

Figure 43: Increase in GDP Developing & Advanced Economies 2019-2025 Purchasing power parity (PPP); international dollars billion

Source: Calculated from IMF World Economic Outlook October 2020

developing countries will be 29 trillion in PPP terms, while the increase in advanced countries will be 11 trillion. That is, the expansion of the size of developing economies in PPP terms will be almost three times as much as the increase in advanced economies.

China's contribution to world growth

Taking the global situation in the short-term China's contribution to world growth will be overwhelming. The IMF projects than in 2019-2021 China will contribute 63% to world growth compared to 9% by the US. Over the medium-term period 2019-2025 China's contribution to world growth will also be overwhelmingly the largest of any individual country - as shown in Figure 44. The IMF projects China will contribute 31.3% of world growth in 2019-2025 – more than three times as much as second placed India (11.0%) and the third placed US (10.9%).

In 2019-2025, China will contribute more to world growth than the US, India and EU combined. In terms of individual countries China will contribute more to world growth than the next six countries combined (India, the US, Indonesia, Germany, Russia and Japan). In summary the contribution

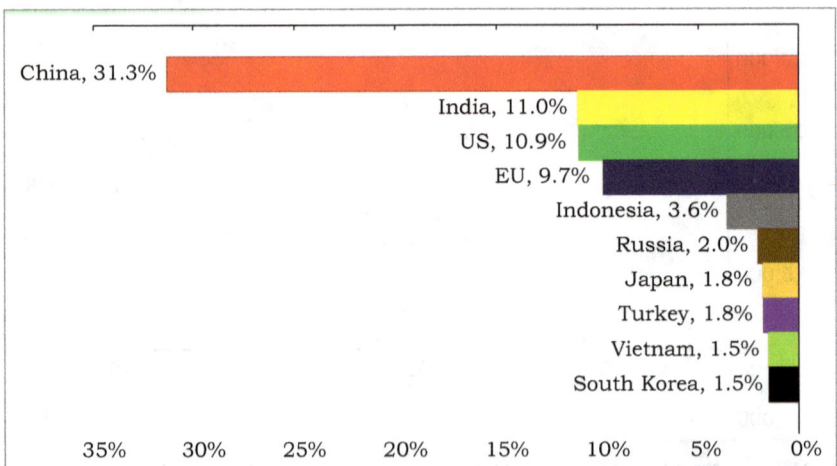

Figure 44: % Contributions to World Growth 2019-2025 in purchasing power parities (PPPs)

Source: Calculated from IMF World Economic Outlook October 2020

to world growth of China in the next five years will be hugely larger than any other individual country.

China, advanced countries, and developing countries

Turning to the comparison between growth in China and that in advanced and developing countries this is shown in the Figure 45. This shows that on the IMF's projections China's growth in 2019-2025 will be larger than all advanced economies combined. However, growth in all other developing countries taken together will be somewhat larger than in China – although as already noted China's growth will be almost three time as large as any other individual developing economy. It is evidently striking that the combined contribution to world growth of China and other developing counties will be almost three times as large as that of the advanced economies.

Shift in the centre of world economic gravity to developing countries

The result of much more rapid growth in developing that advanced economies is necessarily to create a change in the global relation of economic forces. In PPP terms the IMF projects by 2025 developing countries will account for 60.5% of world GDP compared to 39.5% for advanced economies.

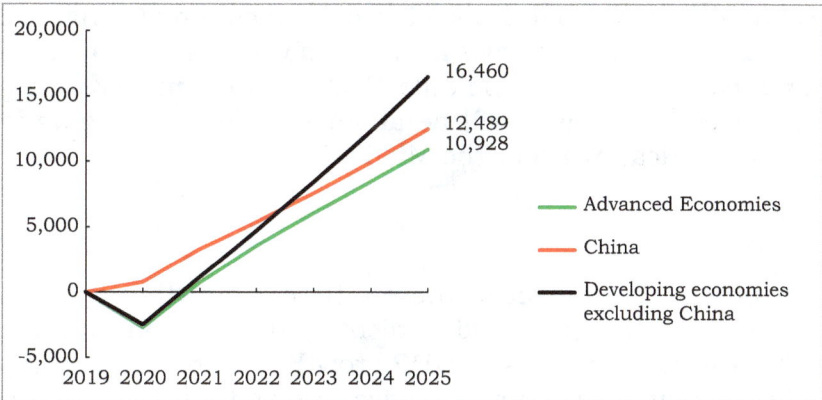

Figure 45: Increase in GDP Developing & Advanced Economies 2019-2025 Purchasing power parity (PPP); international dollars billion

Source: Calculated from IMF World Economic Outlook October 2020

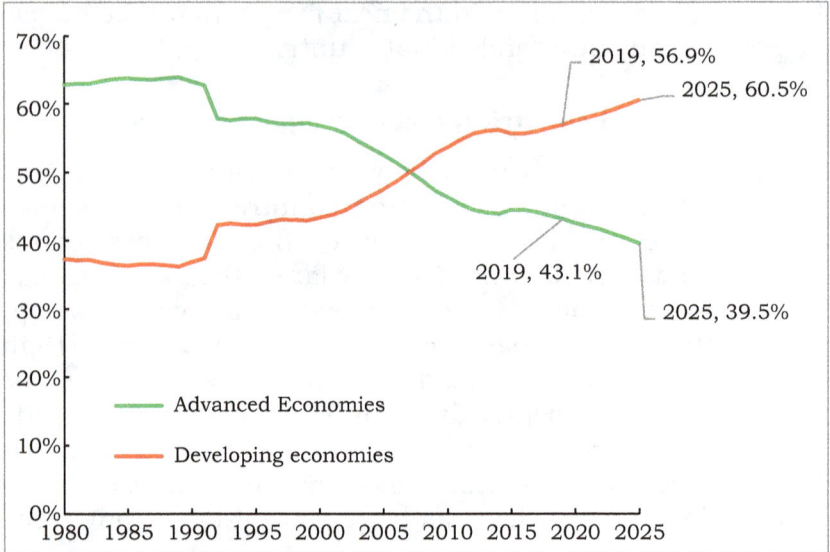

Figure 46: % of World Economy - Developing & Advanced Economies Purchasing power parity (PPP); international dollars billion

Source: Calculated from IMF World Economic Outlook October 2020

Dominance of economic growth in developing Asia

Finally, in terms of contributions to world growth, it should be noted that within the overall greater contribution of developing economies, Asia plays by far the dominant role. Figure 47 shows that developing Asia, including China, will account for about 10 times as much of world growth as Latin America, Africa or the Middle East. Growth in developing Asia excluding China will be about five times as big as in Latin America, Africa or the Middle East.

Trade

Turning to the impact of these different growth trends on trade, the IMF's projected percentage trends confirms the PPP projected patterns of GDP growth. The result of sharp differences in growth between advanced and developing economies is a marked difference in the possibilities for countries to increase their economic growth via exports and trade. Figure 48 shows that the IMF projects that the increase in the volume of goods imports by advanced economies between

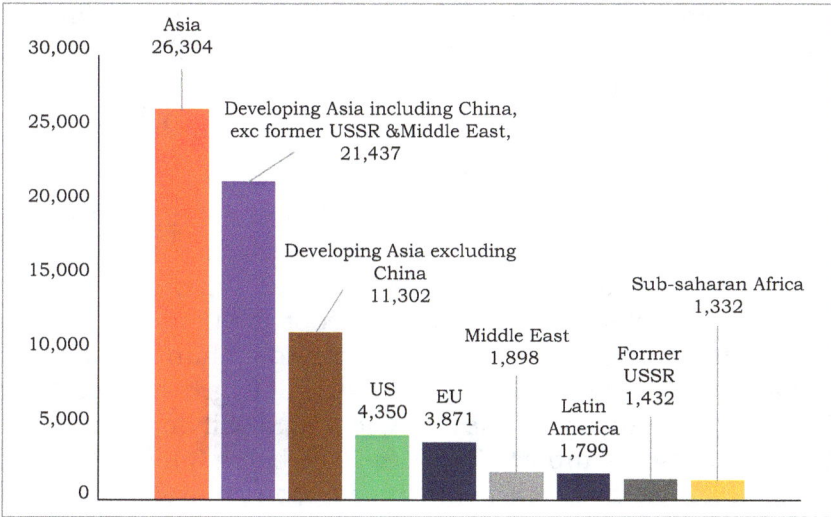

Figure 47: IMF projection of Increase in GDP 2019-2025
Purchasing power parity (PPP); international dollars billion
Source: Calculated from IMF World Economic Outlook October 2020

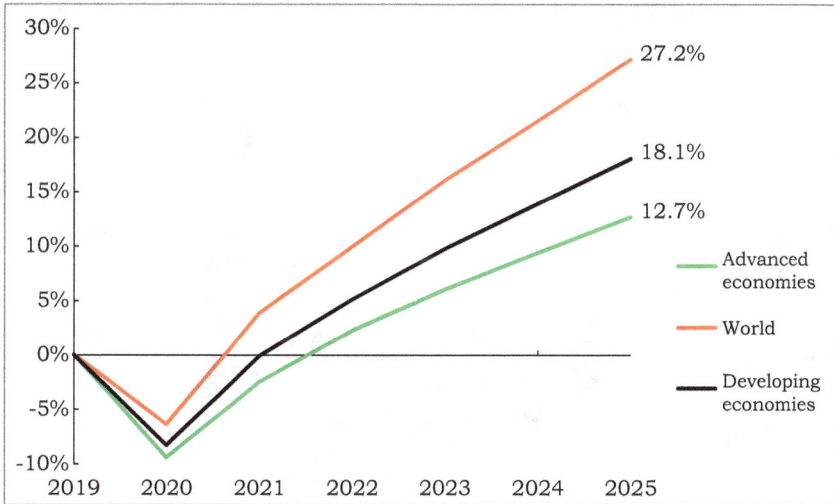

Figure 48: Imports of Goods Volume % change
compared to 2019
Source: Calculated from IMF World Economic Outlook October 2020

2019 and 2025 will be 12.7%. In contrast the volume of
imports of goods by developing economies will be 27.2% -
more than twice as high.

In summary, the rate of increase in the possibility of exports to developing economies will be more than twice as fast as exports to advanced economies.

Dominance of developing Asia in trade

Analysing these trade trends in further detail, Figure 49 shows the increase in imports among the main regions of the world economy. This confirms that imports by every region of developing economies, except for the Middle East and Central Asia, will grow more rapidly than imports by advanced economies. But, in line with GDP growth trends, it is the developing economies in Asia which will dominate with their increase in imports in 2019-2025 being 34.7% - almost three times as fast as the advanced economies. The second most rapidly growing region, at 29.1%, is in sub-Saharan Africa.

It is, of course, in line with these trends in global trade that ASEAN has overtaken the US and EU as China's main trade partner. The significance of RCEP, which includes most of the main developing Asian economies, with the exception of India, is clear from this trend.

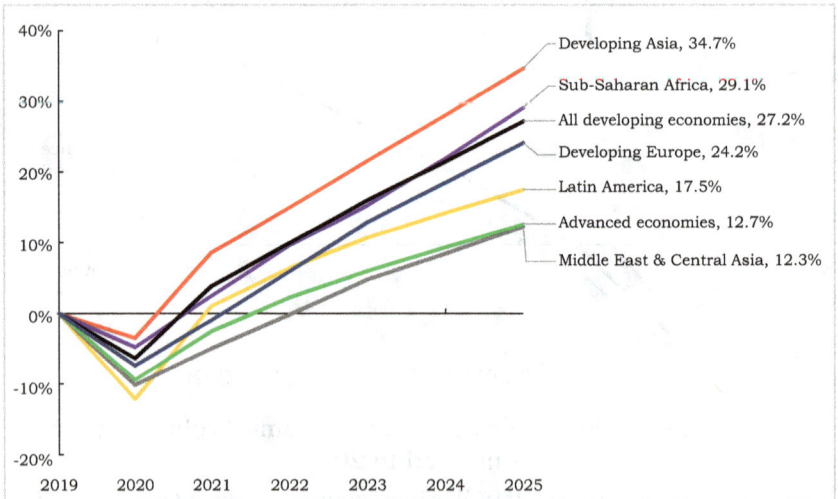

Figure 49: Imports of Goods Volume % change compared to 2019

Source: Calculated from IMF World Economic Outlook October 2020

Economic conclusion

The conclusion of this global situation in economic terms is therefore extremely clear.

- In terms of individual countries world economic development in the NEXT period will be overwhelmingly dominated by China. China will contribute more to world economic growth than all advanced economies combined and three times as much as the US. This of course gives to China a major economic advantage in global competition and makes it highly attractive for economic cooperation.
- In terms of different degrees of development of countries, the global situation will show sharp differences. The combined contribution to world growth of developing countries will not merely be larger than the advanced economies but also somewhat larger than China itself. If the US or advanced economies were able to gain an advantage in economic relations with developing countries other than China then the US and advanced economies would at least to some degree be able to offset China's advantage. Similarly, if China is able to establish the closest relation with other developing countries it will have a very large economic advantage compared to the US.

In summary the world economic situation, in terms of growth and trade, will involve a competition between China and the US, and to some degree other advanced economies, for economic relations with other developing countries. That is, the relation of China and the 'Global South', as non-socialist developing countries are known in the West, is a decisive area of competition between China and the US. To succeed in this struggle China has to develop, and has the possibility to develop, real 'win-win' relations with developing countries – which the US is less able to offer because of the slow growth in its economy.

This means that relations between China and developing countries has a quite different significance to that, for example, at the time of the Bandung conference in 1955 or early meetings of the Non-Aligned Movement. These meetings were politically significant but did not have great weight in the world economy. Today the combination of China and other developing countries is overwhelming the biggest contributor to world economic growth. A combination of China and the other developing countries would have a crucial weight in the world economy and would be far more dynamic than the US/advanced economies. This would appear to give a very strong position to China.

That, however, is the economic development. To understand the overall global situation, however, is necessary to analyse other aspects of the situation, including military and political ones. This produces a somewhat different view of the situation.

Part 3 - Global geopolitics

Politics comes before economics, that is the ABC of Marxism

The economic aspects of the present international situation analysed above has a major impact on international geopolitics and are clearly favourable to China and the common interests of humanity. However, in order to accurately assess the global situation:

- first, there are some features of the global situation that are rooted in much long-term processes than the immediate Covid19 crisis or even the extended slowing of the US economy. The most fundamental of these, due to its increasing urgency, is climate change - which interacts with the situation in all countries.
- Second, it must never be forgotten that in Lenin's words: 'Politics must take precedence over economics. To argue otherwise is to forget the ABC of Marxism.' [181]

It is therefore necessary, in order to understand geopolitical trends, in addition to the economic development, to analyse the political situation in different countries and in different regions.

US policy is against the interests of numerous other countries

In analysing this political situation in different regions of the world it is widely understood in China that the US has launched aggressive policies to attempt to block China's national rejuvenation. But, in terms of international relations and alliances, it is also crucial to grasp that the means used by the US to attack China also attack the populations of other countries - due to the measures/policies the US pressures them to adopt. That is the US pressures other countries to take measures which are irrational from the point of view of their own economies and which, therefore, involve attacks on their own populations. This latter process then determines the situation in different countries.

Merely to take a few major examples of these attacks on their own populations to carry out US policies – numerous others could be given.

- Even within the US itself the Western economic consultancy Oxford Economics calculates that imposing tariffs on all goods from China, due to the price rises created, would cost the average US household over $800 a year.
- In India banning China's software applications such as TikTok not only deprives its people of a source of entertainment but destroys local Indian companies which developed to meet TikTok's users' needs.
- The UK's ban on Huawei means higher prices and later delivery of 5G for British mobile phone users.

In addition to these specific attacks other policies of Trump, such as withdrawal from the Paris Climate Change Accords, constituted an attack on the population of all countries - with not a single other country being prepared to follow the US in this (although this is one policy of Trump that Biden has pledged to reverse).

The fact that anti-China policies to meet US demands damages countries pursuing them, and thereby risks unpopularity and problems for governments following them, is exacerbated by the Covid19 created recession analysed above. US aggression against China therefore does not affect only China and the US but affects the situation in every country – although to different degrees as will be analysed. Any country subordinating economic policy to the US suffers damage from orienting itself to a much more stagnant economy than China.

US situation

Starting the analysis of these impacts with the US, and the question of what is specific about the present overall international situation, the global 2020 Covid19 crisis evidently coincided politically with the defeat of the Trump administration and Biden's election as US President. These two events were inextricably interrelated as it was the Covid19 crisis which led to Tump's defeat, not only via its direct impact but through its overall effect on US society - as was analysed in 大选"押宝"特朗普？其实你不懂美国和"美式民主"[182].

But the effects of the Covid19 crisis, globally and in the US are far greater than those of a short term conjunctural or business cycle change. The Covid19 disaster in the US and Europe, following only a little over a decade after the 2008 international financial crisis, has produced the most general global economic and social crisis of 'the West' since World War II. Given the large scale of this crisis it is necessary to analyse not merely its short term but also its medium/long-term effects. Most immediately what will be the dynamics that follow from Biden becoming president in the midst of the most general Western crisis for over 70 years?

To analyse this first the short-term situation of the Biden administration will be examined and then it will be analysed against the global economic processes over the next five years noted above.

The Biden presidency's domestic position

Starting with the domestic political situation of the Biden presidency the first specific feature of the 2020 Presidential election was the extremely high voter turnout – the highest percentage voter participation in a US presidential election for 120 years. Such a high participation in elections is a symptom of a high degree of social/political tension. Furthermore, throughout the period since 1996, with the sole exception of 2012, percentage voter participation in every US presidential election has been higher than in the previous one. This indicates that political tension in the US has been rising for the last quarter of a century and the 2020 election represented simply a sharp increase in that process. A major change in the situation would therefore be required to lower this rising US political tension – and this is improbable given social tension created by the slow growth of the US economy already analysed. This increasing social tension evidently spilled over into the extraordinary events of the mob storming of the US Congress on 6 January.

Within this framework Biden won the presidency because of the huge increase in voter turnout for the Democratic Party. Trump's vote rose by 11.2 million in 2020 compared to 2016, a significant advance, and one refuting an analysis that Trump's base was demoralised, but this was overwhelmed by the 15.6 million increase in Biden's vote in 2020 compared to Clinton's in 2016.

Social trends in Biden's victory

Analysing in more detail the social trends producing this electoral result by a large margin higher paid Americans voted for Trump and lower paid for Biden [183]. These facts show that claims that Trump represented a 'working class revolt' of those 'left behind' is a pure myth with no basis - except that of ripping individual anecdotes out of context (that is to use exaggeration and one sidedness of the type attacked by Mao in 'On Protracted War'). Such entirely false Trump propaganda should therefore not be repeated in China's media. Biden had a very large lead over Trump among households with an income of less than $50,000 a year (55%-44%), and those with incomes of $50,000-$99,000 (57%-42%), while Trump had a massive lead among households with incomes of over $100,000 (54%-42%). In short Trump was based among the well off and Biden among the less well off. The participation of some 'lumpen mob' elements among the few thousand who stormed the US Congress on 6 January does not alter this overall social situation as revealed by the more than 150 million Americans who voted.

Overlapping with this difference in incomes Biden had a massive lead among women[184] voters (57%-42%) and among Black voters (87%-12%), Hispanics (65%-32%), and Asian Americans (61%-34%). Particularly decisive, compared to 2016, was a much higher voter turnout among Black voters - which delivered victory to Biden in key states. This was then continued into the Senate run off races in Georgia in January, in which an extremely high turnout of Black voters delivered victory to the Democrats – striking a severe blow against the Republicans by depriving them of control of the Senate.

These electoral patterns directly resulted from Trump's policies – which were openly racist, coupled with an economic policy based on tax reductions focused on the best off. These social trends were further deepened by Trump's disastrous policies on Covid – as both the death rate and the effects of the mass unemployment hit the low paid and ethnic minorities worst. Trump's policy was based on a calculation that a white racist coalition, led by the better off, would defeat the lower paid sections of the population, the majority of whom are ethnic minorities and women. This analysis of the social relation of forces turned out to be a serious error by Trump - the lower paid and ethnic minorities substantially outvoted Trump's better off racist coalition. Instead of a triumph of Trump's white racist coalition an unprecedentedly high level of voting by lower paid and ethnic minority voters defeated Trump.

Republican strength in the non-democratic US constitutional system

But analysing beyond the electoral trends - Biden's lead of over 7 million votes compared to Trump and 306 votes to 232 in - the position of Biden in terms of institutional strength within the US is not extremely strong. The Republicans/ Trumpites maintain significant institutional advantages. Only the exceptionally high turnout of the vote for Biden in 2020 allowed these Republican institutional advantages to be overcome. In particular:

- The US constitution is deliberately aimed to favour rural smaller states compared to large cities - which tend to vote for the Democrats. This is shown graphically in the fact that the Republicans are a clear minority party in Presidential election terms, losing the popular vote in seven out of the eight last US Presidential elections, but in both 2000 and 2016 they secured the presidency on a minority of the popular vote due to the Electoral College system. The US Presidential system therefore has an inbuilt anti-democratic bias in favour of the Republican Party.

- Pro-right wing/Trumpite Republicans also now hold a 6-3 majority in the US Supreme Court – which can overturn Presidential actions and laws passed by Congress.
- The Republicans hold strong positions in governorships and legislatures in the individual states.
- In addition to this institutional strength Trump raised $250 million for political campaigning after his defeat in the Presidential election.

In the short term the Republicans have certainly suffered a major defeat in losing not only the Presidency but control of the Senate. But Biden's strength is only based on popular mobilisation and voter turnout and the Republican strength is institutional. This situation is one reason why, for the first-time, a number of Republican politicians turned against Trump after the mob storming of Congress on 6 January. These Republicans were against any attack on the institutions which express their strength – they were therefore prepared to dump Trump, although not Trumpism, in order to protect the institutions which give the Republicans a strength which they do not possess in terms of the US popular vote. So far, all leading Republicans clearly aiming to try to win the next Presidential nomination, such as Mike Pence or Ted Cruz, are presenting themselves as 'Trumpism without Trump.' They propose essentially the same domestic and international policies as Trump, but reject Trump's willingness to challenge US institutions (the mob violence of 6 January) as this threatens a central issue for the Republican Party – how a Party which repeated presidential elections show is a minority in the US can maintain political power.

This Republican institutional strength means that if the enthusiasm/mobilisation of Biden's voters falls the Republicans will be strengthened. Faced with the anti-democratic features of the US political system Biden can therefore only maintain his position if he can retain the high level of mobilisation of less well off, female and ethnic minorities – and he is unlikely to do this for reasons analysed below. If this popular mobilisation is not maintained the institutional strength of the 'Trumpite' forces is likely to defeat Biden.

Therefore, while at present the Republicans/Trumpites have suffered a serious defeat, their position is actually much stronger than a superficial examination of the situation and the immediate aftermath of the dramatic events of 6 January would indicate.

The international situation and the overall relation of forces facing Biden

Turning to the international situation, and how this affects the US, the core of Trump's foreign policy was its anti-China agenda and a tactical estimate of how best to attack China. Obama had tried to form a broad international 'anti-China' united front. To attempt to achieve this Obama had been prepared to make concessions to US partners in Asia, in trying to create a TransPacific Partnership (TPP) including the US, and in Europe - particularly to Germany. In contrast Trump's 'America First' policy analysed that the US could not afford such concessions and that instead US allies should be pressured to transfer resources to the US so that it could directly attack China. The result was that Trump followed a confrontational policy primarily against China but also therefore against some US allies – withdrawing from the TPP and attempting to pressure Europe.

Biden may be expected to reverse Trump's policy and to return to the Obama strategy of attempting to creating a broad anti-China front – this is the meaning of numerous of his proposals including convening a so called 'summit of democracies'. But while significant changes in tactics may be anticipated there is no indication that Biden will reverse the US's strategic overall aggressive policy towards China.

In March, Biden himself wrote in Foreign Affairs that he wanted to project U.S. power on the world. Vijay Prashad has well analysed[185] the views of Biden's nominee for Secretary of State Antony Blinken: 'In September, Blinken said that "China poses a growing challenge, arguably the biggest challenge we face from another nation state: economically, technologically, militarily, even diplomatically."... Unlike Trump's Secretary of State Mike Pompeo, Blinken admits that this relationship will have "adversarial aspects, competitive aspects, but also cooperative ones"; it is this last form, the cooperative, that differentiates Pompeo from Blinken, although the only examples here (climate change, non-proliferation, global health) do not come to the main issue that will divide the U.S. from China, namely China's technological advance.

'What is the strategy to deal with China's technological advance? Blinken said the U.S. had to assemble a "league of democracies," basically the old European allies and Japan—the G7 and NATO—that will stand against China. He has a small supplement to the old idea of "league of democracies"... Blinken wants to create a league of "techno-democracies" and position them against "techno-autocracies, like China". The U.S., he said, had to "do a much better job in leading, coordinating, working with the other techno-democracies to make sure that we carry the day and not China".'

The anti-China stance of Blinken is reinforced[186] by Biden's appointment of Kurt Campbell, a veteran US foreign policy specialist, to oversee US Asia policy. Campbell's views were summarised in the Financial Times as follows: 'He... led the so-called 'pivot' to Asia in the Obama administration, which was largely about pushing back against Chinese coercion in south-east Asia... Mr Campbell... is viewed as being one of the more hawkish Democrats on China.' Gady Epstein, the Economist magazine's China affairs editor, commented[187]: 'This is about as hawkish a China team as one could expect from Biden.'

In summary, Biden is likely to change some US tactics towards China and may well accept cooperation in certain specifically delimited fields, as analysed below, but will not change the fundamental aggressive policy of attempting to block China from becoming an advanced technology and therefore prosperous country.

The relation of forces in the US

Summarising both the domestic and international trends affecting the US, Trump's policy was simultaneously an assault on the worst-off sections of the US population and an international attack particularly on China but also on other countries - China's position and the less well-off sections of the US population were objectively aligned. Trump, however, turned out to have seriously misjudged the relation of forces – a simultaneous domestic attack in the US and internationally was beyond the US strength and resulted in Trump's defeat in the 2020 election. This, therefore, determines the domestic and international contexts in which Biden came to office.

What policy is rational for Biden?

As Trump was defeated because he confronted too many enemies simultaneously, the rational policy for Biden to succeed would be seek to reduce the number of enemies - by some combination of concessions to the US population and lessening the number of international enemies.

Objectively, there are certainly potential ways to achieve this. To take one, Trump, as part of his aggressive international policy, reversed Obama's policy of reducing military expenditure as a proportion of the US economy. Under Trump US military spending increased by over $115 billion, in today's prices, between his assuming office in January 2016 up to the 2nd quarter of 2020 - from 3.9% to 4.5% of US GDP. To reduce social strain the US should therefore reduce its burden of military expenditure as a proportion of its economy. This was Obama's policy and helped underpin his electoral successes in 2008 and 2012. Such a policy would release resources to transfer directly to the US population and to invest in infrastructure, training and R&D to reinvigorate the US economy.

There are forces in the US that feel objective pressure towards such a rational policy. For example, the Wall Street Journal[188] analysed one aspect of this military/foreign policy under the self-explanatory headline: 'Biden to Review U.S. Nuclear-Weapons Programs, With Eye Toward Cuts': 'The incoming Biden administration is planning a review of the nation's $1.2 trillion nuclear-modernization program with an eye toward trimming funding for nuclear weapons...

'President-elect Joe Biden promised during the campaign to reduce the U.S.'s "excessive expenditure" on nuclear arms and criticized President Trump's decision to develop new sea-based weapons, including a submarine-launched cruise missile.

'The new administration is also likely to review the Pentagon's decision to develop a new land-based intercontinental ballistic missile, which is estimated to cost more than $100 billion when its warhead is included, some former officials said.

'"We have to modernize our deterrent," said one former official. "But we cannot spend the amount of money that is currently being allocated."'

Relations with China

US military policy, however, is one of many aspects of US international relations which interrelates with China. China is in a clear position to work with and aid any rational policies by Biden in 'win-win' ways – as China's Foreign Minister Wang Yi made clear in his speech to the New York-based Asia Society on 18 December. This speech was almost universally interpreted in the West as an explanation of China's policy to the new Biden administration.

Wang Yi noted that Biden has outlined four priorities for his administration – dealing with the Covid19 pandemic, fighting climate change, achieving economic recovery and working for racial equality in the US. Wang Yi pointed out that US agreement with China can significantly aid on the first three of these priorities (the fourth follows from the domestic needs of Biden in the US due to the assault on ethnic minorities mounted by Trump which was already analysed). Wang Yi pointed out that China follows a foreign policy based on the five principles of peaceful co-existence and has no intention to compete for hegemony. China also does not seek to export its system or model - instead, China's framework is to focus on its national development and on win-win cooperation with other countries.

Possibilities of China-US cooperation

It is indeed possible, as well as desirable, that cooperation will take place between China and the US on some of the issues prioritised by Biden. Biden has announced that one of his administration's first actions will be to re-join the World Health Organisation (WHO) – facilitating co-operation in fighting the pandemic. Biden has also announced that the US will re-join the Paris Climate Change Accords – opening the way for a common framework on fighting climate change. Biden has not yet announced whether he will abandon Trump's policy of attempting to sabotage the World Trade Organisation (WTO) by vetoing new judges for its appeals machinery, but it is to be hoped this will occur. It would, of course, be even better if the Biden administration went beyond these steps and established a real win-win relation with China.

China is rightly taking steps to propose cooperation regardless of whether the Biden administration accepts or not. This corresponds to the common interests of humanity – indeed it is an excellent example of the 'common destiny of humanity'. Best of all, of course, is that Biden takes up such win-win cooperation. But China's proposals are in the interests of the American people, and of other countries, and are therefore best placed to gain support even if Biden turns them down. China's approach is therefore also the best judged to affect US public opinion confronted with the 'new cold war' hysteria which was whipped up by Trump. China's proposals, because they are in the interests of both the American and the Chinese people, as well as other countries, will therefore also constitute a positive pressure regardless of which path the Biden administration takes.

Who really takes decisions in the US?

The difficulty in the present situation, however, is that decisions in the US are not taken by the American people, and in their interests, but by the US capitalist class – contrary to myths about US 'democracy'. This is currently dramatically illustrated, for example, on US health care. Opinion polls[189] show large majorities of Americans want universal state provided health care ('Medicare for all') but the majority of the US capitalist class does not want this as it would deprive US companies of a lucrative source of profits – around one sixth of the US economy is devoted to health care. So, both Republican and Democratic Parties oppose 'Medicare for all' despite it being overwhelmingly supported by the US population. Similarly, whether the US will follow a win-win policy with China, or a cold war orientation, will not be decided by the American people but by the US capitalist class - via the political establishment in both Democratic and Republican parties which it controls.

Furthermore, the US political establishment, is desperate to conceal the global reality of what has occurred during Covid19. The objective reality is that China protected its population from Covid19, with less than 5,000 dead, while the US suffered a medical catastrophe – with almost 400,000 dead already. China's socialist system was shown to be far superior to the US capitalist one including in the sphere of 'human rights' - staying alive is the foundation of all other human rights! But it would be ideologically and politically catastrophic for the US political establishment if this reality were understood by the US population. Therefore, the US is intent on launching the most intense possible campaign of lying and ideological attacks on China to conceal this reality from its population. It is this which explains the new McCarthyism, that is increase witch hunts, censorship, and attempts to block any objective discussion of China which Wang Yi noted in his speech to the Asia Society.

Given this situation the correct analysis, which can of course be checked against facts as events proceed, is that the Biden administration will retreat from Trump's policies on certain fields – on the WHO, on the Paris Climate change accords, possibly on the WTO, possibly on the nuclear deal with Iran. But it will not change the overall anti-China policy of the US, although it is likely it may change tactics in this in a return to the 'broad anti-China alliance' approach of Obama.

Furthermore, it is an illusion to believe that China can stop this aggressive US policy by an influence on US public opinion by China's English and other foreign language media, by 'soft power', or by any other means. While the 2020 Presidential election showed clearly that anti-China could not be made the main focus of the US, the election was fought out on domestic issues and Trump's attempt to turn it into an anti-China election failed, the US political establishment is quite strong enough to prevent mass active opposition to its anti-China policy. This does not mean that attempts to promote an objective view about the situation in China, or China's 'soft power', in the US is unnecessary but this will not be able to offset the power of the US ruling class within its own country – US 'soft power' is based on US 'hard power'.

This US power is also seen in its ability within the advanced countries to disorientate even parts of movements whose interests are very clearly objectively aligned with China – the US political establishment naturally plays particular attention to this. To take one clear example of this consider the environmental movement. China in fact has the most progressive positions on environmental policy of any major country but this does not stop the US pulling parts of this

movement into anti-China campaign – while other environmental organisations maintain an objective, and therefore
favourable, attitude to China's policies in this field.

The US capitalist class will consequently retain control of
the overall ideological situation in the US. China will therefore have greater possibilities to strengthen its positions
in other parts of the world rather than this making great
progress in mass opinion in the US itself – although naturally every opening to improve the situation in the US must
be pursued and there are forces in the advanced capitalist
countries who are against the new US cold war. In military
terms China will not be able to change opinion in the US
primarily by 'frontal assault' but by 'flank attacks' – that is
building up its position outside the centres of US power. Or,
in other famous expression of Mao, the 'countryside' (the
regions outside the US) will have to surround the 'cities' –
the US. Outside the US and its closest allies, the fact that
China's interests correspond to those of humanity will however create a different situation – as analysed below.

Naturally, the author would be extremely pleased if this
analysis were incorrect, and it was possible for China to take
strong steps forward in winning over public opinion in the US
and advanced capitalist countries – this would correspond to
the overall interests of humanity. But in very serious matters it is necessary not to proceed from what is desirable but
from what is realistic – to 'seek truth from facts.'

Consequences for the Biden administration

The US situation in the US in turn has implications for the
future of the Biden administration itself, including for its
popularity and for its ability to sustain itself against the
Republican assault - which as already analysed is certain
to come. If Biden does not pursue a rational foreign policy,
and continues an aggressive international policy, the lack
of sufficient reduction in international tension will reduce
Biden's ability to give concessions to the population in the
US - thereby undermining its domestic support and ability to maintain the high level of mobilisation of Democratic
Party voters on which his electoral victory in 2020 rested.
An aggressive international policy by Biden will therefore
significantly increase the likelihood of the Democrats defeat

in the mid-tern Congressional elections in 2022 and in the 2024 Presidential race.

Given the strength of the institutional obstacles facing the Biden administration already analysed, international forces must therefore prepare for future weakening and defeats of Biden within the US if he merely changes a few tactics but fundamentally pursues an aggressive international policy – which for reasons already outlined is likely. At present Biden is focussing on increasing the number of women and people of colour in his Cabinet, to better reflect the social forces which elected him, but this will not be sufficient to maintain mobilisation of Democratic voters unless real gains are delivered to the mass of the US population including women and Black people. So far Biden has not proposed policies which would deliver this – and maintenance of an aggressive US foreign policy would directly cut across this.

Therefore, to summarise this dynamic within the US, there is a real possibility of improvement of relations between the US and China in certain fields, but overall the Biden administration will continue to pursue an anti-China course. Furthermore, the fact that Biden will continue to pursue a policy which is not rational either domestically or internationally creates a significant danger of his being undermined before or at the next US elections. It is necessary to be clear internationally that in the medium term, because it is not pursuing rational policies, that Biden administration will be undermined in the US.

It is irrational to give in to US demands – but some countries will

Turning to overall international trends, how does this situation in the US interrelate with China and the rest of the world?

From the facts analysed in detail above it follows clearly that it is economically irrational for any country to give in to US demands. But for a number of countries considerations of political and military links with the US will take priority over rational economic policy – that is politics will come before economics. Australia, for example, has pursued a provocative policy towards China, despite China being its largest trading partner. Canada sabotaged its previous attempts to develop good economic relations with China via actions such as the arrest of Huawei's Chief Financial Officer Meng Wanzhou.

But the balance between economically rational policies and political pressure from the US varies sharply in different parts of the world. In most developing countries governments do not have the economic room for manoeuvre to pursue economically irrational policies which put up prices, limit trade opportunities etc which would directly harm their populations. Therefore, in most of developing Asia (except for India), in the Middle East, in Africa, in the former USSR, the great majority of countries clearly refuse to implement US anti-China policies. At the other extreme, within the US the ruling class feels confident in its ability to control the population and anti-China policies are easily adopted - the US also can impose such a policy on some of its closest allies such as Canada and Australia.

This therefore leaves two large regions of the world in which the outcome of the orientation of governments and of public opinion between China and the US is not clear – Latin America and Europe (excluding Russia). The situation in Latin America was analysed in detail in Guancha in 美国想搞"反华阵线"？可拉美早已不是那个"后院"了 [190] and this is therefore not dealt with here. The other key area where the outcome is not determined, Europe, will therefore be analysed.

The situation in Europe

In terms of the relation of forces between economic interests and the political offensive of the US Europe is one of the world's more most complex situations. The EU is one of the three great world economic centres, together with the US and China, and therefore it has a strong interest in trade and investment with China. Due to Covid19's impact, in the first three quarters of 2020 China became a larger trade partner for the EU than the US. Economically it is therefore highly logical for the EU to seek good relations with China.

Nevertheless simultaneously the EU believes it must rely on the US for military protection – permitting the US to apply pressure. The perceived military enemy of the EU is Russia - China is too geographically distant to be a military threat to Europe. This EU perception is in fact largely delusion - Russia has no interest to be a military threat to the rest of Europe. Nevertheless, this delusion largely dominates European policy in a commitment to military subordination to the US in NATO.

The result of this conflict between the EU's economic interests and its military subordination to the US is that the EU attempts to strike a path which combines the following elements:

- The EU tries to follow a relatively independent economic policy from the US – hence, for example, at the end of 2020 the signing of the Comprehensive Agreement on Investment with China despite US opposition.
- The EU refuses to join US inspired political provocations against China of the Australian and Canadian type.
- The EU simultaneously seeks to avoid any central political clash with the US.

An exception to this overall situation within Europe is the UK – which has left the political structures of the EU if not yet, in reality, its economic framework. Britain's situation is far more subordinate to the US than the key EU powers of Germany and France. From the late 19th century onwards a declining Britain, which had formerly been the world's greatest power, decided that it could only preserve its international interests via subordinating itself to the rising US. Even when Britain was part of the EU, from 1973 onwards, it was always the most pro-US major country within it. In a US-EU clash Britain would take the fundamental side of the US.

Britain's medium sized economy cannot pursue an independent path from the two huge economies of the US and EU. As US-EU tension rose Britain again chose the side of subordination to the US – that was Brexit's real content. As the US currently wants an aggressive policy towards China the UK pursues this far more than the EU.

The New Year message for 2021 issued by Nigel Farage, the historic leader of the pro-Brexit movement in Britain, encapsulated this: 'A lot of people are asking me: what next, what do you do next?... I will tell you what the next big challenge is – and in some ways it is an even bigger challenge that the European Union was... it is China... China are doing their absolute best to take over the world... We need to wake up to the threat that is posed by China. And 2021 begins my next campaign. And that is to make sure we are no longer dependent on China.'

The overall global situation

Finally, what are the conclusions? And why is it clear that 'On Protracted War' is such a fundamental text to study?

Starting from the methodological principle that it is necessary to understand what is specific in time and place about anything being studied, it is necessary to be clear that what is involved in the present international situation is not a war. Certainly if it were not for the existence of nuclear weapons, and the PLA's strength, it is possible that the US would attempt to carry its aggression against China to the point of war – Iraq, Libya, Vietnam and other cases show the US is ruthless enough to consider this. But, fortunately, China's nuclear weapons and the PLA's power mean that the US understands that its own losses in such a war would be so great that no significant body of opinion in the US advocates war with China. This overall situation naturally does not mean that there will not be individual local wars, or possibly proxy conflicts, but there will not be a general war between China and the US unless the US were able to establish a decisive technological advance that protected itself from attack. Ensuring China is never qualitatively left behind in such a race is therefore vital for world peace. The actual subject of 'On Prolonged War', a full-scale/global military conflict, is therefore not a feature of the present situation – Mao was fully aware that China's military defence against Japan would become part of an even wider international conflict, and that was part of his analysis of why China would prevail in such a prolonged war. But while the subject of the present situation is not identical to the subject of 'On Protracted War' the method of analysis fully applies.

What, therefore, are the most essential specific features of the present situation - from which flows, In another of the most famous fundamental question asked by Mao, 'Who are our enemies? Who are our friends? This is a question of the first importance.'[191] In the present situation who are China's enemies, who are potential allies, and how does this interrelate with the common destiny of humanity? To answer this, it is necessary to summarise the chief features of the world situation which were examined at length above and to accurately judge the weight of elements within it.

The continued strength of the US

Starting with the US, to analyse its real situation, to compare its present degree of crisis with those of the past, it is necessary to analyse the core of its state power - its military. It is correct to state that the present political turmoil shows that the US has entered into its greatest crisis since the Vietnam war. But statements[192] such as that the US faces 'the worst political crisis since the Civil War' are exaggerated. The US loss of the Vietnam war greatly disorganised the US military, and greatly undermined political support for its use internationally - making it almost impossible for the US to actively wage war abroad for several years (the 'Vietnam syndrome'). Today no such crisis of the US military exists – it has been regularly used internationally in the last thirty years. Events such as the storming of Congress on 6 January are spectacular, but they do not indicate any problem of the ability of the US to use its physical, that is ultimately military, power either domestically or internationally – unlike the situation after its defeat in Vietnam.

Turning to the US economy, the crisis unleashed by Covid19 is certainly the worst since World War II. But it clearly does not match the scale of crisis of the Great Depression and its outcome in World War II. The US also possesses overall technological superiority compared to China. Certainly, it is true, and significant, that in some specific areas (supply of 5G telecommunications equipment, cashless payments etc) China is genuinely ahead of the US. But it would be to make the error Mao warns against of 'one-sidedness', of looking at individual aspects of the situation and not the total one, not to see the overall technological superiority of the US. Even using PPP measures, the level of productivity of the US economy is more than three times that of China – an index of the technological lead of the US, its long-accumulated advantage in the size of its capital stock etc.

In addition to military and economic factors, in neither the US nor any advanced capitalist country has the ruling class lost political control of the situation. Even left reformist attempts to seriously challenge that political hegemony, for example by Sanders in the US or Corbyn in Britain, were comprehensively defeated. Pressure by the population within the advanced capitalist countries can be significant in limiting the room for action by the US – as was seen dramatically after Vietnam and on a lesser scale by the general US assessment that the invasion of Iraq turned out be an error. But as long as the US retains overall political control within its own country it can always strike back against threats to its key policies – and no Marxist party capable of challenging ruling class control has anything other than marginal support in either the US or any other advanced capitalist country. Furthermore, in the short/medium term, Biden is unlikely to maintain the domestic mobilisation of the US population – opening the way for the return of strongly anti-China Republican forces of the Trump type (with or without Trump). In summary, the political defences and reserves of the US and other advanced capitalist classes remain very strong.

Ability of the US to create alliances with advanced capitalist countries

US military superiority, and its advanced technological character, also means that the US continues to possess great reserves not only domestically but also in terms of ability to create, or to compel, international alliances – in particular with advanced capitalist countries. Despite US short-term political chaos this indicates that the US for military/political reasons will continue to maintain major allies in the 'Global North', that is the advanced capitalist countries. This will continue even if the policies the US aims for them to adopt are economically irrational from the viewpoint of their own interests. Biden will doubtless attempt to use this advantage to the maximum – the interests of the population of these countries, as well as China, on the contrary has every interest in attracting advanced capitalist countries of course to purse an economically rational policy of good relations with China.

In summary, both the domestic and international reserves of the US capitalist class are great and it is an error to overestimate its current problems – just as Mao insisted it was an error to refuse to acknowledge that in 1938 in an immediate sense Japan was stronger than China. Regrettably, it is not possible for China to overtake the US in comprehensive power in a short period. This conclusion on US strength gives the same answer as Mao in 'On Protracted War' – China cannot win quickly no matter how desirable this would be for humanity. Therefore, for this reason the present competition will be prolonged.

A prolonged period of US aggression

A consequence of this is also that the world must prepare for an overall prolonged period of aggression by the US against China – although there may be periods within that prolonged situation in which relations are primarily cooperative and also, even in periods of tension, definite areas in which cooperation is possible.

The US is a capitalist/imperialist state and therefore fundamentally aggressive. This is confirmed not merely theoretically but factually – the US has been at war for 227 out of the 244 years of its history. History has shown clearly the only situation in which the US becomes in overall terms 'peace loving' is when it has suffered defeats and weakness - while when it resumes its strength it returns to aggression. Thus, for example, after its defeat in Vietnam the US pursued for a period of years a policy of 'détente', while after it had regained strength, from the late 1970s, it resumed a policy of aggression against what it saw as its main enemy the USSR (China was not particularly attacked at that time simply because it was not seen as the US's main competitor). Similarly, during and immediately after the 2008 international financial crisis, when the US felt seriously weakened, it adopted a policy of collaboration with China and the G20 – until the US felt it had recovered its strength by 2016, when it began a policy of aggression against China.

The weaknesses of the US and China's strengths

But in contrast to these features showing the continuing strength of the US, and therefore the 'prolonged' character of present competition, it is also necessary to understand the weaknesses of the US – why, therefore, unless it makes mistakes, China will prevail in this prolonged competition and why this is in the interests of humanity.

The first feature showing this is a central contradiction which, as already noted, is key to understanding the global situation.

- The slow growth of the US economy simultaneously makes the US adopt an aggressive policy towards China as the US in its 'zero sum' framework is incapable of speeding up its own economy and therefore it seeks to slow China.
- But in the US this slow growth simultaneously makes it less attractive as a partner for other countries. Furthermore, such a slowing of the world economy is against the interests of humanity – as achieving economic development remains the most decisive task for the overwhelming majority of countries and of humanity.

This central contradiction makes clear with the relation of forces moves gradually against the US and also makes clear that not only for China domestically, but internationally, the most important factor is China's success in achieving its own development – notably its much more dynamic economic development compared to other major economies. This success in economic and social development is determined in the last analysis by China's socialist character – a product of the great struggles and sacrifices of the Chinese people to create the People's Republic of China and the CPC, and their successes in socialist construction since 1949. The superiority of this system has again been confirmed by the way in which China came through both the international financial crisis of 2008 and the Covid19 crisis of 2020 far more successfully than any other major state.

Of course, if socialism were overthrown China would suffer the same catastrophe as the USSR and China's national rejuvenation would be blocked – which would be a disaster not only for China but for humanity. But for this to occur the CPC would have to make disastrous mistakes of which there is no sign.

China and the 'Global South'

But while China's own development is the most important factor in the situation the international processes analysed mean that China possesses the potential to create very great reserves of allies in the 'Global South' – that is among developing countries. The Global South is very large in size, two thirds of humanity even excluding China, and possesses the large common interests with China. This Global South is much more rapidly growing economically than the advanced countries. This means that the situation may, of course, change in individual South countries, for example the present negative turn in India, but due to its size and dynamics overall very great possibilities exist for China to form alliances with the Global South. If difficulties exist with one country these can frequently be compensated for with another – for example the current government of Brazil has been less politically favourable to China than in the period of the presidencies of Lula and Rousseff but Argentina, which can supply many of the same products to China as Brazil, has recently taken steps to more actively engage with China. Furthermore, the size of the Global South makes it impossible for the US to concentrate its forces against a single enemy.

At the political level, these relations of China with the global South are shown regularly in the United Nations. Here a regular voting pattern has been established with Global South countries voting against, giving China a majority against, the attempts by the US and its allies to attack China on issues such as Hong Kong and Xinjiang. This has given China a significant majority on such issues in the UN. Russia, formerly a socialist country, and now economically a developing one, frequently votes with China at the UN and its military power is also a major deterrent to US adventurism. Global South countries have refused to go along with US provocations such as attempts to stir up tensions in the South China Sea. All major developing countries in East Asia signed RCEP despite US opposition to this. Furthermore, these Global South countries are now growing much more rapidly economically than the advanced capitalist countries – therefore good relations with Global South countries are increasingly important for China not only politically but economically.

China possesses allies in the Global South not only among the governments but among the people of these countries – although the US is, of course, making sustained efforts to undermine this diplomatically and by every available means. The US is attempting to compensate for its limited ability to offer any real economic gains to developing countries by spending literally billions of dollars in a public relations offensive against China. This has to be very actively countered – China's diplomacy and numerous forms of media and public relations therefore has a crucial role to play. Steps such as that the first international visit each year by China's foreign minister being to Africa of course is a symbol of such understanding. China must not only aid the population of developing countries, and to offer win-win perspectives, but these need to be clearly understood internationally.

In addition to the possibilities for win-win relations with governments in the Global South there are also much greater objective possibilities to win over support among their populations. As already analysed the US capitalist class possesses sufficient resources that it can control the ideological/political situation both within its own borders and in many of its allies among advanced capitalist countries – only external objective blows and gradual weakening of US power relative to China will reduce this. Therefore, while every effort to win over sections of the population, or economic interests, in advanced countries is valuable at a certain point it runs up against an impenetrable wall – it is simply not possible at the present stage of world development for China to win over a majority of the population in the US or other advanced countries to an objective view of relations with China against determined opposition by the ruling classes of these countries. In contrast among developing countries, in the Global South, there are a significant number of objective opportunities not only to form very good relations with governments but for the majority of the population to have an objective/favourable view of China and relations with it.

This political situation in the 'Global South' is of course complex. China, rightly, does not advocate that other countries follow its 'model' – although it cannot prevent countries from learning from China's success and some of them will do so. The great majority of countries in the Global South will remain capitalist, although some countries will move towards socialism – these latter will be particularly close allies of China. But for the reasons already analysed the great majority of developing countries do not wish to pursue the anti-China policies which the US attempts to impose. These Global South countries therefore form a very large series of allies for China - and the international relation of forces is moving towards them. The combination of, as the main factor, the strength of China's own development, but also the growth of the Global South economies, means a slow but growing shift in the relation of forces towards China. The conclusion that flows from that is clear and the same as, in a difference context, that noted in 'On Protracted War' – China cannot win quickly, but it will prevail. Furthermore, it is in the overall interests of humanity that China should prevail.

This, therefore, again comes back to why 'On Protracted War' has become such a fundamental text to study to aiding understanding the present situation in two senses. First, because while what is involved with the US is competition, and not war, the same conclusion is arrived at – this will be a protracted struggle. Second, the method of 'On Protracted War', as with Mao's other writings, shows the highest method to analyse any situation. It confirms Mao Zedong Thought is not only for historical study but is a vital practical guide to current reality.

Section *6*

Explanation of China's economic policy in terms of Marxist and 'Western' Economics

Deng Xiaoping and John Maynard Keynes

December 2010

Introduction

The present importance of China's economy is twofold. The first is the scale of China's economic achievement, its impact on the international economy, and the consequences of this for the improvement of the social conditions of China and the world's population. The second is the universalisable character of China's economic system. No country can mechanically copy another's economic system – as China insists, its economy has unique "Chinese characteristics" and there is no "Chinese model". But the elements of which this economic system is composed are universal. As analysed below China has solved in practice problems stated in general macro-economic theory. For that reason these elements, in quite different forms and combinations, are of major importance for economic policy elsewhere. This article deals with both aspects in that order. In particular it relates China's economic performance to more familiar Western economic theory.

China's economic and social achievement

In the last twenty-five years China has lifted more than 620 million people out of absolute poverty. That is, according to the calculations of Professor Danny Quah of the London School of Economics, 100% of the reduction in the number of those living in absolute poverty in the world.[193] No other country, therefore, even remotely compares to China's contribution to the reduction of world poverty – a fact which places legitimate, and illegitimate, criticism of China in an appropriate qualitative context.

Furthermore, not only China's rate of increase of GDP but also its increase of consumption, both individual and total consumption including government spending on education and health, is the highest of any major country – see Table 8.

The basis of the very high rate of increase in China's living standards is extremely rapid growth of GDP. Average annual GDP growth since 1978 is 9.9% a year according to World Bank data. As is well known, over a 30-year period this is the highest of any major economy – see Figure 50.

Since 2007 the annual dollar increase in China's GDP, even at official exchange rates, has been higher than the annual increase in the US. This is likely to continue for the foreseeable future. On conservative assumptions - an annual China GDP growth rate of 8.0% and a US growth rate of 3.0% - China's economy would overtake that of the US to be the largest in the world in Parity Purchasing Power

Table 8

Annual Rate of Growth of Household Consumption and Total Consumption 1978-2008		
	Household Consumption	Total Consumption
China	7.9%	8.5%
Indonesia	6.7%	6.0%
Singapore	5.6%	5.8%
India	4.9%	5.6%
South Korea	4.6%	5.6%
US	3.1%	2.9%
UK	2.9%	2.5%
Japan	2.3%	2.4%
France	2.1%	2.1%
Germany	1.6%	1.6%
Source: Calculated from UN National Accounts Main Aggregates Database/World Bank DataBank		

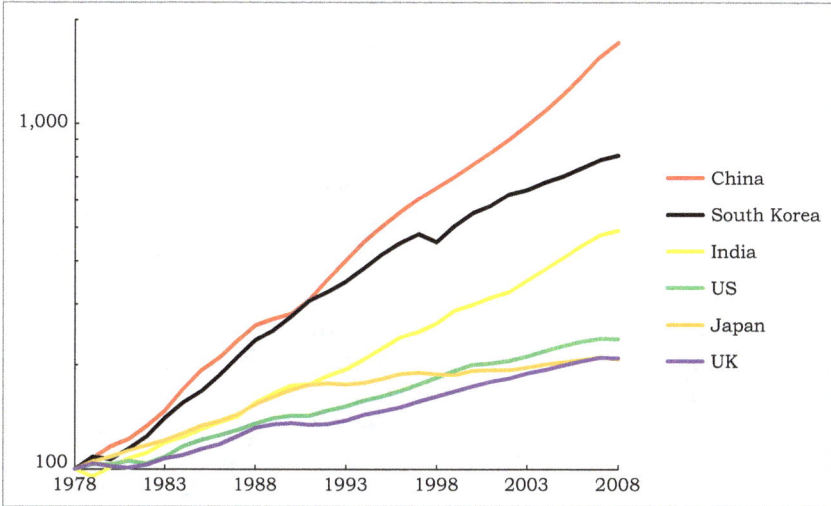

Figure 50: GDP Growth Inflation adjusted prices,
1978=100, log scale

(PPP) terms, in approximately 2019. On actual current five-year moving average annual growth rates - China 9.9%, US 2.5% - China would overtake the US in PPP terms in 2017. The widely quoted Goldman Sachs estimate that China's GDP would overtake the US, at official exchange rates, in approximately 2026 was made before the financial crisis and is outdated – the gap between Chinese and US economies closed by $700 billion in 2009 alone. PWC's estimate that China's economy will overtake that of the US "before 2020" is more accurate.

Given such rapid rises in living standards it is therefore unsurprising that in China this spring, according to Pew Global Attitudes Project, when asked the question "is the country's economic situation good or bad" more than 85% answered "good" compared to less than 20% in the US and UK.[194] The Economist Intelligence Unit, in a report published in August, found that 91% of China's population were optimistic about the future.[195]

China and macro-economic theory

Turning to policy, China's "reform and opening up" process under Deng Xiaoping was, of course, formulated in a Marxist economic framework. It can indeed be outlined in those terms, but an alternative statement of the same issues in Western economic terms, those of Keynes, is given below.

Stated in Marxist terms, China's policy started with a critique of Soviet economic policy. This stated that Soviet economic policy from the introduction of the First Five Year Plan (1929), and by implication Soviet economic policy afterwards, had made the error of confusing the "advanced" stage of socialism, in which production is not market regulated, with the "primary" developing stage of socialism during which the transition from capitalism to an advanced socialist economy takes place.[196] Such a transition should be conceived as extending over a prolonged period – many decades. The final formulation arrived at was that China's was a "socialist market economy with Chinese characteristics".

This debate was framed in Chinese terms, without primary reference to previous economic theory in other countries. The approach, in a Chinese phrase repeated by Deng Xiaoping, was to "seek truth from facts". The discussion, in fact, dealt with themes analysed not only in Western economics but in debates which took place in the early USSR – which Stalin "resolved" by killing the economists who disagreed with him. However, the framework of discussion was indeed primarily China.

In practical terms, the conclusion of such an analysis meant abandonment of an administratively planned economy (e.g. in the USSR it was illegal to sell a pencil at a different price in Moscow and Vladivostok) and the substitution of a market economy in which the state would control certain key macroeconomic parameters – in particular in regard to investment. In terms of economic structure and the state sector it led to "Zhuada Fangxiao" – grasping large state firms and releasing small ones to the non-state/private sector. Those who wish to follow the early stages of this debate, as formulated in Marxist terms, may read Robert Hsu's book on the issue. [197]

Restatement of Chinese economic policy in terms of Keynesian economics

Most people in the West are however unaware of, or disagree with, Marxist economic categories. Therefore, to make the essential points clear, this article will put them in the more familiar terms of Western economics – those of Keynes. The proviso needs to be made, however, that this is the actual Keynes of *The General Theory of Employment Interest and Money* and not the vulgarised version that appears in economics textbooks. Geoff Tily's *Keynes Betrayed* is one of the latest and best in a series of works outlining the difference between the two and the contrast is crucial for understanding China.[198]

For example, budget deficits play only a marginal role in China's stimulus packages – even during 2009's maximum anti-crisis measures China's budget deficit was only 3% of GDP. The core of Keynes *General Theory* itself, as opposed to vulgarisations, however itself also centres on the factors determining investment. It is therefore through this optic that both Keynes's and Chinese economic strategy can be best approached.

The rising proportion of the economy devoted to investment

Already in the founding work of classical economics, *The Wealth of Nations*, Adam Smith analysed that a necessary consequence of the increasing division of labour was that the proportion of the economy devoted to investment rose with economic development: "As the accumulation of stock must, in the nature of things, be previous to the division of labour, so labour can be more and more subdivided in proportion only as stock is previously more and more accumulated... As the division of labour advances, therefore, in order to give constant employment to an equal number of workmen, an equal stock of provisions, and a greater stock of materials and tools than what would have been necessary in a ruder state of things must be accumulated beforehand."[199] As is relatively well known Marx followed Smith in concluding that the contribution of investment rose as an economy developed – describing this process as a "rising organic composition of capital".

Keynes also held that the proportion of the economy devoted to investment rose with economic development. The explanation he offered was, however, somewhat different as he ascribed it to the consequences of rising savings levels accompanying increasing wealth. As the percentage of income consumed fell with increasing wealth the proportion devoted to saving necessarily rose proportionately. As

Keynes stated in the *General Theory*: "men are disposed... to increase their consumption as their income increases, but not by as much as the increase in their income... a higher absolute level of income will tend, as a rule, to widen the gap between income and consumption."[200]

A necessary consequence of an increase in the proportion of the economy devoted to investment is that the impact of any decline in investment will have increasingly serious consequences as an economy became more developed: "the richer the community, the wider will tend to be the gap between its actual and its potential production... For a poor community will be prone to consume by far the greater part of its output, so that a very modest measure of investment will be sufficient to provide full employment; whereas a wealthy community will have to discover much ampler opportunities for investment if the saving propensities of its wealthier members are to be compatible with the employment of its poorer members. If in a potentially wealthy community the inducement to invest is weak, then in spite of its potential wealth, the working of the principle of effective demand will compel it to reduce its actual output, until, in spite of its potential wealth, it has become so poor that its surplus over its consumption is sufficiently diminished to correspond to the weakness of the inducement to invest."(p31)

In the mid-20th century attempts were made to factually dispute the conclusion of classical economics that the proportion of the economy devoted to investment rose with economic development - Milton Friedman devoted an entire book, *A Theory of the Consumption Function*, to attempting to refute Keynes regarding this. However the findings of modern econometrics are conclusive – the definitive demonstration, as usual on matters of long term economic growth, being given by Angus Maddison.[201] Factually, as classical economics including Keynes analysed, the trend is for the proportion of the economy devoted to investment to rise.

To illustrate this, Figure 51 shows the proportion of the economy devoted to fixed investment of the leading economies of successive periods of more rapid growth over the 300-year period for which meaningful statistics can be found.

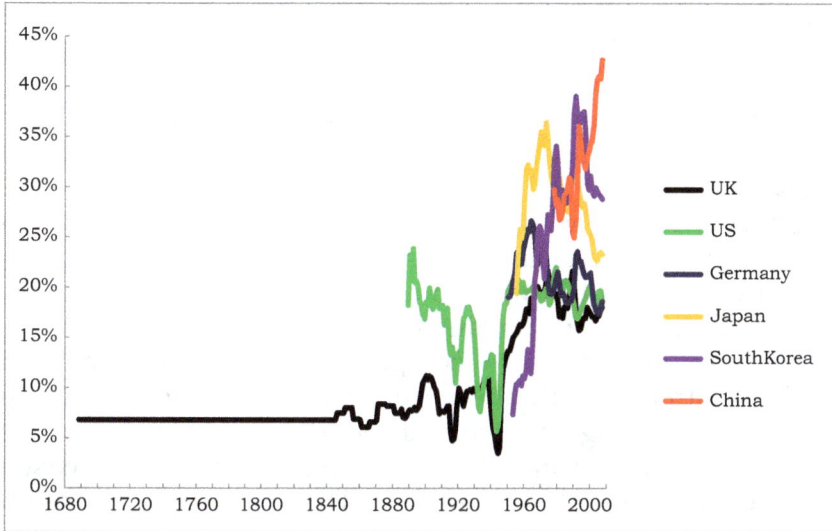

Figure 51: Fixed Investment % of GDP

Source: Deane and Cole, British Economic Growth 1688-1959, The
Economist 100 Years of Economic Statistics, World Bank World
Development

The potential destabilising consequences of the rising proportion of investment

A reason Friedman attempted, unsuccessfully, to refute Keynes over the rising proportion of the economy devoted to investment was that such a trend had the conclusion that any disturbance to the investment mechanism has increasingly destabilising consequences. Friedman noted of this analysis of Keynes that: "the central analytical proposition of the [theoretical] structure is the denial that the long-run equilibrium position of a free enterprise economy is necessarily at full employment."[202]

It is evident that there is a parallelism between the analysis of Keynes and that of Marx regarding the role of profit and investment. Marx noted that, in the absence of offsetting factors, a rise of the proportion of the economy devoted to investment would lead to a falling rate of profit. This is a necessary consequence of a situation whereby the capital stock rises relative to the profits stream. In short, the increasing division of labour, through its consequence in raising the proportion of the economy devoted to investment, the process analysed by Adam Smith, created a tendency of declining rate of profit which Marx analysed as a "barrier to the development of the productive forces."[203]

Keynes also approached economic fluctuations via the profit rate: "The trade cycle is best regarded, I think, as being occasioned by a cyclical change in the marginal efficiency of capital." (p313) However Keynes specific development was to approach the potentially destabilising consequences of the rising proportion of the economy devoted to investment via the angle of effective demand.

Effective demand was composed of both consumption and investment, with the latter tending to rise relative to the former during economic development: "when aggregate real income is increased aggregate consumption is increased but not by as much as income... Thus to justify any given amount of employment there must be an amount of current investment sufficient to absorb the excess of total output over what the community chooses to consume when employment is at the given level... It follows, therefore, that given what we shall call the community's propensity to consume, the equilibrium level of employment, i.e. the level at which there is no inducement to employers as a whole either to expand or to contract employment, will depend on the amount of current investment." (p27)

No automatic mechanism however ensured that the necessary volume of investment would occur: "the effective demand associated with full employment is a special case, only realised when the propensity to consume and the inducement to invest stand in a particular relationship to one another... It can only exist when, by accident or design, current investment provides an amount of demand just equal to the excess of the aggregate supply price of the output resulting from full employment over what the community will choose to spend on consumption when it is fully employed.' (p28) Put bluntly: "An act of individual saving means – so to speak – a decision not to have dinner today. But it does *not* necessitate a decision to have dinner or buy a pair of boots a week hence or a year hence." (Keynes, The General Theory of Employment, Interest and Money, 1936, p. 210). Or in more sophisticated terminology: "The error lies in proceeding to the ... inference that, when an individual saves, he will increase aggregate investment by an equal amount." (p83)

A shortfall of investment would be amplified by the well-known economic "multiplier" into much stronger cyclical fluctuations: "It is... to the general principle of the multiplier to which we have to look for an explanation of how fluctuations in the amount of investment, which are a comparatively small proportion of the national income, are capable of generating fluctuations in aggregate employment and income so much greater in amplitude than themselves." (p122) The outcome of the fluctuations in investment, combined with consumption, in turn determined employment: "The propensity to consume and the rate of new investment determine between them the volume of employment." (Keynes, The General Theory of Employment, Interest and Money, 1936, p. 30)

In turn: "the inducement to invest will be found to depend on the relation between the schedule of the marginal efficiency of capital and the complex of rates of interest." (p27) The reason for this was that the marginal efficiency of capital was "equal to the rate of discount which would make the present value of the series of annuities given by returns expected from the capital-asset during its lift just equal to its supply price." (p135) Consequently "the inducement to invest depends partly on the investment-demand schedule and partly on the rate of interest." (p137)

From this analysis Keynes derived key policy conclusions.

Budget deficits

One, which is well known, is the use budget deficits confronted with recession – the vulgarisation of Keynes lies in *reducing* Keynes theories to support for budget deficits, not in the fact that he supported deficit spending. Keynes analysed budget deficits in general terms of what he termed "loan expenditure": "'loan expenditure' is a convenient expression for the net borrowing of public authorities on all accounts, whether on capital account or to meet a budgetary deficit. The one form of loan expenditure operates by increasing investment and the other by increasing the propensity to consume." (p128)

Therefore, in one of his most famous passages: "If the Treasury were to fill old bottles with banknotes, bury them at suitable depths in disused coalmines which are then filled up to the surface with town rubbish, and leave it to private enterprise on well-tried principles of laissez-faire to dig the notes up again... with the help of repercussions, the real income of the community, and its capital wealth also, would probably become a good deal greater than it actually is. It would, indeed, be more sensible to build houses and the like; but if there are political and practical difficulties in the way of this, the above would be better than nothing." (p130)

Such a general view of deficit spending, did not, of course mean that Keynes was indifferent to what deficits should actually be spent on, and his contempt for double standards regarding when budget deficits were justifiable was scathing: "Pyramid-building, earthquakes, even wars may serve to increase wealth, if... our statesmen... stands in the way of anything better. It is curious how common sense, wriggling for an escape from absurd conclusions, has been apt to reach a preference for wholly 'wasteful' forms of loan expenditure rather than for partly wasteful forms, which because they are not wholly wasteful, tend to be judged on strict 'business' principles. For example, unemployment relief financed by loans is more readily accepted than the financing of improvements at a charge below the current rate of interest...wars have been the only form of large-scale loan expenditure which statesmen have thought justifiable." (p129)

Interest rates

While Keynes supported budget deficits, nevertheless the fundamental cause of recession lay in more fundamental factors affecting investment, which in turn were affected by the rate of interest: "we shall show that the succession of boom and slump can be described and analysed in terms of the fluctuations of the marginal efficiency of capital relatively to the rate of interest." (p144)

As investment was affected by interest rates, therefore, a crucial issue in raising investment was a sufficiently low rate of interest. This problem, in turn, tended to become more acute because of the rising proportion of the economy devoted to investment: "Not only is the marginal propensity to consume weaker in a wealthy community, but owing to its accumulation of capital being already larger, the opportunities for further investment are less attractive unless the rate of interest falls at a sufficiently rapid rate; which brings us to the theory of the rate of interest and to the reasons why it does not automatically fall to the appropriate levels." (p31)

The aim of low interest rates was to relaunch investment by ensuring that the return on investment was above the rate of interest plus whatever was the required premium to overcome liquidity preference. But as Keynes openly acknowledged, such low term interest rates destroy the ability to live from income from interest – which is why, in his famous phrase, Keynes foresaw "euthanasia of the rentier." (p376) He concluded: "I see... the rentier aspect of capitalism as a transitional phase which will disappear when it has done its work." (p376)

"A somewhat comprehensive socialisation of investment"

Despite support for low interest rates Keynes, however, did not consider it likely that these would be sufficient by themselves to overcome the effects of an investment decline. It would therefore be necessary for the state to play a greater role in investment: "Only experience... can show how far management of the rate of interest is capable of continuously stimulating the appropriate volume of investment... I am now somewhat sceptical of the success of a merely monetary policy directed towards influencing the rate of interest... I expect to see the State... taking an ever greater responsibility for directly organising investment." (p164)

This led Keynes to support a "somewhat comprehensive socialisation of investment': "It seems unlikely that the influence of banking policy on the rate of interest will be sufficient by itself to determine an optimum rate of investment. I conceive, therefore, that a somewhat comprehensive socialisation of investment will prove the only means of securing an approximation to full employment." (p378)

Keynes noted that this "somewhat comprehensive socialisation of investment" did not mean the elimination of the private sector, but should mean socialised investment operating together with a private sector: "This need not exclude all manner of compromises and devices by which public authority will co-operate with private initiative... the necessary measures of socialisation can be introduced gradually and without a break in the general traditions of society... apart from the necessity of central controls to bring about an adjustment between the propensity to consume and the inducement to invest there is no more need to socialise economic life than there was before.... The central controls necessary to ensure full employment will, of course, involve a large extension of the traditional functions of government." (p378)

Keynes held this was necessary because: "It is certain that the world will not much longer tolerate the unemployment which, apart from brief periods of excitement, is associated – and, in my opinion, inevitably associated – with present capitalistic individualism." (p381)

Summing up

It is now possible to clearly see the structure of Keynes argument. The rising proportion of the economy devoted to investment meant any downturn in investment would have increasingly destabilising consequences. This could be dealt with to some degree through budget deficits, but given that the key element was investment, and investment was determined by the interaction between profit and the interest rate, a policy of low interest rates was necessary. This would lead to the "euthanasia of the rentier" – for which read state ownership of banks. However it was unlikely interest rates would be sufficient by themselves and therefore the state would need to step in with "a somewhat comprehensive socialisation of investment" which would however work alongside the private sector.

But tracing this argument has now actually arrived at a "Chinese" economic structure - although approaching it via a Keynesian and not a Marxist framework. "Zhuada Fangxiao", grasping large state firms and releasing small ones to the non-state/private sector, coupled with abandonment of quantitative planning, means that China's economy is not being regulated via administrative means but by general macro-economic control of investment – as Keynes advocated.

Implications

What is the overall significance of this? Deng Xiaoping's most famous economic statement is of course "cats theory" –

"it doesn't matter whether a cat is black or white provided it catches mice". But "cats theory" can also be applied to economics itself – it doesn't matter whether something is described in Marxist or Western economic terms provided the same economic structure and policies exist. Zhuada Fangxiao is a conclusion that may be arrived at from either a Marxist or a Keynesian framework.

But while one may be indifferent to the colour of theoretical cats evidently it is not possible to be indifferent as regards policy measures to be taken – precise measures in terms of interest rates, investment etc are required. There is a radical difference in what is being carried out in practice between the US and Europe on one side and China on the other as regards the potential policy measures which have been outlined. In the US and Europe budget deficits certainly have been utilised – although they are coming under increasing attack. Low central bank interest rates have been pursued and some small forms of quantitative easing, that is driving down long term interest rates through central bank purchases of debt, have been used. But no serious programmes of state investment have been launched – let alone Keynes's "somewhat comprehensive socialisation of investment".

In China, in contrast, budget deficits have been combined with lower interest rates, a state-owned banking system ("euthanasia of the rentier") and a huge state investment programme. While the West's economic recovery programme has been timid, China has pursued full blooded policies of the type recognisable from Keynes *The General Theory* as well as its own "socialism with Chinese characteristics." Why this contrast and why has China's stimulus package been so much more successful than that in the West?

Because in the West, of course, it is held that the colour of the cat matters very much indeed. Only the private sector coloured cat is good, the state sector coloured cat is bad. Therefore even the private sector cat isn't catching insufficient mice, that is the economy is in severe recession, the state sector cat must not be used to catch them. In China however both cats have been let loose - with the result that far more mice are caught.

The recession in all the Western economies is driven by a decline in investment – in most countries the decline in fixed investment accounts for two thirds to more than ninety per cent of the decline in GDP. Keynes's calls for not only budget deficits and low interest rates but also for the state to set about "organising investment" are evidently required. But this is blocked because the state coloured cat is not allowed catch mice.

To put it another way, the US and Europe insist on participating in the race while hopping on only one leg – the private sector. China is using two legs, so little wonder it is running much faster than the West.

To turn from metaphors to economic measures, a large scale state house building programme, or large scale expansion of the transport system, of the type being followed in China as part of their anti-crisis measures not only delivers goods that are valuable in themselves but boosts the economy through its macro-economic effect in boosting investment. But in the West such state investment is blocked as it creates competition for the private sector. As the top aim in the West is not to revive the economy, but to protect the private sector, therefore such large-scale investment must be undertaken.

It is an irony. Keynes explicitly put forward his theories to save capitalism. But the structure of capitalism has made it impossible to implement Keynes policies even when confronted with the most severe recession since the Great Depression. The anti-crisis measures of China's "socialist market economy" are far closer to those Keynes foresaw than any capitalist economy. Whereas in the US, for example, fixed investment fell by almost thirty percent during the financial crisis in China urban fixed investment rose by over thirty percent. Consequently there is nothing mysterious whatever about the relative success of the two economies in emerging from the financial crisis – China's economy having grown by seventeen percent in two years and the US remaining below its previous level of GDP.

Deng Xiaoping famously said his death was "going to meet Marx". But Deng may also be having an intense talk with John Maynard Keynes.

And Keynes would be very interested to discuss with Deng's two cats – who appear to have read the General Theory more closely and accurately than any administration in the West.

China's Socialist Economy Explains Its Superior Anti-Crisis Economic Performance

*One of the most striking proofs of the superiority of the social-
ist character of China's economy compared to capitalism is its
performance when faced with global economic crises. This was
dramatically demonstrated during the international financial
crisis after 2007 - and is being shown again during the Covid19
global economic downturn. China came through these global
crises far more strongly than capitalist countries and indeed
both produced dramatic shifts in the international economic
relation of forces in favour of China.*

*The reason China has such superior economic performance
during global economic crises is due to the core of the socialist character of its economy – its large state sector. This allows
China to regulate its overall investment level – whereas in a
capitalist economy the overall investment level is determined by
private capital. That is, in line with its socialist market economy,
China's macro-economic system does not 'administer' its economy, that is regulate all its details, but it does determine key
macro-economic variables of which a crucial one is the investment level – as was examined in earlier sections. This detailed
comparison of the performance of socialist China and the main
capitalist economies during the international financial crisis is
an excerpt from 'Lessons of China's economic development for
Latin America' – originally published in September 2016.*

The socialist character of China's economy

A failure to correctly understand the superiority of China's
economic system, that is a failure to understand that China

is not a capitalist but a 'socialist market' economy, inevitably leads to misunderstanding of the relative dynamics of China and Western economies. The differences in economic structure between China and the West is evident. To take a few key macro-economic features:

(i) China uses direct state methods to alter its investment level, in addition to fiscal and monetary policy, whereas the US rejects state investment and relies for macro-economic management almost solely on fiscal and monetary policy.

(ii) China's level of fixed investment, as a percentage of its economy, is much higher than the US.

(iii) In order to regulate its investment level, China has a large state sector, in addition to a private one, whereas US does not – the US rejects the state sector on ideological grounds.

(iv) China's economy is more open to international trade than the US.

But it has been China's economy which has outperformed, and Western economies have grown far more slowly in comparison. It is precisely these differences in structure which explain why China's economy has grown so rapidly and the West has not. As will be seen, China's economic policy and structure produced better economic growth than the West because China's economic structure and policy more correspond to the forces producing economic growth than does the West's. In summary, it is not the structure of China's economy which is the problem but the West's.

China's superior macro-economic management

The issues of China's long-term growth, which has already been analysed elsewhere, and its shorter term macro-economic management are interrelated and furthermore clearly show the socialist and non-capitalist character of China's economic structure. It will be demonstrated below that China's economic structure generates not only better long-term growth than the West but also creates much superior and more powerful shorter term macro-economic tools for managing its economy than the Western capitalist economies. This explains not only China's much more rapid economic growth than the Western economies but also its great economic outperformance of the US and other Western economies – which in turn resolves key questions in economic theory. To illustrate the superiority of China's system of macro-economic management, the facts regarding the business cycles in the US and other Western economies will first be established and then the superior alternative made possible by China's economic structure will be analysed. This will demonstrate the superiority of China's 'socialist market' macro-economic structure compared to the West not only in ability to generate rapid economic development but in its shorter term ability to regulate business cycles. These issues are integrated in the socialist character of China's economic system.

What drives business cycles?

In order to analyse short and medium term macro-economic management it is necessary to note that it is an elementary arithmetic error to believe that because consumption constitutes the largest part of US GDP, and also of any Western economy, therefore changes in consumption control the US and Western capitalist business cycle. In reality because relative percentage shifts in fixed investment are much greater than changes in consumption, it is fluctuations in investment which primarily determine changes in the economy during major business cycle fluctuations.

This reality of the business cycle may be seen clearly in the most classic of all economic downturns – the US Great Depression after 1929. The post-1929 crash was driven by a severe fall in US fixed investment. As Figure 52 shows, between 1929 and 1933, the period of economic collapse inaugurating the Great Depression, US private fixed investment fell by 69% - a decline more than twice as severe as the fall in US GDP. In contrast the decline of US household consumption was only 18% - less than the 26% fall in US GDP in the period. Figure 52 also shows that by 1938, the last year prior to World War II, regarding trends in different components of US GDP:

- US household consumption and government expenditure had already risen above 1929 levels,
- US private fixed investment remained 39% below its 1929 level.

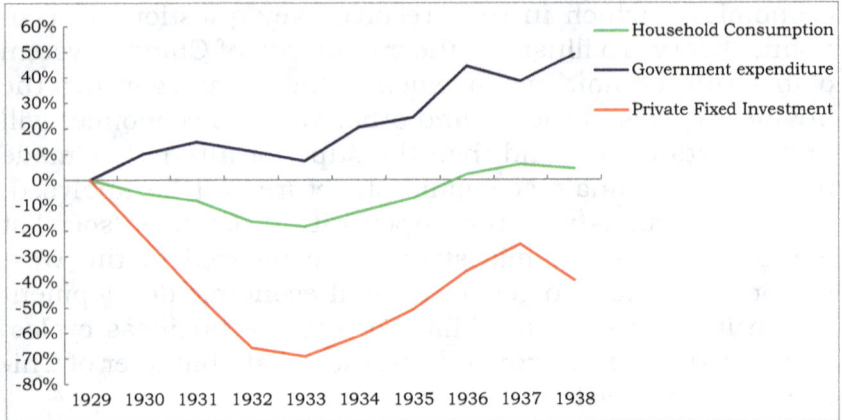

Figure 52: Components of US GDP $ change on 1929 - at 2009 prices

Source: Calculated from Bureau of Economic Analysis NIPA Table 1.1.3

The combination of a recovery in consumption, but a failure of recovery in private investment, explains why in 1938 US GDP was only 2% above its 1929 level – an average annual growth over almost a decade of merely 0.2%. Changes in private fixed investment therefore controlled not only long term US economic growth but the fluctuations in its business cycle - the Great Depression was driven by the collapse in US private fixed investment.[204] US consumption during the Great Depression fluctuated in percentage terms less than GDP, but the percentage fluctuation in fixed investment was far greater than the changes in GDP. It will now be demonstrated that the same process operated in the Western economies during the post-2008 international financial crisis.

What happened in the post-2007 crash – the US

Analysing first trends during the international financial crisis, i.e. the facts which must be explained, Figure 53 shows the changes in major components of US GDP between 2007, the last year before the international financial crisis, and 2009 - the trough of the 'Great Recession'. In inflation adjusted prices by 2009, compared to 2007:

• US GDP by 2009 was $455 billion, or 3.1%, below its 2007 level.

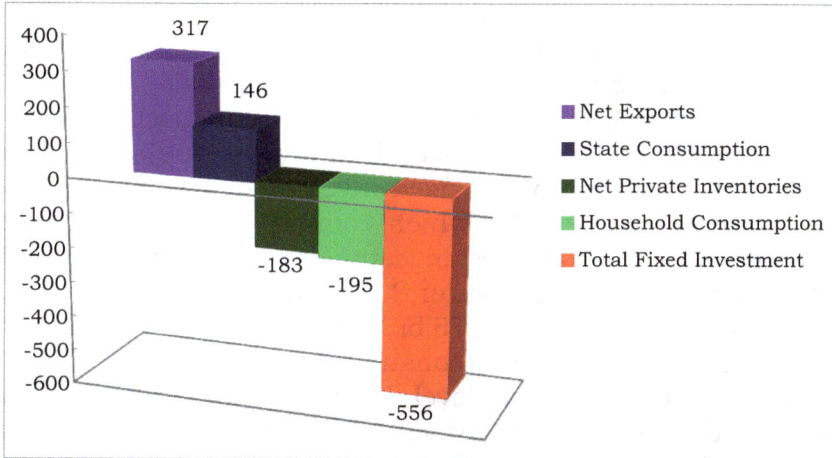

Figure 53: Change in Components of US GDP 2007-2009
$ bn 2009 prices

Source: Calculated from US Bureau of Economic Analysis NIPA
Table 1.5.6

- US household consumption was $195 billion, or 1.9%, below 2007 levels;
- US net exports were $317 billion up;
- US government consumption was $146 billion, or 4.6%, up;

Total US consumption, private and government, therefore only fell by $48 billion or 0.4% in 2007-2009. In contrast:

- US private inventories were $183 billion down;
- But US private fixed investment was $766 billion, or 22.4% below 2007 levels and state fixed investment was only $28 billion, or 4.5%, above – overall fixed investment was approximately $556 billion, or 17.2%, below 2007 levels.[205]

This therefore clearly confirms that after 2007 the same pattern existed in the US 'Great Recession' as with the Great Depression. Despite the fact that consumption is a higher percentage of GDP than investment the percentage decline in fixed investment was over forty times as large as the total percentage fall in consumption, 17.2% compared to 0.4%, while the total decline in fixed investment in inflation adjusted dollar terms in percentages was more than 11 times a severe as the fall in consumption- $556 billion compared to $48 billion. It was therefore the severe fall in US fixed investment which explained the depth of the 'Great Recession.'

Figure 54 also shows that the US 'new mediocre', that is slow growth by historical standards, after 2007 was also caused by a failure of US fixed investment to rebound. By 2014, the latest year for which comparisons can be made with China, US total fixed investment in inflation adjusted terms was only $71 billion, or 2.2%, above its 2007 level. In contrast US GDP was $1,475 billion, or 9.9%, above its 2007 level while US household consumption was $1,172 billion, or 11.7%, above its 2007 level. In short it was the very slow growth of US fixed investment that determined the 'new mediocre'.

The advanced economies as a whole

To show that the same process of fall in fixed investment as in the US operated in the other major Western advanced economies during the Great Recession, Figure 55 shows the changes in components of GDP for the total OECD economies between 2008, the peak of the pre-crisis OECD business cycle, and 2013. In that time OECD GDP grew,

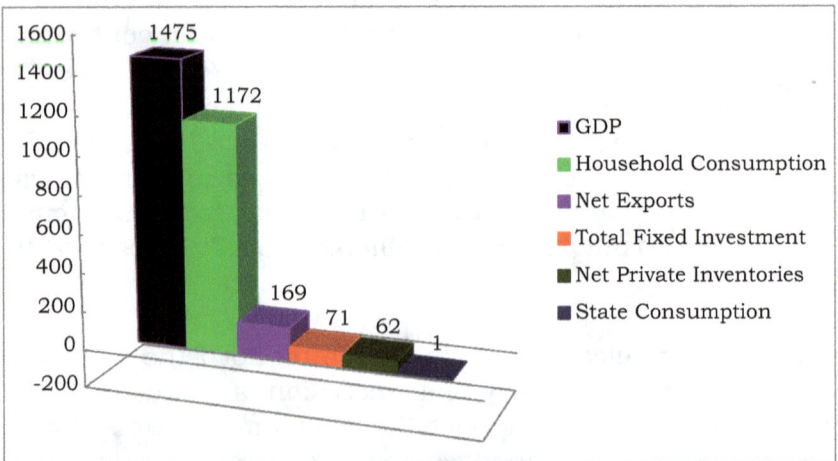

Figure 54: Change in Components of US GDP 2007-2014 $ bn 2009 prices

Source: Calculated from US Bureau of Economic Analysis NIPA Table 1.5.6

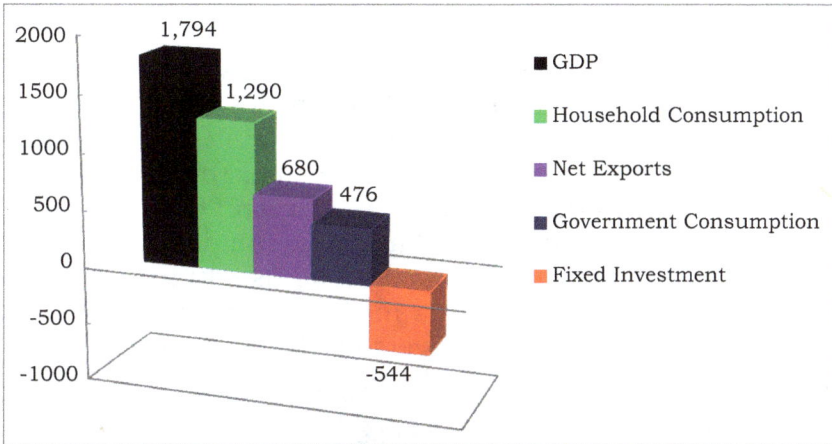

Figure 55: Total OECD -Change in Components of GDP
2007-2013 Total OECD Economies - Constant Price
PPPs US$ bn

Source: Calcuated from OECD Quarterly National
Accounts

due to decline and weak recovery, by only an annual average
0.7%. Figure 55 shows that by 2013:

- OECD household consumption, government consumption and net trade were all above pre-crisis levels.
- OECD fixed investment in inflation adjusted PPPs was
  $544 billion below 2008 levels.

The decline in fixed investment, as with the US, was therefore the fundamental factor depressing overall OECD GDP
during the post-2007 international financial crisis.

The data therefore clearly demonstrates that the same
pattern existed in all G7 advanced economic centres during
the post-2007 international financial crisis as in the US. As
in the Great Depression of the 1930s, the domestic driving
force of the post-2007 Great Recession was the fall in fixed
investment. Fixed investment therefore constituted not only
a key factor in long term growth rates but also determined
the shorter term dynamic in the business cycle. The Great
Recession might, in fact, be properly termed the 'Great Investment Fall'. It is the failure of fixed investment to recover that
created low growth in the Western economies.

China

The contrast to China is striking and shown in Figure 56. Data for net trade in constant price terms for 2014 is not available, but current price data for China shows clearly any shift will have been insufficient to alter the fundamental situation. Taking domestic trends between 2007 and 2014, the latest available data for changes in components of GDP China's GDP increased, in inflation adjusted terms by 16.5 trillion RMB. Overall changes in that period in inventories were negligible. The three drivers of China's GDP expansion were therefore, in inflation adjusted terms:

- Government consumption rose by 2.1 trillion RMB;
- Household consumption rose by 5.7 trillion RMB;
- Fixed investment rose by 8.6 trillion RMB.

Whereas the Great Recession in the US, and the rest of the West, was driven by the fall in fixed investment, in China fixed investment therefore constituted the largest part of rapid economic growth.

China's macroeconomic control of investment

It is also clear from the above data which macro-economic mechanisms allowed China to grew so much more rapidly than the US and other Western economies not only over the

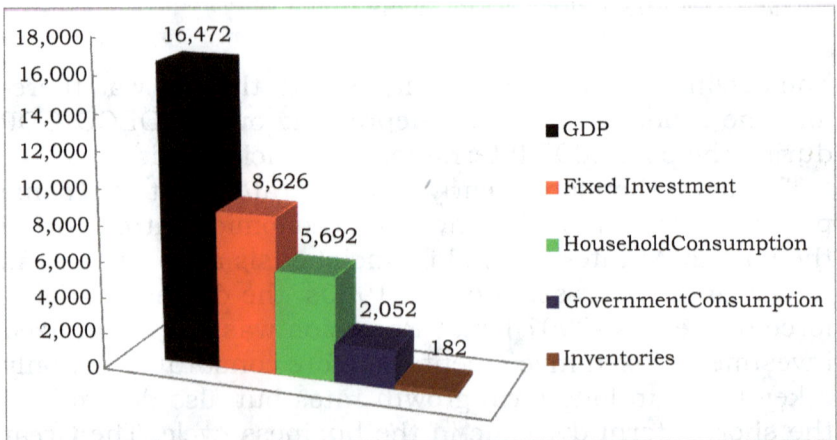

Figure 56: China -Changes in Domestic Components of GDP 2007-2014 Inflation adjusted RMB prices

Source: Calculated from World Bank World Development Indicators

long term but in particular after the international financial crisis. China's rapid growth, and slow US and Western growth, was due to China's fixed investment rising strongly, while US fixed investment fell sharply. Factually, and without understanding the significance of what it was saying, the *Wall Street Journal* summarised the reasons for China's superior performance entirely accurately:

> Most economies can pull two levers to bolster growth: fiscal and monetary. China has a third option. The National Development and Reform Commission can accelerate the flow of investment projects.[206]

China's system of macro-economic regulation, its 'socialist market economy' therefore showed its strength in ability to counter negative trends in business cycles – in the case after 2007 confronted with the biggest business cycle since the Great Depression. The mechanisms by which China achieved fast growth, whereas the US experienced slow growth are clear - they were explained by the different trends in fixed investment. But the question that must be answered is what conclusions can be drawn from the fact that China has mechanisms of macro-economic regulation that are so much stronger than the US?

Why China did not have an investment crisis

The reason China did not suffer fixed investment problems of this US type clearly flows directly from China's different economic structure to the US. In particular:

- China's economy possesses a large state sector, which can be instructed by the government to increase fixed investment.
- China's core banking system is state-owned, and can therefore be instructed to lend for investment.

China's economy, unlike the US, therefore possessed state mechanisms which can ensure available funds are utilised for investment. During the international financial crisis, China was therefore able to expand fixed investment, allowing continuing strong economic growth, whereas in the US fixed investment fell sharply - producing first the Great Recession and then the 'new mediocre'.

NOTES

1   The scale of what is involved is, however, significantly concealed when all that is mentioned are relative percentage economic growth rates between states. The reason is that one inhabitant of the Vatican City or Tuvalu, the world's two small countries in population, is exactly equal to the value of one person from China and the impact of economic development on the individuals in these countries is not dissimilar. But the impact of rapid economic growth in China or Tuvalu has entirely different impacts on the world economy and humanity's overall well-being. Only India matches the population of China - and it is for this reason that China and India will dominate the 21st century with the US eventually becoming world no.3 - no.4 if Europe can unite itself.

2   This is of course rapid growth by the standards of the relevant period.

3   The international impact of the Soviet Union, including on China, can be clearly understood by the fact that until 1949 the USSR was by far the biggest impact of industrialisation, in terms of the proportion of the world's population affected, in history. Almost three times as large a proportion of the world's population were directly affected by the industrialisation of the USSR as by the rapid economic growth of the US.

4   Only if India can sustain the rapid economic growth which commenced in the late 1980s/early 1990s, in a country with 16% of the world's population, will anything resembling the scale of China's impact on the world's population and living standards have been seen. So far, regrettably, the long term sustainability of India's rapid growth has still to be proven by the test of time. Hopefully this will soon be overcome.

5   Calculated from (The Conference Board, 2013) Calculated in EKS PPPs.

6   In terms of other determining indicators of economic development the results are equally striking. In constant price PPP terms, during the period 1990-2010 China contributed 57.1%, that is the majority, of the world's growth in fixed investment growth. In 2000-2010 this reached 63.9% (Vu, 2013, pp. 99-100)

7   Maddison made his calculations in 1990 Geary-Khamis dollars – that is a parity purchasing power with the US dollar in 1990. The fact that the calculations to calculate growth rates are necessarily in constant prices has the effect of making China's GDP for the period after 1990 a somewhat higher percentage of that of the US that current price measures. However the fundamental trends and comparative growth rates of China and the US economies are not altered

8   (Maddison, 2010) calculates the US economy was six times larger than China's. The Conference Board calculate eight times (The Conference Board, 2014). Given the extreme dislocation of China after Japanese invasion and civil war there is evidently a significant range of variation in the estimate. However for present purposes either figure establishes the qualitative situation.

9   Xue Muqiao estimates the losses in the Great Leap Forward in the following way: 'During the national economy's "Great Leap Forward" between 1958 and 1960, heavy industry grew excessively. The number of employees rocketed from 24.5 million to 50 million. In contrast, the number of agricultural

workers decreased by 23 million... Since agricultural production declined dramatically, while other economic sectors grew disproportionately, Chine encountered "three difficult years" from 1959 to 1961... the national economy began to improve in 1963. It resumed full vitality in 1965. This tremendous setback in our national economy had severely tested our mettle.' (Xue, 2011, p. 16)

10   (Maddison, 2010) World Bank data is for 2011 PPPs.

11   It is stressed that this refers to short time frames, which in this context includes five years. It does not apply to medium or long term trends, during which major structural changes altering the growth rate can occur.

12   Deng Rong, Deng Xiaoping's daughter, noted: 'After the People's Republic was established, we had more than seven years of successful socialist reform and construction.' (Xi, 2017 17 January, p. 1) The impact of the pre-1978 period on life expectancy is analysed below.

13   On both the data of (Maddison, 2010) and (The Conference Board, 2014).

14   The data in the World Bank World Development Indicators is given in constant price 2005 US dollars. The data in the Conference Board is in 1990 Geary Khamis dollars (The Conference Board, 2014). Maddison died in 2010 and therefore his data is not available for the most recent period.

15   Wishful thinking in light of this fact helped generate the prolific, if factually disreputable, genre of 'the coming China catastrophe' which has already been referred to.

16   The official criteria used by the World Bank for country classifications in 2013 were low income – Gross National Income (GNI) less than $1,035, lower middle income GNI $1,036-$4,085, high income greater than $12,616. GNI's are calculated according to World Atlas methodology. For a detailed explanation see http://data.worldbank.org/about/country-classifications/world-bank-atlas-method.

17   World Bank PPPs are not available for 1978 but taking 1980, the first year for which World Bank PPP measures are available, still less than 1% of the world's population lived in countries with lower per capita GDPs than China while 74% lived in countries with a higher per capita GDP.

18   This shows that the deviation of PPPs from current exchange rates is on average similar in most developing countries. Therefore comparing Chinese PPPs with its current exchange rate to attempt to claim justification for revaluation of the RMB is illegitimate. The divergence of China's current market exchange rate from its PPP exchange rate is approximately the same as the average for developing economies.

19   (The Economist, 2015)

20   A detailed analyst, such as Andrew Smithers on his Financial Times blog, concludes that the trend growth rate of the US may be as low as 1.5-1.6% a year (Smithers, 2015).

21   See (Ross, 2011). In this field, the target should not be increase in GDP, but the maximum sustainable rate of growth of living standards – 'sustainable' being used in the sense of environmentally sustainable, defensible against external threats, and of being able to maintain such a growth rate of living standards over a prolonged period.

22   Deng Xiaoping outlined the relation between the two as follows: 'We can only improve our standard of living gradually, on the basis of expanded production. It is wrong to expand production without raising the people's standard of living; but it is likewise wrong – in fact impossible – to raise the people's standard of living without expanding production.' (Deng X. , 16 January 1980, p. 243) And: 'Marxism attaches utmost importance to developing the productive forces... This calls for highly developed productive forces and an overwhelming

abundance of material wealth... the fundamental task... is to develop the productive forces... As they develop, the people's material and cultural life will constantly improve. One of our shortcomings after the founding of the People's Republic was that we didn't pay enough attention to developing the productive forces.... Our political line is to focus on the modernization programme and on continued development of the productive forces. Nothing short of a world war would tear us away from this line.' (Deng, 30 June 1984, p. 73)
23   In addition to longer life being a virtually universal human desire!
24   (Sen, 1998, p. 6)
25   India is the most relevant comparison because it is the only country comparable in size to China in terms of population, because its achievement of independence from Britain occurred in 1947, at almost the same time as the creation of the People's Republic of China, and because its life expectancy at that time was close to China's.
26   Calculated from http://mappinghistory.uoregon.edu/english/US/US39-01.html
27   Calculated from 'Life Expectancy: Past and future variations by gender in England and Wales' Longevity Science Advisory Panel, London 2012.
28   Calculated from http://www.mortality.org/
29   A typical example is (Dikötter, 2011) which makes no attempt to assess the dramatic increase in life expectancy at all compared to his claim 'China descended into hell'. (Dikötter, 2011, p. xi)
30   (Xi, Uphold and Develop Socialism with Chinese Characteristics, 2012 January 5, p. Location 476)
31   'In the last 3 decades, China alone has lifted more people out of extreme poverty than the rest of the world combined. Indeed, China's ($1/day) poverty reduction of 627 million from 1981 to 2005 exceeds the total global economy's decline in its extremely poor from 1.9 billion to 1.4 billion over the same period.' (Quah, 2010)
32   The number of people emerging from poverty was less than the population increase due to the rise in the number of those living in extreme poverty in sub-Saharan Africa.
33   (Sen, 1998, p. 9)
34   The shortest life expectancy being Sierra Leone's 48 years and the longest being Hong Kong and Switzerland's 83 years.
35   (Pilling, 2013)
36   In some countries people live longer than would be expected from its level of economic development, while in others lives are shorter than would be expected purely from per capita GDP.
37   For example, taking countries with continuous data records back to 1960, on the data published by the World Bank in 2014 Zambia ranks 99th in the world in GDP per capita, but 111th in life expectancy – its life expectancy is lower than would be expected given its level of economic development. Spain, ranks 24th in GDP per capita but 5th in life expectancy – its people live significantly longer than would be expected given its economic development level. Such differences indicate that the consequences of health care, environment etc. are better in Spain, and worse in Zambia, than would be expected from their overall level of economic development.
38   This was pointed out numerous times by Deng Xiaoping. For example as put by Deng Xiaoping in 1979: 'The aim of our revolution is to liberate and expand the productive forces. Without expanding the productive forces, making our country prosperous and powerful and improving the living standards of our people, our revolution is just empty talk. We oppose the old society and the old system because they oppressed the people and fettered the productive forces.

We are clear about this problem now. The Gang of Four said it was better to be poor under socialism than to be rich under capitalism. This is absurd.

'Of course, we do not want capitalism, but neither do we want to be poor under socialism. What we want is a socialism in which the productive forces are developed and the country is prosperous and powerful. We believe that socialism is superior to capitalism. This superiority should be demonstrated in that socialism provides more favourable conditions for expanding the productive forces than capitalism does.' (Deng, 1979)

39 For countries for which data existed it was 22.8%. However as almost all the countries for which no data existed were extremely poor their GDP per capita in the great majority of cases may be taken as lower than China's.

40 This lower than the most recent figures as the World Bank uses period averages for the calculations.

41 GNI is GDP plus factor incomes (profits, income from employment) earned by foreign residents, minus the income earned in the domestic economy by non-residents. It therefore is a wider measure of total income in the economy as it does not include only income generated within the domestic economy.

42 https://www.learningfromchina.net/deng-xiaoping--john-maynard-keynes/

43 https://www.learningfromchina.net/wrong-analyses-of-china---listed-by-author-and-date/

44 ttps://www.learningfromchina.net/deng-xiaoping--john-maynard-keynes.html

45 http://www.marxists.org/archive/marx/works/1848/communist-manifesto/ch02.htm

46 https://www.marxists.org/archive/marx/works/1875/gotha/ Critique of the Gotha Programme

47 (Xi, 2016 July 1, p. 33)

48 (Xi, 2017 November 3)

49 (Xi, 2012 January 5)

50 It should be noted that even if the extraordinary situation of Japan's recovery from wartime devastation is taken, when in 1945 the Japanese economy was only 49% of its size in 1940, Japan's fastest ever growth over a 39-year period was 1,728% from 1945-1984 - still only about half the growth of China's 3,453% in 1978-2017.

51 But it should be noted that even if the extraordinary situation of Germany's recovery from wartime devastation is taken, when in 1946 Germany's economy was only 38% of its size in 1940, Germany's fastest ever growth over a 39-year period in 1946-1985 was 820%, or an annual average 5.5% - less than a quarter of China's total growth of 3,453% in 1978-2017.

52 (Xi, 2016 July 1, p. 38)

53 (Xi, 2016 July 1, p. 40)

54 For example, taking the 'Asian Tigers', which after China experienced the most rapid economic growth of any countries, Taiwan Province of China's annual GDP growth was only 8.0% in 1950—60 compared to 9.6% in 1960-70 and 9.8% in 1980-1990; in Singapore annual average GDP growth was only 5.3% in 1950-60 compared to 9.2% in 1960-70 and 9.0% in 1970-80; in Hong Kong SAR annual average GDP growth was only 6.9% in 1950-60, compared to 8.9% in 1960-70 and 9.0% in 1970-80; in South Korea annual average GDP growth was 5.%% in 1950-60, 8.7% in 1960-70, and 8.4% in 1970-80.

55 (Deng, 30 June 1984)

56 It should be noted that because this chart measures from the maximum number in poverty to the latest data the numbers for certain countries differs from those for the period 1981-2013, but it clearly does not alter the overall pattern in any significant way.

57   (Marx K., 1875)
58   (Marx & Engels, 1848, p. 504)
59   (Marx K., 1875, p. 85)
60   (Marx K., 1875, p. 86)
61   (Marx K., 1875, pp. 86-87)
62   (Marx K., 1875, p. 87)
63   More precisely Deng stated: 'We were victorious in the Chinese revolution pre-
      cisely because we applied the universal principles of Marxism-Leninism to our
      own realities.' (Deng, 28 August 1985)
64   (Deng, 28 August 1985)
65   (Deng, 29 August 1987)
66   (Deng, 28 March 1978)
67   (Marx K., 1867, p. 750)
68   (Deng, 30 June 1984)
69   (Marx K., 1867, p. 750)
70   (Marx K., 1867, p. 751)
71   (Marx K., 1844, pp. 211-228)
72   "http://blog.sina.com.cn/s/blog_9893ebc80101lpng.html"
73   (Marx & Engels, 1845, pp. 32-34)
74   (Marx & Engels, 1845, pp. 32-34)
75   (Marx & Engels, 1845, pp. 67-70)
76   (Marx & Engels, 1845, p. 74).
77   (Xi, 2017, 17 January). In consequence of this dynamic: 'Economic global-
      ization, a surging historical trend, has greatly facilitated trade, investment,
      flow of people, and technological advances. Since the turn of the century...
      1.1 billion people have been lifted out of poverty, 1.9 billion people now have
      access to safe drinking water, 3.5 billion people have gained access to the
      internet, and the goal has been set to eradicate extreme poverty by 20130. All
      this determines that globalization is generally good. Of course, there are still
      problems, such as development disparity, governance dilemma, digital divide,
      and equity deficit. But they are growing pains. We should face these problems
      squarely and tackle them. As we Chinese like to say: "One should not stop
      eating for fear of choking."' (Xi, 2017, 18 January)
78   (Costa, 2018)
79   (Rachman, 2018)
80   (Xi, 2014, 23 March)
81   (Xi, 2015, 28 September)
82   (Xi, 2017, 18 January)
83   (McMaster & Cohn, 2017)
84   (CBS News, 2018)
85   (Thatcher, 1987)
86   (Marx K., 1857, p. 36)
87   (Smith, 1776, pp. 14-15)
88   (Marx K., 1844, p. 221)
89   (Marx K., 1867, p. 344)
90   (Marx K., 1867, p. 360)
91   (Jorgenson, Gollop, & Fraumeni, 1987, p. 200)
92   (Jorgenson D. W., 1995, p. 5)
93   (Pyo, Rhee, & Ha, 2007)
94   (Liang, 2007)
95   (Ren & Sun, 2007)
96   (OECD, 2017, p. Location 1233)
97   (OECD, 2017, p. Location 1233)
98   (OECD, 2017, p. Location 1236)

99   Calculations from data in (Milne, 2010)

100   (Chang, 2010, p. 159)

101   Calculations from data in (Milne, 2010)

102   (Jones, 2008, p. 2)

103   (Jones, 2008, p. 2)

104   (Marx, 1894, pp. 210-211)

105   http://rdcy-sf.ruc.edu.cn/displaynews.php?id=15011

106   It should be noted that due to lack of data this breakdown is not available for six developing economies in that group – Angola, Iraq, Myanmar, Nigeria, Sudan and Uzbekistan – which slightly affects the exact data, but it will be seen that the difference between advanced and developing economies is so large as to leave no doubt as to the overall situation.

107   The data appears to add up to slightly over 100% merely due to decimal rounding issues

108   (Marx & Engels, 1848, pp. 487-488)

109   (Xi, 2013 April 28, pp. Location 755-Location 761)

110   (Keynes, 2013, p. 283)

111   (Friedman, 1957, p. 5)

112   'Estimates of savings in the United States made by Kuznets for the period since 1899 revealed no rise in the percentage of income saved... despite a substantial rise in real income. According to his estimates, the percentage of income saved was much the same over the whole of the period.' (Friedman, 1957, pp. 3-4)

113   (Barro & Sala-i-Martin, 2004, pp. 15-16)

114   (Keynes, 2013, p. 31)

115   (Keynes, 2013, p. 27)

116   (Keynes, 2013, p. 28)

117   (Keynes, 2013, p. 210)

118   (Keynes, 2013, p. 83)

119   (Keynes, The General Theory of Employment Interest and Money, 2013, p. 122)

120   (Keynes, The General Theory of Employment Interest and Money, 2013, p. 30)

121   (Keynes, 2013, p. 144)

122   (Keynes, The General Theory of Employment Interest and Money, 2013, p. 31)

123   (Keynes, The General Theory of Employment Interest and Money, 2013, p. 64)

124   (Keynes, The General Theory of Employment Interest and Money, 2013, p. 320)

125   (Keynes, The General Theory of Employment Interest and Money, 2013, p. 325)

126   (Keynes, 2013, p. 378)

127   (Keynes, The General Theory of Employment Interest and Money, 2013, p. 378)

128   (Orlik, 2012)

129   (CPC, 2014)

130   (Xi, 2013 November 9, pp. 1262-1274)

131   (Xi, 2013 November 9, pp. 1262-1274)

132   (Hutzler, 2015)

133   (Xi, 2016 July 1, p. 37)

134   (Xi, 2017 November 3)

135   (Xi, 2012 November 17)

136   (Xi, 2012 November 17)

137   (Xi, 2017, 17 January). In consequence of this dynamic: 'Economic globalization, a surging historical trend, has greatly facilitated trade, investment, flow of people, and technological advances. Since the turn of the century... 1.1 billion people have been lifted out of poverty, 1.9 billion people now have access to safe drinking water, 3.5 billion people have gained access to the internet, and the goal has been set to eradicate extreme poverty by 20130. All this determines that globalization is generally good. Of course, there are still

problems, such as development disparity, governance dilemma, digital divide, and equity deficit. But they are growing pains. We should face these problems squarely and tackle them. As we Chinese like to say: "One should not stop eating for fear of choking."' (Xi, 2017, 18 January)

138 (Marx K. , 1867, p. 750)
139 (Marx K. , 1867, p. 751)
140 (Marx K. , 1844, pp. 211-228)
141 (Xi, 2014, 23 March)
142 (Xi, 2015, 28 September)
143 (Xi, 2014, 27 March)
144 (Xi, 2017, 18 January)
145 (Xi, 2014, 27 March)
146 (Leibniz, The Monadology, 1989, p. 214)
147 (Leibniz, On Nature Itself, 1989, p. 164)
148 (Leibniz, Discourse on Metaphysics, 1989, p. 41)
149 (Leibniz, 2000, p. 22)
150 (Leibniz, Discourse on Metaphysics, 1989, pp. 41-42)
151 (Marx K. , 1867, pp. 47-48)
152 (McMaster & Cohn, 2017)
153 (CBS News, 2018)
154 (Thatcher, 1987)
155 https://twitter.com/martjacques/status/1347137399927828481"
156 (Mao Zedong, 1938, Section 15)
157 (Mao Zedong, 1938, Section 1)
158 (Mao Zedong, 1938, Section 1)
159 (Mao Zedong, 1938, Section 1)
160 (Mao Zedong, 1938, Section 30)
161 (Mao Zedong, 1936)
162 (Mao Zedong, 1938, Section 1)
163 (Mao Zedong, 1938, Section 1)
164 (Mao Zedong, 1938, Section 8)
165 (Mao Zedong, 1938, Section 2)
166 (Lenin, Statistics and Sociology' January 1917, https://www.marxists.org/archive/lenin/works/1917/jan/00d.htm
167 (Mao Zedong, 1938, Section 1)
168 (Mao Zedong, 1938, Section 6)
169 (Mao Zedong, 1938, Section 6)
170 (Mao Zedong, 1938, Section 24)
171 (Mao Zedong, 1938, Section 26)
172 (Mao Zedong, 1938, Section 27)
173 (Mao Zedong, 1938, Section 27)
174 (Mao Zedong, 1938, Section 27)
175 (Mao Zedong, 1938, Section 32)
176 (Mao Zedong, 1938, Section 36)
177 (Mao Zedong, 1938, Section 37)
178 (Mao Zedong, 1938, Section 38)
179 (Mao Zedong, 1938, Section 46)
180 (Mao Zedong, 1938, Section 81)
181 Lenin' 'Once Again On The Trade Unions, The Current Situation and the Mistakes of Trotsky and Buhkarin' https://www.marxists.org/archive/lenin/works/1921/jan/25.htm
182 https://www.guancha.cn/LuoSiYi/2020_11_20_572052.shtml
183 https://www.nytimes.com/interactive/2020/11/03/us/elections/exit-polls-president.html

184 https://www.nbcnews.com/know-your-value/feature/how-women-voters-decided-2020-election-ncna1247746

185 https://frontline.thehindu.com/world-affairs/us-foreign-policy-under-joe-biden-presidency-will-not-be-greatly-different-from-that-of-the-past/article33416309.ece

186 https://www.ft.com/content/ac4c02f4-48a7-49f3-9a06-0c3879750b37

187 https://twitter.com/gadyepstein/status/1349387532623114240

188 https://www.wsj.com/articles/biden-to-review-u-s-nuclear-weapons-programs-with-eye-toward-cuts-11608805800?mod=hp_lead_pos4

189 https://www.newsweek.com/69-percent-americans-want-medicare-all-including-46-percent-republicans-new-poll-says-1500187

190 https://www.guancha.cn/LuoSiYi/2020_12_07_573698.shtml

191 (Mao, 1926)

192 https://www.globaltimes.cn/page/202101/1212221.shtml

193 (Quah, The Shifting Distribution of Global Economic Activity, 2009)

194 (The Economist, 2010)

195 (Waldmeir, 2010)

196 (Hsu, 1991, p. 11)

197 (Hsu, Economic Theories in China 1979-1988, 1991)

198 (Tily, 2007)

199 (Smith, 1999, p. 372)

200 (Keynes, The General Theory of Employment, Interest and Money, 1936, pp. 96-97). All page references are to this edition.

201 (Maddison, 'A long run perspective on saving', 1992)

202 (Friedman, 1957, p. 237)

203 (Marx, 1981, p. 350)

204 Keynes was entirely correct in his analysis of this and he made full use in *The General Theory of Employment Interest and Money* of Kuznets calculations on this (Keynes, 1936, pp. 386-392)

205 The word 'approximately' is used because it is not possible to mechanically add chained constant price data. However, over such a short period of time the difference is unlikely to be extremely significant.

206 (Orlik, 2012)

Articles

1. China's is the Greatest Economic Achievement in World History
   Published in April 2016 (Chapter 2 of "The Great Chess Game")
2. China's Achievement in Living Standards
   Published in April 2016 (Chapter 3 of "The Great Chess Game")
3. Other countries can learn from China's socialist development strategy
   Published 15 August 2016
4. Why China is a socialist country – China's theory is in line with Marx
   Published 12 September 2017
5. The triumph of Chinese Marxism -'reform & opening up' to 19th Party Congress
   Published 24 March 2018
6. Deng Xiaoping – the world's greatest economist
   Published 14 August 2014
7. Xi Jinping's 'a common future for humanity' – its relation to Marx's Capital
   Published 18 July 2017
8. China and South-South Cooperation in the present global situation
   Published 14 January 2021
9. Explanation of China's economic policy in terms of Marxist and 'Western' Economics
   Published December 2010
10. China's Socialist Economy Explains Its Superior Anti-Crisis Economic Performance
    Published July 2016

Bibliography

Barro, R. J., & Sala-i-Martin, X. (2004). *Economic Growth*. Cambridge, Massachusetts, US: MIT Press.

Bukharin, N. (1925). 'Critique de la plate-forme économique de l'opposition'. In L. Trotsky, E. Préobrajensky, N. Boukharine, Lapidus, & Osttrovitianov, *Le Débat Soviétique Sur La Loi de La Valeur* (1972 ed., pp. 201-240). Paris: Maspero.

CBS News. (2018, January 26). *Trump sends "warmest regards" to Africa after "sh*thole countries" row*. Retrieved March 3, 2018, from CBS News: https://www.cbsnews.com/news/donald-trump-rwanda-paul-kagame-african-union-warmest-regards-shithole-countries/

Chang, H.-J. (2010). 23 Things They Didn't Tell You About Capitalism. London: Allen Lane.

Costa, R. (2018, January 20). *Bannon calls Trump's speech "Jacksonian"*. Retrieved March 3, 2018, from Washington Post: https://www.washingtonpost.com/local/2017/live-updates/politics/live-coverage-of-trumps-inauguration/bannon-calls-trumps-speech-jacksonian/?utm_term=.6e5405e6289c

CPC. (2014, January 16). Decision of the Central Committee of the Communist Party of China on Some Major Issues Concerning Comprehensively Deepening the Reform. Retrieved February 2014, 2014, from China.org.cn: http://www.china.org.cn/china/third_plenary_session/2014-01/16/content_31212602_2.htm

Deng, X. (21 August 1985). Two kinds of comments about China's reform. In X. Deng, *Selected Works of Deng Xiaoping 1982-1992* (1994 ed., pp. 138-9). Foreign Languages Press.

Deng, X. (28 August 1985). Reform is the only way for China to develop its productive forces. In X. Deng, *Selected Works of Deng Xiaoping 1982-1992* (pp. 140-143). Beijing: Foreign Languages Press.

Deng, X. (28 March 1978). Adhere to the principle "to each according to his work". In X. Deng, *Selected Works of Deng Xiaoping* (2001 ed., pp. 117-118). Honolulu: University Press of the Pacific.

Deng, X. (2 June 1978). 'Speech at the all-army conference on political work'. In X. Deng, *Selected Works of Deng Xiaoping 1975-1982* (2001 ed., pp. 127-140). Honolulu: University Press of the Pacific.

Deng, X. (29 August 1987). In everything we do we must proceed from the realities of the primary stage of socialism. In X. Deng, *Selected Works of Deng Xiaoping 1982-1992* (pp. 247-8). Beijing: Foreign Languages Press.

Deng, X. (30 June 1984). Building a Socialism with a Specifically Chinese Character. In *Selected Works of Deng Xiaoping Vol. 3 1982-1992* (1994 ed., pp. 72-75). Beijing: Foreign Languages Press.

Friedman, M. (1957). *A Theory of the Consumption Function.* Princeton: Princeton University Press.

Hornby, L. (2016, July 1). *Xi Jinping pledges return to Marxist roots for China's Communists.* Retrieved March 14, 2018, from Financial Times: https://www.ft.com/content/be1b2528-3f57-11e6-8716-a4a71e8140b0

Hsu, R. C. (1991). *Economic Theories in China 1979-1988.* Cambridge and New York: Cambridge University Press.

Hutzler, C. (2015, September 22). *Despite Slump, China's Xi Jinping Pledges Economic Reforms.* Retrieved March 14, 2018, from Wall Street Journal: https://www.wsj.com/articles/despite-slump-chinas-xi-pledges-economic-reforms-1442894460

Jasny, N. (1972). *Soviet Economists of the Twenties.* Cambridge: Cambridge University Press.

Jones, C. I. (2008). Intermediate Goods and Weak Links: A Theory of Economic Development (Version 2.5). U.C. Berkeley and NBER.

Jorgenson, D. W. (1995). 'Productivity and Postwar US Economic Growth'. In D. W. Jorgenson, *Productivity* (Vol. 1, pp. 1-23). Cambridge, Massachusetts: The MIT Press.

Jorgenson, D. W., Gollop, F. M., & Fraumeni, B. M. (1987). *Productivity and US Economic Growth.* New York: to Excel.

Keynes, J. M. (1936). *The General Theory of Employment, Interest and Money* (Macmillan 1983 ed.). London: Macmillan.

Keynes, J. M. (2013). *The General Theory of Employment Interest and Money* (The Collected Writings of John Maynard Keynes ed., Vol. 7). Cambridge: Cambridge University Press.

Kondratiev, N. D. (n.d.). *The Works of Nikolai D Kondratiev* (1998 ed.). (N. Makasheva, W. J. Samuels, V. Barnett, Eds., & S. S. Williams, Trans.) Pickering and Chatto.

Leibniz, G. W. (1989). Discourse on Metaphysics. In G. W. Leibniz, R. Ariew, & D. Garber (Eds.), *Philosophical Essays* (R. Ariew, & D. Garber, Trans., pp. 35-68). Indianapolis and Cambridge: Hackett Publishing Company.

Leibniz, G. W. (1989). On Nature Itself. In G. W. Leibniz, R. Ariew, & D. Garber (Eds.), *Philosophical Essays* (R. Ariew, & D. Garber, Trans., pp. 155-167). Indianapolis and Cambridge: Hackett Publishing Company.

Leibniz, G. W. (1989). The Monadology. In G. W. Leibniz, R. Ariew, & D. Garber (Eds.), *Philosophical Essays* (R. Ariew, & D. Garber, Trans., pp. 213-225). Indianapolis and Cambridge: Hackett Publishing Company.

Leibniz, G. W. (2000). Leibniz's Fourth Letter, Being an Answer to Clarke's Third Reply. In G. W. Leibniz, S. Clarke, & R. Ariew (Ed.), *Correspondence* (pp. 22-28). Indianapolis and Cambridge: Hackett Publishing Company.

Lenin, V. I. (1917, January). *Statistics and Sociology.* Retrieved from Marxists.org: https://www.marxists.org/archive/lenin/works/1917/jan/00d.htm

Lewin, M. (1975). *Political Undercurrents in Soviet Economic Debates.* London: Pluto Press.

Liang, C.-Y. (2007). 'Industry-Wide Total Factor Productivity and Output Growth in Taiwan, 1981-1999'. In D. W. Jorgenson, M. Kuroda, & K. Motohashi (Eds.), *Productivity in Asia: Economic Growth and Competitiveness* (pp. 146-184). Cheltenham: Edward Elgar.

Maddison, A. (2010). *Statistics on World Population, GDP and Per Capita GDP, 1-2008 AD* . Retrieved January 23, 2011, from Angus Maddison (1926-2010): http://www.ggdc.net/MADDISON/oriindex.htm

Mao, Z. (1926, March). *Analysis of the Classes in Chinese Society*. Retrieved from Marxists.org: https://www.marxists.org/reference/archive/mao/selected-works/volume-1/mswv1_1.htm

Mao, Z. (1936, December). *Problems of Strategy in China's Revolutionary War*. Retrieved from Marxists.org: https://www.marxists.org/reference/archive/mao/selected-works/volume-1/mswv1_12.htm

Mao, Z. (1938, May). *On Protracted War*. Retrieved from https://www.marxists.org/reference/archive/mao/selected-works/volume-2/mswv2_09.htm

Marx. (1894). *Capital Vol.3* (Marx and Engels Collected Works Vol.36 1895 ed.). Moscow: Progress Publishers.

Marx, K. (1844). Comments on James Mill, Élémens d'Économie Politique. In K. Marx, *Karl Marx and Frederich Engels Collected Works* (1975 ed., Vol. 3, pp. 211-228). Moscow: Progress Publishers.

Marx, K. (1857). *Economic Manuscripts of 1857-58* (Vol. Collected Works 28). London: Lawrence and Wishart.

Marx, K. (1867). *Capital Vol.1* (1988 ed.). (B. Fowkdes, Trans.) Harmondsworth: Penguin.

Marx, K. (1867). Capital Volume 1. In K. Marx, *Marx and Engels Collected Works* (1996 ed., Vol. 35, pp. 7-761). London: Lawrence and Wishart.

Marx, K. (1875). Marginal notes on the programme of the German Workers Party. In K. Marx, *Karl Marx Frederich Engels Collected Works* (1989 ed., Vol. 24, pp. 81-99). London: Lawrence and Wishart.

Marx, K., & Engels, F. (1845). The German Ideology. In K. Marx, & F. Engels, *Collected Works* (1976 ed., Vol. 5, pp. 19-539). London: Lawrence and Wishart.

Marx, K., & Engels, F. (1848). Manifesto of the Communist Party. In K. Marx, & F. Engels, *Collected Works* (1976 ed., Vol. 6, pp. 476-519). London, UK: Lawrence and Wishart.

McMaster, H. R., & Cohn, G. D. (2017, May 30). *America First Doesn't Mean America Alone.* Retrieved June 4, 2017, from Wall Street Journal: https://www.wsj.com/articles/america-first-doesnt-mean-america-alone-1496187426

Milne, R. (2010, February 15). *The Cogs are Clogged.* Retrieved September 22, 2010, from Financial Times: http://www.ft.com/cms/s/0/0e5c21aa-1a6a-11df-a2e3-00144feab49a.html

OECD. (2017). *Compendium of Productivity Indicators 2017* (Kindle Edition ed.). Paris: OECD Putlishing.

Orlik, T. (2012, May 29). *Show Me The China Stimulus Money.* Retrieved February 11, 2014, from Wall Street Journal: http://online.wsj.com/news/articles/SB10001424052702303674004577433763683515828

Preobrazhensky, E. (1921-27). *The Crisis of Soviet Industrialization* (1980 ed.). (D. A. Filzer, Ed.) London: MacMillan.

Pyo, H. K., Rhee, K.-H., & Ha, B. (2007). 'Growth Accounting and Productivity Analysis by 33 Industrial Sectors in Korea (1984-2002)'. In D. W. Jorgenson, M. Kuroda, & K. Motohashi (Eds.), *Productivity in Asia: Economic Growth and Competitiveness* (pp. 113-145). Cheltenham: Edward Elgar.

Rachman, G. (2018, January 21). *Trump's speech to set tone at Davos party.* Retrieved March 3, 2018, from Financial Times: https://www.ft.com/content/a9b6a1f6-db74-11e7-9504-59efdb70e12f

Rouen, R., & Sun, L. L. (2005). *Total factor productivity growth in China industries: 1981-2000.* presented at the 5th International Input-Output Coonference, Beijing, China 27 June-1 July 2005.

Smith, A. (1776). *An Inquiry into the Nature and Causes of the Wealth of Nations* (1981 ed.). Indianapolis: Liberty Edition Volume 1.

Thatcher, M. (1987, October 31). Epitaph for the eighties? "there is no such thing as society'. *Women's Own.* Retrieved from http://briandeer.com/social/thatcher-society.htm

Xi, J. (2012 January 5). Uphold and Develop Socialism with Chinese Characteristics. In J. Xi, *The Governance of China (Kindle Edition)* (2014 ed., Vol. 1, pp. Location 450-500). Beijing: Foreign Languages Press.

Xi, J. (2012 November 17). Study, Disseminate and Implement the Guiding Principles of the 18th CPC National Congress. In J. Xi, *The Governance of China (Kindle Edition)* (2014 ed., Vol. 1, pp. Location 165-449). Beijing: Foreign Languages Press.

Xi, J. (2013 April 28). Hard Work Makes Dreams Come True. In J. Xi, *The Governance of China (Kindle Editiion)* (2014 ed., pp. Location 749-819). Beijing: Foreign Languages Press.

Xi, J. (2013 November 9). Explanatory Notes to the "Decision of the Central Committee of the Communist Party of China on Some Major Issues Concerning Comprehensively Continuing the Reform". In J. Xi, *The Governance of China (Kindle Edition)* (2014 ed., pp. Location 1129-1503). Beijing: Foreign Languages Press.

Xi, J. (2014, 23 March). Follow the Trend of the Times and Promote Global Peace and Development. In J. Xi, *The Governance of China (Kindle Edition)* (pp. Location 3972-4094). Beijing: Foreign Languages Press.

Xi, J. (2016 July 1). Stay True to Our Original Aspiration and Continue Marching Forward. In J. Xi, *The Governance of China* (Vol. 2, pp. 32-48). Beijing: Foreign Languages Press.

Xi, J. (2017 17 January). Shoulder the Responsibilities of Our Time and Promote Global Growth Together. In J. Xi, *The Governance of China Col.2* (pp. 519-532). Beijng: Foreign Languages Press.

Xi, J. (2017 November 3). *Full text of Xi Jinping's report at 19th CPC National Congress*. Retrieved March 2, 2018, from Xiinhuanet: http://www.xinhuanet.com/english/special/2017-11/03/c_136725942.htm

Xi, J. (2017, 18 January). Towards a Community of Shared Future for Mankind. In J. Xi, *The Governance of China* (Vol. 2, pp. 588-601). Beijing: Foreign Languages Press.

Xi, J. (2014, 27 March). Exchanges and Mutual Learning Make Civilizations Richer and More Colorful. In J. Xi, *The*

Governance of China (Kindle Edition) (pp. Location 3797-3909). Beijing: Foreign Languages Press.

Xi, J. (2015, 28 September). A New Partnership of Mutual Benefit and a Community of Shared Future. In J. Xi, *The Governance of China* (2017 ed., Vol. 2, pp. 569-575). Beijing: Foreign Languages Press.

Xi, J. (28 September 2015). A New Partnership of Mutual Benefit and a Community of Shared Future. In J. Xi, *The Governance of China* (2017 ed., Vol. 2, pp. 569-575). Beijing: Foreign Languages Press.

Xinhua. (2010, September 24). *Premier Wen expounds 'real China' at UN debate.* Retrieved February 2, 2012, from China Daily: http://www.chinadaily.com.cn/china/2010WenUN/2010-09/24/content_11340091.htm

Xinhua. (2011, July 1). *China still largest developing country: Hu.* Retrieved February 2, 2012, from China Daily: http://www2.chinadaily.com.cn/china/cpc2011/2011-07/01/content_12817816.htm

Xinhua. (2018, February 23). *zhēn lǐ zhī guāng gēng jiā càn làn — — zhuān jiā xué zhě tán « gòng chǎn dǎng xuān yán »fā biǎo 170 zhōu nián.* Retrieved March 3, 2018, from People's Daily: http://world.people.com.cn/n1/2018/0223/c1002-29830764.html

Author Bio

John Ross is Senior Fellow at Chongyang Institute for Financial Studies, Renmin University of China (in Beijing). He was the first non-Chinese citizen to be made a full-time member of one of China's new Think Tanks. Chongyang Institute is one of the most influential Think Tanks/Research Institutes in China.

He was appointed to this position at Chongyang Institute because of his almost 30 years of analysis of China and its relations to the international economy. This started with his 1992 article, originally published in Russian, 'Why the Economic Reform Succeeded in China and Will Fail in Russia and Eastern Europe' - the analysis of which is clear from the title. He is author of over 500 articles, including two best-selling books in Chinese, on China and its relations with the world economy.

From 1992-2000 he lived in Moscow, where he attempted to persuade the Russian authorities to follow a China style economic reform instead of Western shock therapy.

Before becoming employed in China John Ross was Director of Economic Policy for the Mayor of London during the period of Ken Livingstone.

His analyses have been published in English, Chinese, Spanish, Portuguese, French, Russian, German, Indonesian and Polish. Within China his work has been published in People's Daily, Global Times, on China Central Television, on China Radio International and other publications and media. He has over 1.1 million followers on Weibo – the Chinese equivalent of Twitter.

John Ross is the winner of several state and private sector media prizes in China.

www.ingramcontent.com/pod-product-compliance
Lightning Source LLC
Chambersburg PA
CBHW070808270326
41927CB00010B/2349